MEMOIR, LETTERS, AND REMAINS

OF

ALEXIS DE TOCQUEVILLE.

AUTHOR OF *DEMOCRACY IN AMERICA.*

TRANSLATED FROM THE FRENCH
BY THE TRANSLATOR OF *NAPOLEON'S CORRESPOND-
ENCE WITH KING JOSEPH.*

WITH LARGE ADDITIONS.

IN TWO VOLUMES.

VOL. I.

British Library Cataloguing-in-Publication Data
A catalogue record for this book is available from
the British Library

Alexis de Tocqueville

Alexis-Charles-Henri Clérel de Tocqueville was born on 29 July 1805, in Paris, France. He was a highly influential political thinker and historian, best known for his *Democracy in America* (1835-40) and *The Old Regime and the Revolution* (1856). Tocqueville was born into an old Norman aristocratic family; his parents narrowly avoided the guillotine due to the fall of Robespierre in 1794, and after a short exile in England, they returned to France during the reign of Napoleon.

Tocqueville began his political career in 1830, the same year as the establishment of the July Monarchy (1830-1848) of which Tocqueville remained a lifelong opponent. From 1830 to 1851, he served as deputy of the Manche department, and defended abolitionist views and free trade in his parliamentary debates. Tocqueville also supported the colonisation of Algeria though, creating a confused position somewhere in between leftist arguments and more conservative politics. Despite his nonconformist political stances, Tocqueville was also elected general counsellor of the Manche in 1842, and became the president of the department's *conseil général* between 1849 and 1851.

Aside from this political career, he was a prolific traveller, and obtained a mission from the July Monarchy to examine prisons and penitentiaries in America between 1831 and 1833. Whilst Tocqueville did visit some prisons, he travelled widely, taking extensive notes about his observations and reflections.

The result was *Democracy in America*, his most famous work – in which he examined the democratic revolution, a phenomenon that he believed had been cumulatively occurring over the past seven hundred years. Tocqueville also made an observational tour of England and Ireland in the late 1830s, producing the *Memoir on Pauperism* regarding English life, and observations on the appalling living conditions of Irish Catholic tenant farmers. In 1841 and 1846, he resumed his travels, and journeyed to Algeria. These trips inspired Tocqueville's *Travail sur l'Algérie*, in which he criticised the French model of colonisation, based on attempts to assimilate the native population, preferring the British model of indirect rule, which avoided involvement in population politics. He went as far as openly advocating racial segregation between the European colonists and the Arabs through the implementation of two different legislative systems.

After the fall of the July Monarchy during the February 1848 Revolution, Tocqueville was elected a member of the Constituent Assembly of 1848, where he became a member of the Commission charged with the drafting of the new Constitution of the Second Republic (1848–1851). He defended bicameralism (the policy of having two parliamentary chambers) and the election of the President of the Republic by universal suffrage. This position was not just based on humanitarian reasoning however; the more conservative rural population was seen as a good counterbalance to the revolutionary spirit of Paris. In 1849, he was appointed the Minister of Foreign Affairs, and actively supported laws restricting political freedoms, such as the liberty of clubs and freedom of the press. This realpolitik stood in contrast with Tocqueville's defence of freedoms in *Democracy in America,* but he firmly believed that stability in French political life was a necessary prerequisite for such autonomies. His strong theoretical support of political liberty was reflected in Tocqueville's opposition to Louis Napoléon's 1851 coup. As his biographer, Joseph Epstein has concluded, 'Tocqueville could never bring himself to serve a man he considered a usurper and despot. He fought as best he could for the political liberty in which he so ardently believed... He would spend the days remaining to him fighting the same fight, but conducting it now from libraries, archives, and his own desk.' A long time sufferer from bouts of tuberculosis, Tocqueville eventually succumbed to the disease on 16 April 1859. He is buried at the Tocqueville cemetery, Normandy.

PREFACE.

THE original of this work, edited by M. Gustave de
Beaumont, is already well known and widely circulated
in France.

I do not feel that any apology is needed for offering
to the public a translation. M. de Tocqueville's letters
are valuable as sources of information and instruction,
and above all as a moral study. The depth and seri-
ousness of his mind, combined with an almost feminine
grace and delicacy, the elevation which pervaded his
whole character, and which breathes in nearly every
sentence that he wrote, will be peculiarly appreciated
by an English reader.

And yet I feel great diffidence in introducing M. de
Tocqueville's thoughts, clothed in other words than his
own. He attached an almost exaggerated importance
to style; he so shrank from exhibiting his ideas, unless
expressed in the very best language, corrected and reconsidered again and again, that to change their form

is a greater responsibility with regard to him than to almost any other author.

I have been enabled to add to this English version some short specimens of a talent which M. de Tocqueville possessed in as much perfection as that of writing, by the access which Mr. Senior has given me to his journals. They contain notes of his conversations with M. de Tocqueville, and are often referred to in M. de Tocqueville's letters. Mr. Senior has also communicated to me the original letters to him from which M. de Beaumont selected those which are published in the second volume.

From these two sets of documents I have extracted some passages, which will be found in order of date.

The journals are a slight and inadequate, but still the only, record of M. de Tocqueville's conversation.

The new letters, and parts of letters, are political. Those which refer to English politics were, probably, omitted by M. de Beaumont as uninteresting to a French reader; and those which refer to French politics as too offensive to the existing Government in France.

Neither of these objections applies to an English publication.

I was anxious to exhibit M. de Tocqueville in two characters, in each of which he was eminent — that of a converser and that of a practical politician.

M. de Beaumont's book could not show him in the

former. It does show him in the latter; but the representation is rather an outline than a picture. It does justice to his delicate honor, to his ardent love of liberty, to his courage, and to his sagacity; still it wants details.

M. de Beaumont's charming memoir, and the published letters, show principally his general views. The extracts which I have made from Mr. Senior's journals, and from the unpublished letters, contain M. de Tocqueville's feelings and opinions on the public events of France and of England, as they took place. His criticisms of the past, his anticipations of the future, his regrets, his fears, his hopes, and his plans, are expressed too fully, too strongly, and too unreservedly, to be fit for a French publication; but I believe that the English reader will be thankful for them.

By the kind permission of Mr. Mill, I have reprinted the article in the *London and Westminster Review*, mentioned in the Memoir (vol. i. p. 83), and I have also been allowed to add M. de Tocqueville's account of the breaking up of the Assembly, in December, 1851, which appeared in the *Times*.

I take leave of my task with regret. I fear that I never again shall have an opportunity of associating so long and so intimately with such a mind. It seems to me that no one on whom the delightful duty has not been imposed of studying every page of these let-

ters, of endeavoring to extract the heart of each sentence, can thoroughly appreciate them. If I succeed
in introducing them to a larger circle of English readers, it will be some small consolation for the loss of a
dear and highly valued friend.

JULY 23, 1861.

CONTENTS TO VOL. I.

——◆——

UNPUBLISHED WORKS OF ALEXIS DE TOCQUE-VILLE.

FRANCE BEFORE THE CONSULATE.

CHAPTER I.

CHAPTER II.

LETTERS.

LETTERS TO EUGÈNE AND ALEXIS STOFFELS.

LETTERS.

MEMOIR

OF

ALEXIS DE TOCQUEVILLE.

CHAPTER I.

CHILDHOOD — EARLY TRAVELS IN ITALY AND SICILY — ENTRANCE
INTO PUBLIC LIFE — THE RESTORATION (1827-1828) — REVOLUTION
OF 1830 — INTENDED EXPEDITION TO THE UNITED STATES.

ALEXIS CHARLES HENRI CLEREL DE TOCQUEVILLE
was born in Paris on the 29th July, 1805. His mother,
Mademoiselle Le Pelletier de Rosambo, was a grand-
daughter of M. de Malesherbes ; his father, the Comte
de Tocqueville,* was, under the Restoration, successively
Prefect of Metz, of Amiens, of Versailles, and a peer of
France.

Brought up entirely at home, Alexis de Tocqueville
learnt little, if good manners and a high tone of feeling
can be reckoned as little. It is certain that his early education was much neglected ; he commenced his classical
studies at the college of Metz, which he entered whilst
his father was prefect of the town. Though weak at

---

* In the last years of his life, the Count de Tocqueville published
two remarkable works : the title of the first is " *Histoire Philosophique
du règne de Louis XV.*" 2 vols. 8vo.; and that of the second, " *Coup-
d'œil sur le règne de Louis XVI.*" 1 vol. 8vo.

starting in Latin and Greek, he was, from the beginning,
first in French composition, where imagination is of more
importance than correctness; and not long ago the Imperial Academy of Metz recorded with pride, that in the
year 1822 Alexis de Tocqueville, at that time a student
in rhetoric, had carried off the first prize.* After this
brilliant termination of studies in which he often regretted that he had not been grounded, in the year 1826 he
set out on his travels.

Accompanied by his brother Edward,† his elder and
guide, he ran through Italy, visited the principal towns,
and made an excursion into Sicily.   In this tour he
already gave proofs of the eager curiosity and of the
activity of mind which he brought to bear on all subjects.
This is evidenced by two bulky MSS. containing his notes
and the impressions of each day.   Certainly these are
not works of the highest order ; and their author was under no illusion as to the merit of his first-born, for on the
cover of one is written, in his hand, " Very indifferent."
But the criticism is, to say the least, severe ; and even if
it were deserved, it would be, nevertheless, an interesting
study to follow the first steps of so great a writer, to note
the progress of his mind, groping, wandering, erring, and
at length, after many wanderings, recovering the right
path.

It is, indeed, curious to observe the young traveller ;
at first he treats Italy after the fashion of ordinary tour-
ists.   He visits scrupulously every gallery ; does not pass
over one picture, nor omit one medal ; he notes all the

* See the speech delivered on the 15th May, 1859, by M. Salmon,
President of the Imperial Academy of Metz.

† Then Baron, afterwards Viscount de Tocqueville, his second
brother. They were both older than himself.

works of the great masters. He does still more ; he commences a serious investigation of the principles of ancient architecture, of which he undertakes exactly to define the different schools, for the purpose, no doubt, of regulating his taste. He evidently took little pleasure in this study, for it is soon abandoned. Rome, not only rich in works of art, but in which every stone is a record of past greatness, suggests to him his first work of imagination.

The author supposes that at the end of a long walk in the Eternal City, he climbs the Capitol from the side of the Campo Vaccino, and, overcome with fatigue, falls asleep on the ground. In his dream, Ancient Rome appears to him with all her past glory, her heroes, her power, and, above all, her liberty ; he sees defile before him all the great events, and all the great men of Roman antiquity, from the foundation of the Republic to the murder of Cæsar ; from the first Brutus to the accession of Augustus.

Suddenly he is awakened by a procession of barefooted friars ascending the steps of the Capitol on their way to their church, whilst a cowherd rings his bell to assemble the cattle browsing in the Forum.

"I arose," he continues, "and turned slowly towards my home, looking back from time to time, and saying to myself: Poor human nature ; what then art thou ? . . . . "

This sketch, which, to be filled up worthily, would have required all the taste and the imagination that he had, and also the learning which at that time he had not, was not the best adapted to the powers of Alexis de Tocqueville. Still, from this work, in which he dates the downfall of Rome from the day when she lost her liberty, the future character of the man may be predicted.

It is still more perceivable in the tour in Sicily, where, witnessing the misery inflicted on the people by a detestable government, he is led to reflect upon the primary conditions on which depends the decay or the prosperity of nations. His first intention was to describe only the external aspect of the country; but soon he paints the institutions and manners, and ideas take the place of descriptions.

He was finishing in Sicily his travels and his MS., when a royal order of the 5th of April, 1827, recalled him to France. He was appointed *juge auditeur*,* and attached in this capacity to the Tribunal of Versailles, of which town the Comte de Tocqueville was prefect. He

---

* We have in English no exact equivalent for the French terms. I have, therefore, put them into the text without attempting to translate them, hoping that they will be sufficiently explained by the following short sketch of the French system. There are, at present, in France about 6,300 judges, of whom about 2,500 belong to the *Tribunaux de Première Instance*, courts resembling our county courts, and about 360 in number. To every court is attached a *Ministère Public*, consisting of a *Procureur Impérial*, called, when the office was instituted by the law of the 27 *Ventôse an* 8, *Commissaire du Gouvernement*, and afterwards *Procureur du Roi*, and of his substitutes.

The functions of the *Procureur Impérial* are divided into those of the *Audience* and those of the *Parquet;* a distinction corresponding with the division of the duties of an English judge into those performed in court, and those performed in chambers. The substitutes of the *Procureur Impérial* are attached to him some of them as "à l'Audience," and some of them as "Au Parquet." The duties of the *Procureur Impérial* resemble those of our Attorney-General. He represents the Government. His substitutes act for him. Substitutes are also attached to every court, whose duty it is to act for any judge who is absent.

Those attached to the *Cour de Première Instance* were formerly called *Juges Auditeurs*, and are now called *Juges Suppléants*.

The same person may be both *Juge Suppléant* and also substitute of the *Procureur Impérial*. This was the case with M. de Tocqueville. He was *Juge Suppléant* of the *Cour de Première Instance* at Versailles,

was just one-and-twenty, the age required by law for entering the *magistrature*.

If Alexis de Tocqueville had been an ordinary man, his destiny would have been ready traced; his name, his family, his social position, his profession pointed out his path. Grandson of Malesherbes, he would have been sure of attaining the highest places in the *magistrature*, even without an effort, merely trusting to the lapse of time. Young, agreeable, connected with all the great families, fitted to aspire to the most brilliant alliances, of which many had already been proposed to him, he would have married some rich heiress. His life, confined by narrow prescribed limits, would have glided by, at any rate calmly and honorably, in the regular discharge of the duties of his office, in the comfortable enjoyment of a large salary, amidst the narrow but never-failing interests of the judicial bench, and in the sober, peaceful happiness of private life.

This scheme of existence was suited neither to his intellect nor to his disposition; and at starting he resolved to owe his advancement to himself alone; he sought, in the career on which he entered, an opening for the exercise of his talents. It is well known that the office of *juge auditeur*, (since converted into that of *juge suppléant*,) did not involve any very active duty, unless the officer was called to take part in the business of the *ministère public*. This employment Alexis de Tocqueville solicited and obtained. There he found among his colleagues M. Gustave de Beaumont, with

and was also *Substitut du Procureur du Roi* both in that court, and in the *Cour d'Assises*, or the criminal court of the town.

The Judges, and the persons forming the *Ministère Public*, constitute the *Magistrature*, and receive the title of Magistrates. — TRANSLATOR.

whom he commenced an intercourse which soon ripened into intimacy, and became afterwards the closest friendship.

Alexis de Tocqueville had but a few times occupied the seat of the *Ministère public* in the *cour d'assises* of Versailles, when he became distinguished. His grave style of speaking, his serious turn of thought, the ripeness of his judgment, and the superiority of his intelligence, raised him high above the ordinary level. His chief success was not with the crowd, but no important suffrage was ever wanting to him. No doubt was entertained of the brilliancy of his prospects, and more than one *président des assises* foretold his high advancement. It must be admitted, however, that in these predictions Malesherbes was thought of more than Montesquieu.

Yet, though all his qualities were admirably suited to the *magistrature*, that was not, perhaps, the calling most suited to his abilities. Alexis de Tocqueville, possessed in the highest degree the rare faculty of generalization; and, precisely because here lay his superiority, this was the constant tendency of his mind. The judge follows ordinarily an opposite tendency, which he derives from the habits of his profession, which store his mind with what is specific, and with particular cases. Tocqueville's thinking power was cramped by being imprisoned within the bounds of his peculiar duties. This irksomeness increased in proportion to the trifling character of the case. On the other hand, his talent increased in proportion to the importance of the cause, as if the bonds which fettered his intelligence were snapped or loosened.

Need it be added, that a mind so eager for independence and freedom often left the narrow sphere of law to enter the arena, at that time unreservedly open to all questions of general political interest? When their judicial labors were over, when the duties of the *audience* and *parquet* had been fulfilled, the two colleagues, now friends, united as much by the similarity of their tastes as by that of their ideas and opinions, threw themselves into studies of their own selection, especially those connected with history. And then what activity and emulation! how delightful was this laborious life, how sincere their pursuit of truth, and what aspirations after a future — after a future unbounded and cloudless, such as the passionate faith of youth reveals to ardent minds and generous hearts at a season of enthusiastic belief.

Those who did not witness that period (from 1827 to 1828), and who are acquainted only with the languor and the indifference of our own, will hardly comprehend its excitement. Twelve years had elapsed since the fall of the empire. For the first time France had known liberty, and had loved her. This liberty, a comfort to some, the greatest of blessings to others, had created for all a new country. Institutions were substituted for the will of one man; new habits arose amidst profound peace. The development of instincts, feelings, and wants, till then unnoticed, had contributed to awaken a new life in a regenerate nation. Yes, it must be acknowledged that, setting aside the old revolutionary and imperial parties whose liberalism was a lie, and in spite of the disagreements inseparable from freedom, France was at that time sincerely liberal, passionately attached to her new institutions, jealous in maintaining them, quickly alarmed by the dangers which threatened them, and ready to see in their destruction or preservation her own degradation or grandeur. Now, for the first time, the great problem of constitutional liberty was seriously stated in France.

The country seemed to feel the peril of the experiment.
With what anxiety she watched its progress! with what
emotion she looked for the slightest symptoms of a storm,
whether coming from the people or from the sovereign!
What interest was then taken in the smallest incidents
of public life — the arbitrary act of an official, a prose-
cution for libel, the verdict of a jury, a new book, a word
let fall in one of the Chambers, sometimes a newspaper
article!

It was precisely at this moment that the struggle between the parties which divided the Government as
much as the State, was about to assume the most angry
character. A few days more, and between the Government of the Restoration and its downfall, there would
be only the ministry of M. de Martignac, that last
attempt of the moderate party, whose success might have
spared France many misfortunes.

Alexis de Tocqueville looked on at this mighty struggle with the strong feelings common to the young men
of that period, to which he added a wisdom and a store
of observations which were rare. Some of his political
opinions became thenceforth fixed principles. Of these
the chief was, that every people, worthy of the name of
a nation, should participate in the conduct of its own
affairs, and that without free institutions there can never
be any real greatness for a country, or true dignity for
its rulers; his pride would not brook that he should ever
serve a master. This was for him a fundamental truth,
derived both from his head and from his heart. He hated
equally revolution and its offspring, absolute power. Admitting every form of free government, even the republican, he was firmly convinced that the form best suited
to the state of France and the habits of her people was

constitutional monarchy, in which the nation is represented, whilst the authority of the sovereign is preserved; and if he prayed for the maintenance of the elder branch of the Bourbons, it was because he believed its sway to be more favorable to liberty than that of a dynasty ushered in by a revolution.

While however he thought possible, and earnestly desired, the success of those who were endeavoring to reconcile the monarchy with liberty, Tocqueville saw clearly the difficulty of the enterprise, and the depth of the abyss already opening beneath the feet of our generation; and this gave a solemn meaning in his eyes to the great drama, the scenes of which were beginning to unfold themselves.

The ordinary superficial view never satisfied him; he went farther. Already a retrospective glance at our history gave him an insight into the great questions which he afterwards explored while seeking an explanation of his own time. He perceived that, notwithstanding the outward peace which reigned on the surface of French society, we were actually in a state of revolution. But what principally struck him was, the essentially democratic character of that revolution; it was the principle of equality pervading and domineering over the existing society. The great problems, which were to be the business of his life, which he would one day go to a new world to study, already rose to his mind.

How to reconcile equality, which separates and isolates men, with liberty? How to prevent a power, the offspring of democracy, from becoming absolute and tyrannical? Where to find a force able to contend against this power among a set of men, all equal, it is true, but all equally weak and impotent? Was the fate of modern society to be both democracy and despotism ? — These were the questions which from that time filled his thoughts, and disturbed his mind.

It has been said with truth, that Tocqueville was a thinker; he was so, and a thinker whose brain, always at work, never allowed itself a moment's rest. The term thinker would be, however, inappropriate, if applied to him in the ordinary sense of an abstract philosopher who takes pleasure in metaphysical speculations ; who loves knowledge for its own sake, and is enthusiastically attached to ideas and theories, independently of their application. Such is the real philosopher ; such was not Tocqueville, whose speculations had always a practical and definite object. In fact, he was little versed in mental science. He had not much taste for it ; he was imperfectly acquainted with its language ; and whether wrongly or rightly, its controversies always seemed to him more or less barren. At one time, in his early youth, his mind, impatient of doubt, had sought for help in metaphysics ; but in that quarter he had found no aid. His notes of this period bear witness to the painful efforts of his mind, when in the earnest search for truth, he discovers the imperfection and the impotence of the human reason ; he stops short, and seems to give up that chimera in the following sorrowful words : —

"There is no absolute truth ;" and a little farther on he writes still more sadly : —

"If I were desired to classify human miseries, I should do so in this order : —

1. Sickness.
2. Death.
3. Doubt."

As is the case with all minds seeking for light, he began with doubt; but like all strong characters he clung firmly to the principle, which he at length adopted as the best and truest, and made it the absolute rule of his conduct. Slow at first to perceive where his duty lay, he did not hesitate to follow it when once ascertained. He was as resolute in action as he had been slow in resolving. Essentially practical, in all intellectual speculations, he considered the past only as it affected the present, and foreign countries only with a view to his own. Thus his historical studies, and especially those relating to the first French revolution, were all treated in relation to the actual state of France, and to the events of the time, becoming every day more serious, and threatening fresh disturbances, perhaps even another revolution.

This revolution broke out. Without hesitation, but without enthusiasm, Alexis de Tocqueville joined the ranks of the government of 1830. He possessed already a faculty which he always retained, that of seeing quicker and farther than others. The excitement to which a great popular movement gives birth, the enthusiasm, the pleasurable feelings which usually welcome a new *régime*, — to none of these things was he sensible. He considered the revolution of July as a calamity; he feared lest a prince thus raised to the throne should rush into war in order to be feared, or be weakly pacific in order to be pardoned. Still the constitution of 1830 was the second, perhaps the last chance offered to France of the establishment of constitutional monarchy and of political freedom. He could not refuse his adhesion; he gave it with sadness, and six months afterwards he started for the United States.

No powerful link kept him in France, and an irresistible curiosity drove him to America. He thought nothing of his prospects in the magistracy. What chance had the son of a prefect under the restoration of receiving from the government of July a promotion, which the government of the restoration had not bestowed on the grandson of Malesherbes, after four years' service as *juge auditeur* at Versailles? On the other hand, the revolution which he had just witnessed, the violent scenes which it had occasioned, the passions which it had excited, and the strange theories which it had brought to light, served only to increase the interest and the weight of the questions which disturbed his mind. Every day he became more and more convinced that France, in irresistibly drifting into democracy, was also drifting into its perils. He determined to visit the only great country in which those dangers have been conquered, and where perfect equality reigns side by side with liberty. He communicated his scheme to his late colleague at Versailles, then *substitut du Procureur du Roi* in Paris, who was charmed with the proposal. Obstacles, however, stood in their way: as magistrates they both required leave of absence, and a legitimate cause for obtaining it. At that time, as is always the case immediately after a revolution, all innovation was held in honor, and a reform of real but of secondary importance (that of the prisons) attracted public attention. A penitentiary system, which had proved successful in the United States, was talked of. The two young magistrates presented to the then Minister of the Interior, the Comte de Montalivet, a paper in which, after setting forth the question, they offered to study it on the spot, if they might be sent on an official mission. It was granted to them; and the Minister of Justice having consented, the two friends set out with a leave obtained in due form. It has often been said that this mission was the cause of Alexis de Tocqueville's expedition. It was in truth only the pretext. His real and long premeditated object was to study the customs and institutions of American society.

CHAPTER II.

THE AMERICAN EXPEDITION.

ALTHOUGH the inspection of prisons was the pretence rather than the purpose of the journey of the two travellers, they gave to the subject as much serious attention as if it had been their sole object.

They had scarcely reached New York (on the 10th of May, 1831) when they zealously proceeded to discharge the official duties of their mission. Sing-Sing and Auburn in the State of New York, Wethersfield in Connecticut, Walnut-Street and Cherry-Hill in Pennsylvania, all the establishments to which these places have given a name, and many others less celebrated in the annals of penitentiaries, were successively the objects of their conscientious examination. A single example will give an idea of the importance attached by them to this task: the fact which we are about.to mention will likewise throw a curious light on Tocqueville's power of memory,

When they visited at Philadelphia the famous prison Cherry-Hill, where the system of solitary confinement both by day and by night was in full practice, they thought that the way to judge of its effects was to examine not only the physical condition of the prisoners, but besides, and above all, their moral state. It was true that the entry of the Director on every one of them was, "behavior, perfect" — "conduct, excellent;" but the French commissioners could not help asking, what breach

of discipline was possible to a prisoner confined alone between four walls, without any contact with his fellows?
Permission, therefore, was asked to visit and converse
with the convicts separately, without the presence of any
official, in the hope that they would reveal their secret
impressions, and the actual state of their feelings. Leave
was granted, and Alexis de Tocqueville undertook this
delicate duty, unassisted by his companion, who thought,
with him, that a confidence which might be made to one
would not be made to two. He devoted a fortnight to
this minute inquiry, commenced at first from a feeling of
duty, but continued with extreme interest, sometimes
struck by the curious effects of seclusion on the human
mind, and at other times deeply affected by the moral
wretchedness unveiled to him. He often was led on by
the interest of these *tête à têtes* to prolong them beyond
the hours fixed by the discipline of the establishment, and
was always detained by the poor prisoners, ingenious to
prolong the, for them, rare opportunity of conversing with
a man, though they knew not with how great a man.
Tocqueville recorded on the spot, and afterwards revised,
all that passed at these interviews. Soon, however, after
quitting Philadelphia, he sought for these notes in order to
show them to his colleague, but could not find them. He
looked again, but in vain. At last he was convinced that
they were lost. He then put together all that he could
recall, and so deep was the impression which these secret
conversations had made on him, that in a few hours he
had restored to paper every one, without confusion or a
single omission. The next day, when no longer looking
for his notes, he found them. On comparing his recollections with these notes it was surprising to see how they
corresponded, and with what prodigious fidelity his mem-

ory had reproduced the whole that had passed. A few details only had been forgotten, but the leading thought was always there. In the work on the penitentiary system which was afterwards published, these notes appear under the title of "*Enquête sur le Penitencier de Phila-delphie.*" (Inquiry into the Penitentiary of Philadelphia.) Alexis de Tocqueville had no memory for words nor for figures, but he possessed the strongest possible remembrance of ideas; when once grasped his mind retained them forever.

The Inquiry on Penitentiaries being over, Tocqueville turned, it must be owned, with still more eagerness to the study of more general questions; and, assuredly, the political men by whom he had in France been charged with a special and official mission, had no reason to complain of his laying it aside for a time to fulfil the more comprehensive mission which he had imposed upon himself.

A description of this expedition cannot be expected in these pages.* It extended throughout the American Union. Alexis de Tocqueville began by studying New England, of which Boston is the first City; as, in order to have a thorough knowledge of a river, it is necessary to explore its source. Such a narrative would alone fill a whole volume, and would far exceed the limit assigned to this work. Nor could the author record the

---

* Independently of the motives here stated for abridging the account of this journey, there is another which will be, perhaps, better understood by the reader, namely, the success of the book, published by M. Ampère, under the name "*Promenade en Amérique,*" in which, whatever can be suggested by a view of the United States has been detailed in the same spirit as that of the author of this memoir, with a vivacity which belongs to a direct narrative, and which recollection cannot supply.

travels of Tocqueville without describing also his own, for their lives were at that time inseparably united. Might he not thus be carried towards a rock which he is peculiarly anxious to avoid? In spite of the charm of this expedition, connected as it is with the first impressions, and imbued with all the poetry of his youth, he has resolved to set aside all personal recollections, and to think only of the friend, the remembrance of whom ought alone to occupy him. The interest of Tocqueville's journey consists, moreover, less in what he saw, than in his manner of seeing. His mode of observing was peculiar. It is impossible to imagine the activity of mind and body, which, like a burning fever, preyed upon him incessantly. Everything was to him matter for observation. He arranged beforehand in his head all the questions that he wished to solve, to each of which the incidents and conversations of each day bore reference. He never failed to note, then and there, every idea that occurred to him. For he had remarked that the first impression gives itself utterance almost always in an original shape, which, once lost, is not recovered. It is interesting to read now the little note-books which he always carried about with him to receive his first impressions. The germs of the leading thoughts of his work on Democracy are to be found in them; and more than one is transcribed literally. These memoranda are few 'and short. He observed much and noted little.

Whilst Alexis de Tocqueville was travelling over North America to study its institutions, and to penetrate to the very heart of the people, an Englishman, the pleasantest companion possible, was visiting the same country, with no other aim than to discover the varieties of game peculiar to the climate; and especially the different races of wild ducks. There were also two very distinguished Frenchmen, whose society was very agreeable, looking out for picturesque subjects for landscapes.

Of those who passed through, seeing nothing and looking for nothing, not even for wild ducks, it is not necessary to speak. These different modes of travelling are certainly equally fair and lawful; they are not mentioned here in order to censure those who travel for bodily exercise or as an agreeable pastime, but only to show that Alexis de Tocqueville travelled differently. Undoubtedly, between the man who produces a book from his travels, and another who brings back an album, there is an intermediate class neither so earnest as the former, nor so frivolous as the latter. But there is scarcely any traveller, however serious his aim, who does not at times seek for amusement or indulge in repose. Tocqueville, when travelling, never rested.

Rest was foreign to his nature; and whether his body were actively employed or not, his mind was always at work. While he never shrank from any effort which might diminish or use up his strength, he never could be persuaded to do anything to repair it. It never occurred to him to consider an excursion as an amusement, or conversation as relaxation. The two travelling companions conversed incessantly; and if what our good Ballanche says be true, that to discuss a subject well it is necessary to agree, they thought so much the same on all things, that their conversation must have been profitable. But from the first it took a serious turn, and thus could not be considered as rest. For Tocqueville, the most agreeable conversation was that which was the most useful. The bad day was the day lost or ill-spent. The smallest loss of time was unpleasant to him. This notion kept him in a constant state of tension; and in his travels it became such a passion, that he never reached a place without first assuring himself of the means of leaving it, so that one of his friends said that his departure always preceded his arrival.

There are countries in which the most industrious traveller finds, even in spite of himself, some occasions of rest and relaxation. For example: it sometimes happens that he meets one of the frivolous idlers, common enough in Europe, who seek for society in order to consume the time which they know not how to employ, and whose presence, although irritating, forces the brain to rest. In a country where nobody is idle and everybody sensible, Tocqueville could not profit by this salutary diversion. The admirable and universal good sense of the Americans attracted and captivated him. It was for him a mine of inestimable value, which he worked without ceasing; following thus impetuously, without halt or rest, the bent of his inclination.

And when one recollects how frail and delicate was the body which contained this ardent soul and restless spirit, one asks how such physical weakness could sustain so much mental activity! And it is even less easy to understand when one considers that, instead of sparing as much as he could this feeble body, he seemed to delight in submitting it to the severest, and even to the most dangerous trials.

It was thus, that one day, in spite of the obstacles which ought to have stopped him, he resolved to penetrate into the far west till he should reach the wilderness.

It was not on his part a mere vague curiosity — a mere natural desire to go where no one has gone before. His resolution had a more serious motive. Convinced that one of the first conditions of prosperity in America is the immense extent of space as yet unoccupied, he wished at least to make a *réconnaissance* in these regions, — to advance in the forest to the boundary of civilization, — to see the last pioneers and the first wild Indians.

Every journey is easy when one follows the beaten track; out of it there are always difficulties. For a young, robust man, like his travelling companion, such an enterprise, of course, was no sort of risk; but for health so delicate as his it was a real danger. The expedition could not possibly be accomplished unless by taking very long journeys, almost always on horseback, without stopping on the way; it was necessary to pass whole days without rest, and nights without sleep or even shelter. There were to be no more regular meals, no more inns, no more roads. These were certainly reasons sufficient for not undertaking such a campaign; and each one was urged upon him in the most pressing terms. But no resistance withstood his vehemence. It can scarcely be imagined how imperiously, when he wished for a thing, he proved to others and persuaded himself that it was the most reasonable in the world. The thought of danger never stopped him. He often showed his contempt for it, not only in America, but in his other travels — in England, in Ireland, in Algeria, and in Germany — even at times when his failing health required extra care and precaution. However, at the period we speak of, he was right; his excursion to the wilderness was accomplished, though not without much fatigue, yet without great detriment to his health; and none of his travels, perhaps, produced on him such vivid and durable impressions.

It would be a great mistake to suppose that Tocqueville, whom, in his travels, we have seen searching chiefly for ideas, remained insensible and cold before the sublime scenes of nature. On the contrary, no one was more affected and attracted by them. While all his intellectual faculties disposed him to meditation, another tendency of his mind inclined him to be a dreamer; and it was never but by an effort of will that he roused himself from the state of passive impressions to reënter that of active ideas. It was judgment alone that prompted this effort, for the reverie to which he was inclined was for him always full of melancholy, and for that reason he fled from it. Intellectual activity was his refuge from troublesome or painful images. But never, at any period of his life, did Tocqueville allow himself to be so carried away by external impressions as under the irresistible charm of the great deserts of America, where all combined to enchant the senses, and to set thought to sleep. He has described these impressions in a little work called "A Fortnight in the Wilderness," which the reader will find at the end of this memoir. These charming pages have never before been printed, owing to a circumstance which, perhaps, it is best to disclose here.

Whilst Tocqueville gave himself up to the study of American institutions, the occupation of his travelling companion was to collect a few sketches of manners, which he afterwards framed, with more or less success, in a novel entitled " Marie ; " in it he naturally had described the forests, the solitudes, and the very wilderness visited by the two friends ; he had made it the stage of his drama, he had transported thither his own emotions, and had thus attempted to convert his fiction into something real.

When later, however, Tocqueville published the second part of his work, describing the effects of democracy upon manners, he thought of appending this " Fortnight in the Wilderness " to his book ; but when, as usual, he read it aloud to his friend whom he always consulted, the author of " Marie " imprudently predicted for it a far greater success than that attained by his own novel.   At the time Tocqueville said nothing ; but he had made up his mind, and nothing could ever induce him to publish what might trespass on the ground chosen by his friend, or appear as a rival to his work.   There were in his friendship a refinement and a delicacy which demanded the greatest circumspection.

At the end of this memoir, immediately before the " Fortnight in the Wilderness," is placed a pamphlet of only a few pages, published here for the first time, under the title of " Excursion to the Lake Oneïda," and taken, also, from the memoranda of this expedition.   It is an episode of the same kind.   These fragments will show Tocqueville to the public in a new light.   But his intimate friends alone can fully appreciate the sensibility and the poetry of his impressionable nature, united as they were with an intellect of such depth and clearness.

At a later period in their journey, when his health was expected to run no risk, it was exposed to much severer trials.   Winter was approaching, and the travellers had resolved to reach the South before its arrival.   Their plan was to reach the Ohio near Pittsburg, there to embark in a steamer, and to descend the Ohio and the Mississippi to New Orleans ; an extremely simple and easy journey in ordinary weather, even before the existence of railways.   But this year winter came a month

earlier than usual. Besides, in that country the extremes
of heat and cold are great, and succeed each other without interval. A few days after their departure from
Baltimore, where summer still lingered, they found the
Alleghanies covered with the frost and snow which were
to last for the whole winter. But, in order to shorten
this account, which is meant to be only a sketch, it will
be as well, in the absence of the notes of Alexis de Tocqueville, in this instance missing, to reproduce *verbatim*
those which his travelling companion jotted down in
pencil day by day.

"1st *Dec.* 1831. — Left Wheeling, ten miles from Pittsburg, by the steamer. The Ohio is covered with loose
ice; its banks with snow. The navigation is said to be
dangerous at night, especially in a dark night. However, we proceed . . . . towards midnight, an alarm!
— all lost! — it is the captain's voice! We have struck
on a rock (Burlington Bar); our vessel has split; she is
sinking every moment. Awful sensation! — 200 passengers on board, and only two long-boats, each capable of
holding ten or twelve people. The water mounts higher
and higher; the cabins are already full. Admirable
coolness of the American women: there are fifty, and
not one scream in the face of advancing death. Tocqueville and I cast one glance upon the Ohio, which at this
part is more than a mile in breadth, and carries down
large masses of loose ice: we squeeze each other's hands
as a parting token. . . . Suddenly the vessel ceases to
sink: her hull is jammed on the rock which she struck.
What has saved her is the depth itself of the injury, and
the rapidity with which the water, upon rushing in,
makes her settle on the rock. . . . .

"No more danger . . . . but what is to become of us, stranded in the middle of the river, like convicts on a hulk?

"Another steamer, the *William Parsons*, passes and takes us on board . . . . we continue our voyage . . . . The 2d December reach Cincinnati; hasten to quit it again, driven away by the cold. . . . . The 3d, leave Cincinnati; bitter cold. 4th, our vessel is stopped by the loose ice. We pass twenty-four hours in a little creek, where we have intrenched ourselves to wait for the thaw. It does not come. The cold increases.

"The captain determines to put us on shore. We reach it by gradually breaking the ice, and thus opening a passage for our vessel.

"We land at West Port, a little village in Kentucky, about twenty-five miles from Louisville.

"Impossible to find either a carriage or horses to take us to Louisville; we are forced to walk; our luggage is thrown into a cart, which we follow. We walk all day through woods, in half a foot of snow. America is still a vast forest.

"On the evening of the 7th December, arrive at Louisville. Here the same difficulty. The Ohio is not more navigable than at West Port. What is to be done? retrace our steps? revisit places already seen? Not to be thought of. But how to proceed?

"We are saved. We are told that we can travel southwards by land, till we reach a point where the navigation of the Mississippi is never impeded by ice. Memphis is suggested to us, a little town in Tennessee, on the left of the Mississippi, about forty miles off.

"On the 9th, leave Louisville in the Nashville stage-coach, a journey of two days and two nights. On arriving at Nashville, we hear that the Cumberland (a tributary of the Ohio) is frozen over.

"*December* 11.—Departure from Nashville. As we proceed farther south, the cold becomes sharper. Never, they say, in the memory of man, has anything been known like it. So those who come but once are always told.

"Ten degrees below freezing.* The cold continues to increase. Our stage-coach turns into an open *char-à-banc*. Frightful roads. Precipitous descents. No regular highway. The road is only an opening cut in the forest. The stumps of the trees not completely cut away, so that they form so many impediments over which we jolt incessantly. Only thirty miles a day. 'You have, have you not, very bad roads in France?' says an American to me. 'Yes, sir, and you have, have you not very good roads in America?' He does not understand me; American conceit.

"After Nashville, not one town on the road; only a few villages scattered here and there till we reach Memphis.

"*December* 11.—A brace and a wheel, and then an axletree broken. Half the way on foot. We bewail our sad fate. 'Complain away, then,' we are told. 'On the day before yesterday one traveller broke his arm here, and another his leg.'

"On the 12th, cold still more severe; we cross the Tennessee by the ferry; it is covered with huge masses of ice. Tocqueville benumbed with cold; he shivers all over. His appetite is gone; his head affected; impossible to go further; we must stop. . . . . Where? what is to be done? No inn on the road. Extreme perplex-

* Réaumur. — Tr.

ity.   The stage goes on. . . . . Here is a house at last;
Sandy Bridge is its name — the Log House! no matter,
we are set down.

"*December* 13.—What a day — what a night!   Rough
logs of oak piled up form the walls of the room in which
Tocqueville's bed is placed.   It freezes hard enough to
split stones.   I light a monstrous fire ; the flame crackles
on the hearth, fanned by the draft which blows in on all
sides.   The moon shines on us through the crevices of
the logs.   Tocqueville gets warm only by burying himself under the blankets and the multitude of clothes which
I heap upon him.   Our host will not help us.   Entire
isolation and neglect.   What to do ?   What will happen
if the illness increases ?   What is the nature of the illness ?   Where find a doctor ?   The nearest is more than
thirty miles off ; it would take more than two days to go
thither and back ; what should I find on my return ?   The
name of our hosts is Mr. and Mrs. Harris, small proprietors in the Tennessee ; they own slaves ; and, as slave-
owners, they never work.   The husband shoots, walks
about, rides on horseback — gives himself the airs of a
gentleman ; they are little aristocrats on the feudal system, and they dispense hospitality at the rate of a dollar
a day.

"*December* 14.— Tocqueville better.   He will not have
an illness, but he is too weak to leave ; difficulty of finding anything fit for him to eat.   Prodigious diplomacy
employed to obtain from Mrs. Harris a rabbit killed by
her husband.   I give it to my invalid instead of the
everlasting bacon.

"*December* 15.—Great progress ; on the 16th Tocqueville quite well ; his appetite returned ; impatience to
quit as soon as possible this inhospitable place.   The

stage-coach between Nashville and Memphis passes. What a vehicle! Tocqueville climbs into it not without difficulty. The cold is still intense. We travel two days and two nights; renewed symptoms, painful, but with no evil consequences.

"*December* 17. — Reach Memphis. Alas! the Mississippi, too, is covered with ice, and navigation interrupted. Mémphis! — about as large as Beaumont-la-Chartre. What a falling off. Nothing to see — neither men nor things. We roam about the forests of Tennessee; delight of Tocqueville, who kills two parrots with magnificent plumage. We find Shakespeare and Milton in a log hut.

"*December* 24. — The frost suddenly breaks. In the evening a steamer (the *Louisville*) appears, going down the river. In a few days she takes us to New Orleans, where we now are on the 1st of January, 1832."

The remembrance of Sandy Bridge and of a few disastrous days would not now be without a certain charm, if, though as yet Tocqueville does not appear to have had even the seeds of the deadly malady by which he was prematurely cut off, one did not perceive the symptoms of the delicate constitution which was always on the point of breaking down, and which so often stood in his way.

CHAPTER III.

RETURN FROM AMERICA—RETIRES FROM THE MAGISTRACY—
DEMOCRACY IN AMERICA (FIRST PART)—MARRIAGE—ENTRANCE
INTO THE INSTITUTE—THE ACADEMY OF MORAL AND POLITI-
CAL SCIENCE—BECOMES A MEMBER OF THE ACADEMY OF
FRANCE—PUBLICATION OF THE SECOND PART OF THE DEMOC-
RACY—IS ELECTED DEPUTY.

AFTER having passed a year in the United States,
Tocqueville returned to France. From that time his
object was to write the book for which he had already
formed the plan and collected the materials. His attention was diverted for some time by the penitentiary
question, of which our two colleagues had to render an
account to the government and to the public. They did
so in the form of a report addressed to the minister, and
in a book which was their first joint composition and
publication.*

The resumption of his magisterial duties at Versailles
might have proved an obstacle, or at least a rival, to the
progress of the work. An accident removed it. His
friend, M. de Beaumont, who had returned to his official
post, refused to speak on an occasion when the part which

---

* Under the title of *The Penitentiary System in the United States,
and its application in France*, 1 vol. 8vo.; 2d edition, 2 vols. 8vo.; 3d
edition, 1 vol. 8vo. Translated into German by Dr. Julius of Berlin,
and into English by Francis Lieber of Boston, the distinguished author of many publications, among others of a book entitled *Political
Ethics*. He is now a member of the Institute.

the *ministère public* had to play appeared to him discreditable, and had, for this reason, been dismissed. Tocqueville, considering himself affected by the blow which struck his friend, immediately sent in his resignation in these terms: —

"Toulon, May 21st, 1832.

"Monsieur le Procureur-General,

"Being now at Toulon, engaged in inspecting the Bagnio and other prisons of the town, it was only to-day that I learnt, from the *Moniteur* of the 16th of May, the severe and, I venture to say, unjust sentence pronounced by *M. le Garde des Sceaux* on M. G. de Beaumont.

"Long united in intimate friendship with the person who has just been dismissed from his functions, whose opinions I hold, and whose conduct I approve, I think myself bound voluntarily to share his lot, and to abandon with him a career in which neither active service nor upright conduct is a security against unmerited disgrace.

"I have the honor, therefore, to request you, *M. le Procureur-Général*, to have the goodness to lay before *M. le Garde des Sceaux* my resignation of the office of *juge suppléant* at the Tribunal of Versailles.

"I have the honor to be," &c.

In fact this proceeding was a greater loss to the magistracy than to Tocqueville. By giving up his office he became once more absolute master of his time, of which he was about to make such admirable use.

He composed his two first volumes of the *Democracy in America* from the year 1832 to 1834. These two years were probably the happiest of his life. Not only he devoted himself with ardor to his book, but he was able to do so without a single anxiety.

Free from all professional duties, not yet married, but already attached to her who was to be his wife; his mind at rest, and his heart satisfied; he was in a state so rare and always so short-lived, in which a man, freed from every obligation, every restraint, every care, taking part in the affairs of the world and of his domestic circle only as much as he chooses, free, in short, without being solitary, is in full possession of his intellectual independence.

The life of Tocqueville during these two years, austere yet full of passionate excitement, could not be contemplated without deep interest. He took refuge during the whole day in a lodging, of which the secret was known to few, where he gave himself up to the intense and unmixed satisfaction of intellectual creation. Separated by only a few moments from the torrent of success which was soon to carry him away — to delight and, at the same time, to enslave him; he was at this time rejoicing, without a care, in the seclusion which belongs only to obscurity; as great as he ever became, but unknown to the world and to himself, full of hope, though not without a certain misgiving, on the point of being illustrious, though still unknown. No work of genius has ever been created in the midst of the distractions of the world. Woe to the writer who cannot raise himself above the earth, and create for himself an atmosphere of thought! That pure atmosphere Tocqueville found in his self-made existence, between the labor which elevated his mind and the tender feeling which impassioned his heart.

The two first volumes of the *Democracy in America* appeared in the month of January, 1835.

An analysis of this book is not within our limits. It

is in the hands of every one, and may be judged by every one.* Here it is enough to record its immense success — a success which, perhaps, cannot be compared with any other in our time. Every one knows the remark of M. Royer-Collard : " Since Montesquieu there has been nothing like it : " and, " twenty years later, we repeat the same judgment," said, on a great occasion, a celebrated historian and distinguished statesman — M. de Barante.† The most remarkable characteristic of this success was its universality. There is, perhaps, no other instance of a book which, addressed to the highest intellects, has made so much progress with the public in general. The first sign of popular success appeared in the office in which the book was printed. The workmen engaged in its production, from the overseer and the correctors of the press down to the simple compositors, bestowed upon their work unusual care, expressed to the author their sympathy, and seemed eager for the success of a book, to which each thought it an honor to have contributed. It was a good omen, and all the more encouraging, as the editor, an intelligent man, who could not, of course, have read his MS., had consented, with extreme reluctance, and on the refusal of another publisher, to bring out the book.

Edition followed edition with incredible rapidity, almost all in the cheap form suitable to an extensive demand ; and the book has now reached the fourteenth. The success still continues ; and if the expression of a sincere conviction be permitted to the author of these

---

* See the excellent work of M. de Laboulaye on the " Life and Writings of A. de Tocqueville," and the Criticism on M. de Lacy. — *Variétés Littéraires*, vol. ii. s. 67.

† Historical Society of France. Meeting of the 2d May, 1859.

pages, he ventures to say that from year to year its reputation will increase ; and that it will find in its duration
the consecration which belongs exclusively to works of
genius.

No surprise need be excited by the fact that this success made all parties desirous of appropriating the book
and its author. Some declared Tocqueville to be a demo-
crat; others said that he was an aristocrat.   He was neither. Born in the ranks of the aristocracy, but with a
love for liberty, Tocqueville had found modern society in
the hands of the democracy ; and, considering this to be an
established fact, which it was no longer possible to question, he thought that to the absolute equality thus produced it was essential to add liberty; for without liberty
equality has no check to its impulses, no counterpoise to
its oppressions; and he judged this union so necessary,
that he saw no aim in the present time more important
to pursue, and to it he therefore devoted his whole life.
This is the leading idea of the book ; and, we may add,
of those which followed it.

All great political writers have written with some
such object in view. That of Tocqueville was to unite
liberty to the already existing equality; and he not
only searched eagerly in a democratic country for the
fundamental conditions of liberty, but it may even be
said that he discovered and pointed them out. In the
lowest order a municipal power firmly rooted, between
the commonalty and the ruling order, trial by jury,
and a judiciary power strong enough to arbitrate with
steady impartiality between the rulers and the people ;
local privileges placed out of the reach of the perils
which always threatened the general political freedom,
so that in case of its overthrow these shall not perish

with it. He was the first to understand and point out the protection afforded to liberty by judicial institutions, and the peculiar importance of these institutions to a democracy. All this is prominent in every page of his *Democracy in America.*

The brilliant success of the *Democracy* was not confined to France; it was equally striking abroad; and the book was immediately translated into every language. But what is above all worthy of remark, is the sensation which it excited in the very country which it described and criticised. The Americans could not understand how a stranger, after a residence among them of only a year, could, with such marvellous sagacity, master their institutions and manners; enter into the spirit of them; and exhibit, in a clear and logical form, what they themselves had, till then, only vaguely apprehended. There is not one eminent man in the United States who does not acknowledge that M. de Tocqueville revealed to him the constitution of his country, and the *esprit des lois* of America.

And it is no less worthy of remark, that while he produced this impression on the most democratic people in the world, he found equal favor in the most aristocratic, namely, in England. There also his book met, in every rank of society, in periodicals, in drawing-rooms, in the Houses of Parliament even, with universal approbation, of which he received the tokens in person; for, at this time (May, 1835), with the companion of his American tour, he visited England. He had done so two years before (in 1833); he had been received with kindness, but with the ordinary kindness due to his name and to his letters of introduction. The comparison between these two receptions measured the revolution in his existence made by a single day, and he delighted in a change for which he had to thank only himself.

Such was the moral weight which the publication of Tocqueville's book had given to him, that a House of Commons committee on bribery at elections took advantage of his presence in London to obtain the benefit of his information. His evidence on this occasion was quoted, five months afterwards, in the House by Sir R. Peel, in support of his own opinions, and appealed to at the same time by the other side of the House.

One characteristic of Tocqueville's book, which belongs to all great intellectual works is, to take a place above the narrow views of party, the accidents of the day, and the passions of the moment. For this reason, it was from the beginning, and will long continue to be, quoted as an authority by the holders of the most opposite opinions; and this explains the success obtained by it in the country where aristocracy has the ascendant, as well as in that where democracy rules.

Tocqueville derived another advantage from his visit to England; it was for him the beginning of personal relations with some of her most distinguished men, with many of whom he formed a friendship that lasted during his whole life.

On his return from this visit, full of lively impressions and flattering recollections, he married, in the month of October, 1835, the young English lady, Miss Mary Mottley, with whom he had long been deeply in love. Thus two great events took place in the same year — the success of his first book, an immense success, which threw him at once into public life; and marriage, which settled the destiny of his private life.

Of a man's own acts there is not one that exercises a greater influence on all the rest of his life than his marriage; nor is there any which more fully lays open the depth of his real character. Miss Mottley had scarcely any fortune, and the worldly-wise did not spare their objections. These objections acquired new force from the recent success of Tocqueville, which added one more advantage to those of his birth and fortune. But he did not hesitate. Intellectual superiority would, indeed, hardly be worth having, if the moral feelings and character were to remain on the ordinary level. Although Tocqueville's reason had imbibed democratic notions, he retained aristocratic sentiments; and there is none so aristocratic as a contempt for money. Though sensible of its value as a means of action in this world, Tocqueville considered money as of secondary interest. He did not admit the possibility of risking for it honor and happiness; and differing from the majority, who in marriage seek chiefly to make a good bargain, he wisely and proudly followed the dictates of his mind and heart. He did not act thus from mere impulse; he was deeply convinced of the moral influence exercised over the entire existence of a man by the character of her whom he has chosen for a companion. He knew that in public as well as in private life, the most upright conscience and steadfast independence are liable to totter if they have not at their side an auxiliary force to rest upon; he knew that a fall is certain to the man who allies himself with weakness; in fact, he knew himself, and that he could only find happiness in union with a wife who would merge her existence in his, and who would entirely unite her life to his, to his tastes, pursuits, and convictions, so far removed from the tastes and convictions of the world.

He had discovered all these qualities in her whom he loved, and from that moment his determination was irrevocable.   How often has he said to the writer of these lines, that his marriage, censured by the prudent, had been the most sensible action of his life.   Perhaps the friend to whom he confided his most secret thoughts, best knows all that the tender and faithful companion of his life was to him during a union of twenty-five years; sympathizing intensely with his success, cheering him when he lost heart, soothing and tranquillizing him when he was in sorrow or depression; full of care, devotion, and energy in all his trials.

A year after his marriage, on his return from a tour of some months, which he had been making with his wife in Switzerland, he wrote to the oldest friend he had,* a letter, of which one passage proves, better than anything which could be said here, his opinion of her to whom his fate was united.

"Nacqueville,† October 10th, 1836.

" . . . . I cannot tell you the inexpressible charm which I have found in living so continually with Marie, nor the treasures which I was perpetually discovering in her heart.   You know that in travelling, still more than at other times, my temper is uneven, irritable, and impatient.   I scolded her frequently, and almost always unjustly; and on each occasion I discovered in her inexhaustible springs of tenderness and indulgence.   And then, I cannot describe to you the happiness yielded in

---

* Count Louis de Kergorlay.

† Nacqueville, near Cherbourg, is the château of Tocqueville's eldest brother, Count Hippolyto de Tocqueville, with whom he was then staying.

the long run by the habitual society of a woman in whose
soul all that is good in your own is reflected naturally,
and even improved. When I say or do a thing which
seems to me to be perfectly right, I read immediately in
Marie's countenance an expression of proud satisfaction,
which elevates me still higher ; and so, when my conscience
reproaches me, her face instantly clouds over. Although
I have great power over her mind, I see with pleasure
that she awes me ; and as long as I love her as I now do,
I am sure that I shall never allow myself to be drawn
into anything wrong.

"Not a day passes when I do not thank Heaven for
having thrown Marie in my way, or without my thinking
that if anything can give happiness on earth, it is the
possession of such a partner. . . . "

What he then felt and wrote, he felt and wrote still
more strongly twenty-five years later, when, in the midst
of many vanished dreams and disappointed expectations,
his only complete and lasting satisfaction was that afforded
by his marriage.

In the mean time the success of the *Democracy*, confirmed by the public, soon received a more distinguished
sanction. It carried its author to the Institute, which
may be said to have opened wide to him her doors. Already in 1836, the Academy of France, that every year
crowns the works of the greatest moral utility, had on
this account accorded to the *Democracy in America* an
extraordinary prize raised from 6,000 fr., which in general is the maximum, to 8,000, in order to mark an especial distinction.* In 1838, Tocqueville was elected a

* At the sitting of the 11th of August, 1836. The prize was award-
ed on the report of the Villemain, who thus concluded an analysis of

member of the Academy of Moral and Political Science,
and the circumstances of his election prove the eager
desire of the Institute to receive him into their body.
The vacancy to be filled was that made by M. de Romi-
guière, who belonged by his labors to the philosophical
section. The vacant seat was therefore in that section,
and Tocqueville, whose claims were of another order, did
not seem the man to fill it. To prevent objection and
disappointment, the Academy removed one of its members, M. Jouffroy, from the moral section, in which he
was well placed, to what suited him perhaps still better,
the philosophical section. A seat in the moral section
was thus rendered vacant, and Alexis de Tocqueville,
well fitted for it by his talents and his works, was called
upon to fill it. But in 1841, when the death of M. de
Cessac left unoccupied a *fauteuil* in the Academy of
France, the member elected was Tocqueville.*

The publication, in 1840, of the last two volumes of
the *Democracy in America*, which complete the work by
describing the influence of democracy on manners, now
raised still higher Tocqueville's reputation and claims.

I have abstained from criticising the first two volumes.
I shall be equally reserved as to these. It is enough to
state, that they cost their author much more time and
much more exertion than their predecessors. He felt the
obligations imposed by success. He resolved not merely
not to sink, but to rise. He used to say that a writer

the *Democracy*. "Such is M. de Tocqueville's book: talent, good
sense, elevation, a simple, unaffected style, and the love of virtue elo-
quently expressed, are its characteristics; and they give the Academy
little hope of crowning a work with similar claims."

* In the *Moniteur* of the 22d of April, 1842, may be found the remarkable speech, on his reception, by Alexis de Tocqueville, and the
reply of Count Molé.

ought to aim, not at making a good book, but an excellent
book—a maxim, not of vanity, but of severe self-exaction,
which he applied as much to his lightest as to his most
important compositions. In preparing these volumes, he
gave still deeper meditation to his matter, and still more
exquisite polish to his style. He had written admirably
before he had reflected deeply on the secrets of the art
of writing. Glimpses of them he got while he was working. He was convinced that they must be thoroughly
mastered by the writer whose works are to live. He
felt that every creation of the mind, great or small, is a
work of art, and that the force and the effect of a thought
depend on the words in which it is clothed. In the first
two volumes, Tocqueville had frequently been a great
artist without appearing to be one. In the last two he is
always one, but not without a visible effort. If the effort,
however, be visible, so is the fruit. The style approaches
nearer to perfection. In his earnest ambition to attain
that object, he reperused the masters of style, especially
the great men of the seventeenth century. He tried to
discover the rules by which each of them was guided;
but there was no one whom he studied with more perseverance and more interest than Pascal. The two minds
were made for one another. The duty of constant
thought imposed on his reader by Pascal was a charm to
Tocqueville. He perhaps owes to this predilection the
only blame to which he has exposed himself, that of
giving his reader no rest. In some parts of the last two
volumes of *La Démocratie*, thought is linked to thought
without an interval for repose or relaxation. In the first
two volumes, Tocqueville was not open to this charge.
In his animated description of American institutions, facts
are inseparably mixed with speculations. An English-

man, author of an interesting work on the United States, was complimenting him on this part of the work; "What I especially admire," he said, "is, that while treating so great a subject, you have so thoroughly avoided general ideas."

There could not be a greater mistake; but Tocqueville was delighted. It showed to him that the abstractions with which his book is filled, had been so skilfully presented in a concrete form, that an acute, though certainly not a profound, reader did not perceive that the particular facts were only illustrations of general principles. No one can rise from the perusal of the second part of the work with such an impression. In describing the intellectual activity, the feelings, and the manners of the Americans, it was no longer possible to conceal the presence of general ideas, and by introducing them in the form of facts to render them more effective though less obvious. The book is full of reflections upon reflections. A reader incapable of rising to their source, and of feeling in himself the subtlety of their truth, must be fatigued by what may have appeared to him a collection of ingenious propositions, capable, perhaps, of proof, but also, perhaps, of refutation. Vigorous intellects, and only those, understand and admire the power which renders clear and precise, subjects which, to most minds, are vague and obscure. To them these volumes, suggested by no model, appear like a masterpiece of skill, and they rank them even above their forerunners.

We have said that Tocqueville, in his anxiety to develop his intellect and improve his art, had studied earnestly the great writers of the seventeenth century. One intellectual labor leads to another; and he was thus led to fill some gaps in his early education. Delighted

by the historians, he had, perhaps, neglected the great
philosophers and moralists of ancient and modern times.
To read them was a useful preparation for a writer who
had to estimate the influence of democracy on the feelings, the opinions, and the manners of a people. He
may be said to have devoured Plato, Plutarch, Machiavel,
Montaigne, Rousseau, and their fellows.

" I feel," he wrote to a friend, " while reading these
works, of which it is shameful to be ignorant, and which
but yesterday I was scarcely acquainted with, the pleasure with which Marshal Soult learned geography when
he became foreign minister."

The quantity of books of different kinds which he then
read is prodigious. One class only he absolutely avoided;
those which, directly or indirectly, bore on his own
subject. He feared that if his mind had once begun to
tread a path marked out by another, it might not easily
return to its own, and might lose the vigor and the originality which he regarded as the principal merit in literary
composition. All this shows how it was that the second
part of his work cost him five years, the first part having
been finished in two.

His progress was retarded by another cause. His
personal position was altered. The absolute independence, which is the privilege only of early youth, was
gone. Besides the domestic demands of marriage, and
the social ones of literary success, two new elements were
introduced into his life: the interests of a landed proprietor and of a politician.

Country life, without doubt, is eminently favorable to
the soundness and the development of the intellect; that
is, if its seclusion be enjoyed, and its business avoided.
To enable the mind to create and to produce, the condi-

tions are silence, security, the absence of all disturbance,
and the certainty that when the inspiration begins, when
the thought is budding, it shall not be blighted, or broken off, or even kept back by some accidental interloper,
some private business, or some domestic care. This perfect security, not merely undisturbed, but not even in
danger of disturbance, can be found in the country, but
only on the supposition that the author be a visitor.
Tocqueville lived on his own estate. Though he had
two elder brothers, the Vicomte and the Baron de Tocqueville, family arrangements made after the death of
his mother, in 1836, and facilitated by the strong mutual
attachment of the three brothers, made him the possessor
of the old family seat, the chateau of Tocqueville, in the
peninsula which ends by Cherbourg.

It was in bad repair; full of associations and of ruins.
From the upper window are seen the sea and the magnificent coast of La Manche. The fertility of this country
equals its beauty. Nowhere is nature more grand or
more rich. But the traditions which make a country
interesting, and the natural charms which render it
seductive, are as dangerous to the mind as they are
enchanting to the heart. Interests are the enemies of
ideas; and even when the cares and the associations of
property do not enslave the thoughts, its business occupies the time. Tocqueville struggled against these material influences; but perhaps the struggle was weakened
by the feeling that the care of his property, though mischievous to his book, promoted another object, which
already attracted him — the entrance into public affairs.

It is certain that if he had not sought political life, it
would have sought him; for in a free country, anything
that raises a man above the crowd draws to him public

attention, and Tocqueville was already illustrious. But in fact he desired it. Tocqueville had much ambition; not the vulgar ambition which feeds on money or on place, or is satisfied by empty honors — such ambition he knew only to despise it. The ambition which filled and animated him was the manly and pure ambition, which in a free country is the first of public virtues; an ambition which is patriotism, which is eagerness for the grandeur of the country which it aspires to govern through the struggles which belong to liberty, by efforts never suspended, and by successes due only to merit and to talent — a great and noble ambition, not to be blamed, but to be honored, which alone can give brilliancy or dignity to power, and which aggrandizes even those whom it fails to exalt.

Now, to dwell in the country, and to take part in its business, is not merely useful, but necessary to political life. Local interest is created and preserved by residence. On local interest depends election; and in a free country, election is political birth.

To establish local interest in Normandy, Tocqueville had to meet not merely the difficulties opposed to a new candidate, but also some special obstacles. In spite of his father's influence in the province, or rather in consequence of that influence, he found, and it could not be wondered at, a general disposition to attribute to him legitimist opinions. Much time, and much personal intercourse with his countrymen were necessary before this prejudice could be overcome. It was so deeply rooted, that without the assistance of his book, of the acclamation which it obtained in the great world, and which was echoed in every hamlet, it is doubtful whether it would ever have been overcome. The obstacle was

strengthened even by his dignity of character. Desirous
as he was to enter the elected Chamber, he was resolved
that it should be only on the condition of perfect independence. The following anecdote shows the strength
of his feelings on this point.

At the election of 1847, Count Molé, the prime minister, knowing that Tocqueville was a candidate in La
Manche, without his knowledge, officially recommended
him as a government candidate. In so doing, M. Molé
merely yielded to his feelings of sympathy and affection
for a young relation, whose rising reputation delighted
him, and whose attachment to himself would be increased
by his support. Tocqueville, who had offered himself as
an independent candidate, knew only a week or two before the election, that he was recommended by the government. Believing that such a support, while it in-
sured his success, might injure his character, he immediately addressed to Count Molé a vehement remon-
strance. Molé's answer was equally sharp. The correspondence which followed was honorable to them both:
to the candidate, for the frankness and firmness with
which he rejected a patronage that would have secured
his election; to the minister, for the liberality with which
he offered his aid, and for the dignity with which he
withdrew it. The result was that Tocqueville failed;
but as the cause of his failure was known, it revealed his
character. Two years after, at the general election of
1839, he was chosen by a large majority. He was then
fully the master of his constituency.

Every one must feel the disturbance that the efforts
necessary to open the way to political life must have
made in his intellectual existence; how much energy
and strength of will were necessary in order to carry on

together, in spite of the obstacles of a health which was always fragile, the composition of his book, a work for solitude and retirement, and the care of his political ambition, a work to be carried on only in public, and amidst all the cares and obligations of publicity.

He was elected in March, 1839, and it was not until the beginning of 1840, that the last two volumes of his *Democracy in America* were published.

Here ends, for the present, his literary life, to be resumed after an interval of fifteen years — and his political life begins.

CHAPTER IV.

POLITICAL LIFE.

FROM 1839 to 1848, Tocqueville represented uninterruptedly the *arrondissement* of Valognes, and always
voted with the constitutional opposition.

Those times are too near to us to allow his public life
to be freely discussed. Though strongly attached to
constitutional monarchy, Tocqueville resisted a policy
which it would not be advisable to attack now, even if
one wished to do so. Opposed to him were men whom
he respected, and who have ceased to be adversaries.
Anything resembling a reproach addressed to these
statesmen, some of whom are living, would have been
disavowed by him, and would discredit his memory.
Nor would there be any use in reviving questions between
men now united by feelings far more important than their
past differences or their past rivalry.

The time will no doubt come, when the conduct of the
government and of the opposition will be submitted to the
judgment of history. And when this great cause is tried,
among the materials of the pleadings will be taken into
account many of the speeches of Tocqueville, his votes,
his acts, and the moderate but firm resistance to Louis
Philippe's government, which he maintained up to the
24th of February. But that time has not yet arrived,
and any intermediate discussion of the subject would be
premature.

Without offending, however, any person, or wounding

any party, it may even now be said, that Tocqueville passed through parliamentary life with distinction. That his intentions were always upright; that his ambition was always public-spirited; that his views were profound; that his eloquence was grave, often brilliant, often applauded, always listened to with respect; that his powers of judgment and of reasoning were of a high order, and that at a time when no defect escaped notice, his character never met with an attack or even a suspicion.

It must be admitted that in politics he did not, as he had done in letters, assume at once the highest rank. Though possessing the principal qualities which form a great statesman, he wanted some of those which form a great speaker, and in parliamentary government the latter character is necessary to the former. He spoke with ease and with great eloquence, but his voice partook of the general weakness of his body. Perhaps, too, he was too much excited by the discussion. He was too susceptible, too sensitive. The battle of a debate requires from the speaker the vigor which war demands from the soldier, and the coolness which it exacts from the general, for the speaker is both general and soldier; he fights and he commands. Tocqueville had not strength for such struggles, his health always suffered from them. It was seldom, therefore, that he could engage in them; and speaking seldom he could not be a leader.

Tocqueville, as a speaker, had also to contend with his habits as a writer. Examples without doubt may be cited of great writers who have been illustrious as speakers; but it is a general truth, that to write a book is a bad preparation for public and unpremeditated speaking. Literary labor is regular and methodical. The writer proposes to himself an ideal perfection, inconsistent with the unforeseen or accidental turn of a debate. Almost all the merits of a book are defects in a speech. A great book is written for the future. A speech is made for the present. Its business is the business of to-day. A book is thought; a speech is action. What is explained in a book is only hinted in a debate.

Tocqueville brought to the Chamber the habits and the methods of an author. A speech is merely a mode of action; he considered it too much as a work of art. To fit an idea to be presented to_ the Chamber, it-was requisite, of course, that it should be true, but he also required that it should be new. He abhorred commonplaces: an admirable feeling in an author, but most mischievous to one who addresses a large assembly—an audience which delights in commonplace.

Tocqueville had also contracted, both from theory and from practice, another habit, always excellent in a writer, but sometimes bad in a speaker. He never employed more words than were absolutely necessary to convey his thoughts to an intelligent reader.

A speaker ought to let the length of his discourse depend on the impressions produced on his audience. He ought to observe, sentence after sentence, those impressions, to end his explanation as soon as he finds that he is understood, to carry it on in a new shape if he sees that it has not been fully comprehended; and, passing rapidly over what may be offensive, and dwelling on what meets with the sympathy of his hearers, to persevere until their conviction is apparent. All this is opposed to the habits of a writer, and above all, of a good writer. If Tocqueville was not great in the Chamber, it is because he was superior in his own study. His principal defect as a speaker was due to his principal merit as a writer.

This accounts for the cold reception of some of his speeches, which we now read with deep interest. What they lost in immediate effect they will gain in durability.

It may be added that during this whole period, from 1839 to 1848, he was in a position unfavorable to eloquence. He could be eloquent only when impelled, inspired, and sustained by deep and vehement feelings. Such feelings were not excited by the character which his conscience prescribed to him, that of a member of the opposition. He was too cautious, too reserved, perhaps too foreseeing, to act that character well. There was nothing of the tribune in him. Nature formed him rather to act with a government than with an opposition. This was proved at a later period of his political life, and appeared even at this time, when his exclusion from office deprived him of many opportunities for showing his administrative talents. Thus in 1839, soon after his election, having been directed to prepare a report on the abolition of colonial slavery, he not only laid down, ably and firmly, the great principles of justice and humanity, which ultimately gained this sacred cause, but by the respect with which he treated existing interests and vested rights, he prepared the government and the public to make concessions, and the colonists to accept a compromise.

Thus again, in the next year, 1840, charged with a report on prison reform, he carried, first in the committee and afterwards in the Chamber, all the important clauses of a bill, which was, in fact, an application of his own theories on the subject.

Later, in 1846, when the great question of our African empire was before the Chambers, Tocqueville, who, for

the purpose of studying it, had twice travelled in Algeria
(once, at the risk of his life), in the spring of 1841, and
again in the winter of 1845, became a member of the
commission appointed by the Chamber, and prepared,
in the name of the commission, a report, in which the
principles of colonization are so well treated, that even
at this day, the government could do no better than consult it in the framing of regulations, and in the general
management of the colonies. Tocqueville was eminently
practical, to the great surprise, and, perhaps, disgust of
those who maintained that the man of theory must be
inferior in action. He possessed the two principal qualities for a statesman; first, the glance which penetrates
into the future; discovers beforehand the path to be followed, the rocks to be avoided; which sees quicker and
farther than others; a gift not only precious to a minister, but to every chief of a party. Secondly, a knowledge of men. No one knew better how to attach them,
and to make use of them; to discern their talents and
deficiencies, and turn both to account; to ask from every
one the service for which he was best fitted; and when it
was finished, to dismiss his agents, satisfied with him and
with themselves. Very frank, and very discreet; never
reserved, saying only what he intended to say, to the
extent and at the time that he wished to say it, and
expressing it with an exquisite grace, which gave a
value to every word, Tocqueville's capacious mind, eminent talent, and high character, placed him among the
remarkable men who, under a representative government,
and in ordinary times, are formed to take a chief part in
the affairs of their country.

In a speech, pronounced on the 27th of January, 1848,
in the Chamber of Deputies, Tocqueville, with an almost

prophetic voice, announced the revolution which was on the point of breaking out.

".... It is supposed," said he, "that there is no danger because there is no collision. It is said, that as there is no actual disturbance of the surface of society, revolution is far off.

"Gentlemen, allow me to tell you, that I believe you deceive yourselves. Without doubt the disorder does not bréak out in overt acts, but it has sunk deeply into the minds of the people. Look at what is passing in the breasts of the working classes, as yet, I own tranquil. It is true that they are not now inflamed by purely political passions in the same degree as formerly; but do you not observe that their passions from political have become social? Do you not see gradually pervading them opinions and ideas, whose object is not merely to overthrow a law, a ministry, or even a dynasty, but society itself? to shake the very foundations on which it now rests? Do you not listen to their perpetual cry? Do you not hear incessantly repeated, that all those above them are incapable and ·unworthy of governing them? that the present distribution of wealth in the world is unjust, that property rests upon no equitable basis? and do you not believe that when such opinions take root, when they spread till they have almost become general, when they penetrate deeply into the masses, that they must lead sooner or later, I know not when, I know not how, but that sooner or later they must lead to the most formidable revolutions?

" Such, gentlemen, is my deep conviction; I believe that at the present moment we are slumbering on a volcano (murmurs), of this I am thoroughly convinced . . . ." (excitement).

Tocqueville, therefore, was more grieved than surprised by the revolution of the 24th February, 1848; but the pain it gave him was no less great. He had not been bound by any close or peculiar tie to the fallen dynasty, he was attached to it in a merely constitutional point of view; but his great intelligence had, from the first, appreciated the extent of the danger to liberty caused by the revolution.

The danger he considered immeasurable, and the consequent mischief the greatest possible. To avert, in the midst of so much irremediable misery and ruin, this last and greatest danger, seemed to be all that remained for him to attempt. Therefore, after an attentive study of the events passing before him, after considering the raging passions, the divisions of party in the country, divisions which were faithfully represented in the assembly, he became, whether rightly or wrongly, convinced of two things; first, that the only and, perhaps, the last chance of liberty for France, lay in the establishment of the republic; second, that every attempt to prevent its success would end in the ruin of the republic in favor of the power of a single person. In so judging he was assuredly not carried away by enthusiasm. His instinct and his reason were equally offended by the republic of 1848; the violent and surreptitious origin of the revolution, — its authors, — the licentious theories, and even the absurd phraseology that it had brought forth, were thoroughly repugnant to his nature, and would have held him aloof from the republic, had it not been for the extent of the evil from which he thought that the establishment of the republic alone could save France. Tocqueville would have done anything to obviate it, because he felt that its natural consequence would be to drive France into an abyss of misery; but now that the republic was established, he saw safety in its mainte- nance. Was he wrong? Was the permanence of the republic a chimera? One must beware of judging every- thing by the result. Many declared the republic to be impossible, who proclaimed still more impossible the per- manence of absolute power. However that may be, it is essential to make known the convictions of Tocque- ville, as they only can furnish the key to his conduct at this important epoch of recent history. These convic- tions regulated all his acts; and it is remarkable, that in the midst of the most perplexing circumstances, Tocque- ville had not one instant of hesitation or weakness, but appeared invariably more energetic and more resolute than ever.

The department of La Manche sent Tocqueville as its representative to the constituent assembly convoked for the 4th of May. Placed on the committee for the for- mation of a constitution, Tocqueville was penetrated with the sense of its importance; he applied himself conscien- tiously to the ungrateful task imposed on the committee — a task which, considering that it was executed between the 15th of May and the 24th of June, could not but be full of imperfections, some of which would, perhaps, have been avoided had the ideas which Tocqueville in vain tried to introduce been adopted. To quote a single ex- ample : Tocqueville proposed that, instead of being elected by the direct suffrage of the people, the Presi- dent of the republic should, as in the United States, be elected by a limited number of electors, themselves cho- sen by universal suffrage. Instead of one Assembly, he preferred a representation consisting of two Chambers. But although his opinions did not prevail, he continued

to give his most cordial and earnest assistance to the labors of the committee; for he was convinced, that in such
times the immediate success of a constitution depends
less on the principles which it puts forth, than on the men
who have to carry them out. Animated by these sentiments, and with the same singleness of purpose, Tocqueville supported General Cavaignac. He not merely gave
to him his vote, but also his strongest moral support,
though without illusion as to the difficulties of his can-
vass and the decreasing chances of his success. The
sight of this gradual decline, the deep sense of the calamities towards which France was rapidly drifting, excited
Tocqueville's patriotic regret. His opinions at that time
live probably in the memory of many; but they are, perhaps, nowhere better recorded than in his correspondence
with the author of this Memoir, who was at that period
in London, and to whom he despatched a daily report of
the national assembly, the state of the political thermom-
eter, and his own private impressions. At some later
date this extremely curious correspondence may be published; now it is impossible. It paints with wonderful
accuracy the deformities of the times — the defects both
personal and material, as well as the grief which they
produced in Tocqueville.

In the month of October, 1848, two of his political
friends, MM. Dufaure and Vivien, whose wishes and
fears were similar to his, having been admitted to share
the councils of General Cavaignac, Tocqueville was appointed to represent France as plenipotentiary at the
conference of Brussels, the object of which was the mediation of France and England between Austria and
Sardinia. Although this mediation had been formally
accepted by Austria, Tocqueville was already convinced,

from the turn of events both in that country and in France, that there was a great chance that the conference would never take place. He accepted, however, lest, by refusing their pressing solicitations, he should appear to withhold his coöperation from his friends, whom he feared to damage in proportion to his sense of the importance and the difficulty of their undertaking. Finally, when, six months after the presidential election of the 10th December, 1848, renewed disturbances brought back the fear of anarchy, and the necessity was felt of maintaining order under the standard of the republic and of the constitution, the President made an appeal to the men best known for their attachment to the constitution, Tocqueville, who had just been elected a member of the legislative assembly, accepted the portfolio of foreign affairs ; and, with his friends MM. Dufaure and Lanjuinais, became part of the ministry of M. Odilon Barrot, which lasted till the manifesto of the 31st of October in the same year. At the moment when this ministry was formed, Tocqueville was travelling with his wife on the Rhine ; his friends sent for him, and he reached Paris only just in time to assume his duties.

The short period of his ministry of foreign affairs would alone have sufficed to prove the rare practical capacity for business of Tocqueville ; who, in the space of two months, had to settle two great questions, that of Rome, and that of the Hungarian refugees whose extradition was demanded from the Sublime Porte by Austria and Russia.

All who at that time observed Tocqueville, admired the clearness of his views, and the uprightness and firmness of his acts. It has seldom happened to a minister to leave, in so short a time, such brilliant and yet durable traces of his administration, not only at home, but in foreign governments. All the diplomatic agents of France at that time, among whom Tocqueville by his influence had placed two of his personal friends, General Lamoricière at the court of St. Petersburgh, and M. Gustave de Beaumont, at that of Vienna, can bear witness to this fact. From the first they were struck by the elevated and dignified tone of his despatches. Tocqueville, indeed, charmed all who came in contact with him, by the attraction of his moral and intellectual qualities; and when the act of the 31st of October separated him from the head of the government, the President, who as well as others had been captivated, endeavored to attach him to his person, projects, and designs. Without being insensible to these proofs of esteem, the resolution of Tocqueville could not be shaken. He insisted on the preservation of the republic, and all was tending towards the empire, or rather the empire was set up. The Legislative Assembly dragged on, rather than lived for two years ; like a strong man, who though mortally wounded, can neither recover nor die. Tocqueville sat in it to the end, with the thorough disgust and bitter regret caused by the spectacle of its long agony. He had not, however, to reproach himself with a moment's weakness or desertion. To the end he trod firmly and uprightly the path which he had traced for himself. When the question of a revision of the constitution was agitated *in extremis* in the Assembly ; without deceiving himself as to the character of the petitions which demanded this revision, but convinced that the power of the President must be renewed, and that if anything could diminish the fatal effect of this popular *coup d'état*, it would be to render it beforehand constitutional; he voted for the revision, and speaking in the name of the committee, he stated his motives in a report which was his last and one of his most remarkable parliamentary labors. A few days later the parliament had ceased to exist.

Tocqueville, fatigued by his ministerial duties, and with health much impaired, had a short time previously quitted France for a warmer climate: he went to seek rest and sunshine in the neighborhood of Naples, at Sorrento, where he passed the winter, and where he would have had only too good a right to prolong his stay. But, in spite of the charms and the salutary effects of his residence in this delightful retreat, to which the society of a few friends * added the advantages of an intimate and chosen society, Tocqueville instantly quitted it to return to Paris, when he saw the storm gather and ready to burst over the Assembly of which he was a member. He chose to be at his post, and to take his share of the danger in the struggle which he hoped would ensue ; and he was present on the 2d of December, 1851. He was at the meeting of the tenth *arrondissement ;* he approved and signed all its resolutions; and was sent with two hundred of his colleagues to the barracks on the Quai d'Orsay ; from whence, on the night of the 2d of December, they were transferred to Vincennes. Here ends the political life of Tocqueville, together with that of liberty in France.†

The most striking features in Tocqueville's political character are firmness combined with moderation ; and

* M. Ampère, and Mr. Senior, who, with his family, arrived in January.

† An interesting account of these events was written by M. de Tocqueville, and published in the *Times* of the 11th of December, 1851. It will be found in the second volume of this work. — TR.

moral greatness and dignity combined with ambition. In revolutionary times the men who are not violent are often accused of weakness. It is true that Tocqueville had none of the revolutionary energy, produced more by temper than by conviction, which proceeds by fits and starts, and is subject to sudden reaction.

Tocqueville was not violent; but nothing could surpass the strength and constancy with which he held to his opinions. Intrenched behind the line marked out by his reason, and fortified by his conscience, he was invincible; he never quitted it for an instant, either to obtain power or to keep it. And yet the ambition that, as we have seen, fired his mind on his entrance into public life was not extinguished; it continued equally vivid, but it was always of that nobler kind which, counting as nothing empty honor and material advantages, sees in power only a means of accomplishing, if not great things, at least things useful to his country.

Convinced that in a free nation power should always vest in the political party which has the majority, and that there can be neither greatness nor dignity in a government unless the party in power makes known its principles, and remains faithful to them, he did not feel, he could not even understand, ambition except within these limits. It is indeed the lot of all men, whose public ambition is of this kind, to attain office rarely, and still more rarely to keep it. But greatness does not consist in the mere possession of power; and the statesman who desires that his memory may be honored, must, above all, preserve in the conduct of public affairs his personal dignity and self-respect.

Although Tocqueville did not long retain what is called power, he enjoyed a much nobler and more lasting

influence than is obtained by the daily management of
affairs, — the moral influence exercised by his ideas.
By them he exercised, and still exercises, great political influence over his own age. His opinions formed a
school. He is everywhere quoted and considered as an
authority, abroad as well as at home. It was, especially,
this powerful moral influence that made Tocqueville a
politician and a statesman.

CHAPTER V.

EVENTS SUBSEQUENT TO THE SECOND DECEMBER, 1851 — L'ANCIEN
RÉGIME ET LA REVOLUTION — UNPUBLISHED WORKS AND COR-
RESPONDENCE.

AFTER this violent breaking up of his political existence, there was still one tie left which bound Tocqueville
to public life. He was a member, and had for many
years been regularly elected president, of the *conseil
général* of his department (La Manche). Though of a
subordinate nature, it was a tie of deep interest and perhaps nearer to his heart than any other. But as it could
have been preserved only by an oath which his honor
forbade, even this last tie had to be broken.

Notwithstanding this blow, Tocqueville was not cast
down. It was his fate to rise with every trial. He
never displayed more strength and dignity than in these
sad times. Between his intellectual and moral faculties
there was a remarkable correspondence ; as his eloquence
rose with his subject, so the greater the trial the stronger
and firmer it found him. On such occasions his energy
was admirable.

We have said that Tocqueville's political existence
had come to an end : but we were wrong — it continued.
Tocqueville carried it on first by remaining what he had
been ; for in revolutionary times there is but one way to
preserve one's principles : it is, not to change in the midst
of change, to maintain one's character unimpaired ; not
for a single day to give the lie to one's past life ; to en-

dure patiently, nobly, not the displeasure of a sovereign (which would be easy enough), but that of the times, far more painful and oppressive; to see trampled under foot by the people all that one had seen erect and honored by them, without abandoning a particle of it one's self; to witness this apostasy, yet to hold one's faith firmly; and not only hold it, but declare it, profess it, hope for its final triumph, and, with all one's remaining strength, devote one's self to its cause. Even so did Tocqueville after the 2d of December; naturally, without effort, without remission, and with a firmness that did not falter for a single instant.

In the midst of the profound sadness excited in him by the changed prospects of his country, he determined to oppose material force by moral influence; to make a dignified attitude and literary study compensate for the loss of political power; and in the sphere, however narrow it might be, left to independent thought, to endeavor to propagate, or rather to awaken, ideas which may be dormant in the public mind, but can never perish.

Inspired by this sentiment, Tocqueville not only set himself to work, but undertook to animate his friends with ardor similar to his own; and it was a cause of real regret to him that, while they all sympathized deeply with his energy and his success he could not prevail on some of them to resume the intellectual labor of which he set them an example. Assuredly none resisted more frequently his solicitations than he who, by writing these pages, seems now to yield to them. But, alas! he writes only a biography; nor can he help a bitter feeling when he thinks of the price which he pays for the fulfilment of the earnest wishes of his friend.

Immediately after the 2d December, 1851, Tocqueville had retired to his estate in Normandy.

The quiet of the country, and the repose of private life succeeding to the noise of the capital and the disputes of the forum, certainly present a singular charm, intoxicating the mind and lifting it above itself. It is another life, another world, almost another nature; a passion for truth seizes you instead of a passion for victory; the desire of knowledge, not that of success; a proud disdain of the multitude, to which you have been a slave : *Turba argumentum pessimi.* But, in order to enjoy these sensations, the heart must not be full of grief; one must not be an exile in one's own country. Tocqueville's mind was too much troubled, and his moral sense too much in a state of revolt to enjoy the soothing influence of a country life. It was not for this that he went to live on his estate, but in order to work. This work was his last book : *L'ancien Régime et la Revolution.* He first thought of writing this book six months earlier, at Sorrento, in the beginning of the year 1851; a time when, reflecting on the state of France, he saw but too clearly the lot about to exclude a whole generation from public affairs, and thus create a leisure which must be employed. The national assembly was not then extinct; but all its members were conscious of its daily decreasing strength. On the 10th of January, 1851, he wrote the following letter to M. Gustave de Beaumont : —

"Sorrento, January 10th, 1851.

". . . . Sorrento becomes every day more agreeable to me; the beauty of the country and of the climate

---

* "On the State of Society in France before the Revolution," translated by Mr. Reeve. — TR.

is incomparable; our apartments are very convenient. All I wanted was some intellectual occupation; some amusement rather than work for the mind. I am beginning to have it. Before leaving Tocqueville, I had put together some of my recollections of my period of office; and had written down a few of the reflections which occurred to me on the men and things of that time. I have returned to this work; no portion of which, as you are well aware, can now be published in any form. Though I do not feel the same zest and aptitude for it that I had at Tocqueville, still it helps me through the morning hours, at which I am in the habit of administering a certain portion of food to my mind. I will read it to you some day, when we have nothing better to do than to gossip over the past. You are aware that the events of my ministry of five months are of no great importance; but the near view that I had of affairs was curious, and the physiognomy of the persons engaged in them interested me. They are, in general, rather bad subjects, of which I have made but middling pictures; but a gallery of contemporaries often gives the spectator more pleasure than magnificent portraits of even the illustrious deceased. However, this employment, or rather these dreams, are far from calming the restlessness of mind usual to me in solitude.

" I have long, as you know, been engrossed with the thought of undertaking another book. It has occurred to me a hundred times that if I am to leave any traces of my passage through the world, it will be far more by my writings than by my actions. Besides, I feel myself more capable of writing a book now than I was fifteen years ago. I have, therefore, employed my thoughts, in my walks over the hills round Sorrento, in search of a subject. It was requisite that it should be of our own time, and such as to enable me to join facts with ideas, the philosophy of history with history itself. These were for me the conditions of the problem. I had often thought of the empire, that singular act of the drama, yet incomplete, called the French revolution; but I had always been checked by insurmountable obstacles, and especially by the idea that I should appear to wish to rewrite celebrated books already written. But now the subject has presented itself in a form which has seemed to me more approachable; I have been thinking that, instead of undertaking to write the history of the empire, I must try to exhibit and to explain the cause, the character, and the import of the great occurrences which form the chief links in the chain of events of that time; the facts to be no more than a sort of solid unbroken foundation on which to rest all the ideas which I have in my head, not only concerning the empire, but on the period by which it was preceded and succeeded; on its character; on the extraordinary man who was its hero; on the direction given by him to the progress of the French revolution; of his influence over the condition of our nation, and the destiny of all Europe. One might make on these subjects a short book, in one volume, or perhaps in two, which would not be without interest or even dignity. My mind has worked on this new canvas, and under the stimulus has discovered many views which never occurred to me before. All is, as yet, a sort of vision floating before my imagination; what say you of the original idea?"

The cloud cleared away, and Tocqueville on returning to private life set to work. The difficulty is easily understood. In order to describe the revolution and its results,

Tocqueville was obliged first to study the times by which it was preceded; as to understand an effect one seeks for the cause. He set himself to explore and to paint the social and political state of France before 1789. He had, therefore, to perform respecting old France, a task some-what similar to that which he had performed respecting North America. But instead of dealing, as in the United States, with a country and institutions actually before his eyes, he had to describe an extinct society, times and institutions that had passed away; and of which he was forced, as it were, to exhume the skeleton, in order to paint the resemblance. Now it is hard to imagine the toil, even after the lapse of less than half a century, of discovering the traces of what has been destroyed or metamorphosed by a great and sudden revolution. Toc-queville applied to this study all the resources of his powerful intellect; he analyzed with his wonderful sagacity the elements, which before and after 1789, composed civil and political society in France; he made each the subject of a profound and diligent inquiry. He found many materials for his work in the great public libraries of the state; but he, perhaps, nowhere found more valuable documents than among the archives of the old provincial administrations, especially in that of Tours. For the benefit of these researches, as well as that of his health, for which the temperate climate of Touraine was recom-mended, he established himself at St. Cyr, near Tours, for a part of the year 1854.

But in studying his subject, he did not confine himself to France; he wished once more to see Germany, where every trace of the ancient feudal system is not yet effaced, and where, perhaps, better than in any other country, may be seen the characteristics of a nation not yet completely

revolutionized. He performed this journey in the summer
of the year 1855 ; and, as for such an inquiry he wanted
a knowledge of the German language, he had the courage
to learn it ; and he acquired it so rapidly, as soon to be
able to make use of the original documents.

It was in the beginning of 1856 that he published the
first part of this great work, which he was not, alas, permitted to finish. The book met with prodigious success ;
as much abroad as in France. It was immediately translated into every language, noticed in every newspaper
and review, and welcomed by a concert of unanimous
praise.*

Tocqueville's satisfaction at this success was not entirely
personal ; he thought it a good symptom of the public
mind, still capable of appreciating a book full of the passionate love of liberty. If anything in this success troubled
him, it was its universality. It seemed to him that the
natural opponents of his theories ought to have attacked
him ; and he feared that the indulgence with which they
treated his book, might be a proof less of impartiality on
their part, than of a general indifference to politics.
However that might be, the organs of the public press all
agreed, especially on one point ; in their praise of the
work, they pointed out a new step made by the author, a
purer taste, a graver style, a greater steadiness of thought
and self-reliance.

To the twelve years of his public career, Tocqueville
owed a maturity of judgment, and power of observation,
which he could not fail to show in his writings. If it be
true that a literary life is a bad preparation for a political
life, it is no less true that politics are an excellent intro-

---

* See especially M. de Rémusat's remarkable article in the *Revue
des Deux Mondes* of the 1st of August, 1856.

' duction to literary composition; especially to that of a book in which recent facts are mingled with history, and the statesman's experience is of as much importance as the talent of the writer. A retrospective glance thrown over the long interval between 1840 and 1852, during which political action suspended his intellectual creations, would, perhaps, lead us to infer that what Tocqueville gained most from those years, was a greater fitness for the production of this last book.

The account given here of its success is, perhaps, but a feeble reflection of the impression produced on the public by this work. In reading it we feel more than the pleasure of contemplating a beautiful work of art, for our minds become filled with the great interests which occupy the thoughts of the author. We see that he is not merely presenting us with a series of remarkable anecdotes, but that he studies the past with the object of exploring the secrets and unravelling the mysteries of the future. We are aware that our own destinies and the lot of our children are concerned. We read with a solemn feeling, like that of the ancients consulting their oracle. It is more than admiration; it is emotion. The reader thinks as much of himself as of the book; and such is his faith in the penetration of the writer, that while reading the premises he longs to reach the conclusion.

Many persons throughout Europe waited for this conclusion, in order to solve the enigma of our revolution. To this point, Tocqueville directed all the powers of his mind. In fact, the title of the first part, the only part yet published, does not give a true idea of the scope of the whole work. To judge by the title, *L'ancien Régime et la Révolution*, it would seem as if the author assigned, in the order of his thoughts, the same importance to the

study of the *ancien régime* as he did to that of the French
revolution. But such was not the case. His aim was
not to paint the ancient state of society. He used it only
as a background to throw into relief the new state of
things; the year 1789; the revolution, its consequences;
the empire; and, above all, the Emperor. This was the
vital point of his studies, the origin of his reflections, of
his anxieties, of his alternations of hope and depression.
The right name for the book would have been the
" French Revolution;" and Tocqueville would have
chosen it, had he not been afraid of taking a worn-out
title. The French revolution was the subject which filled
his thoughts, and took possession of his mind; the dark
abyss into which he hoped to convey light, the mysterious
problem which he was bent upon solving.

But what was this solution to be? The published
volume does not exhibit and could not contain it; the
author's intention in it being to offer only a summary of
the past. It is most probable, that the whole work would
have extended to at least three volumes. The regret
produced by the interruption of so great a work can now
be understood, especially as the second volume was far
advanced; Tocqueville wanted only a few months more
to finish it. The order of the chapters, and the sequence
of the ideas, was arranged from first to last; some chapters are not mere sketches, they are pictures which have
received the artist's last touch ; and even where the out-
lines are not distinct, they are indicated.

By collating these precious materials, arranging them,
supplying here a few pages, there a few words, it would
no doubt be possible to put this second volume into form,
and make it over to the natural curiosity of the public.
But who would dare to venture on this experiment, espe-

cially considering the importance attached by Tocqueville to publishing nothing which was not as nearly perfect as he was able to make it? Often in the margin of the MS. one sees, in the author's hand, these words : " *To be reconsidered ; to be verified.*" Sometimes a single note of interrogation set against an opinion expresses marks of the writer's doubt, and suggests a reconsideration.

In the presence of so many signs of scruples and fears, who would venture to be bolder than the author himself? Who would dare to solve the questions raised, to touch the delicate points, to end the unfinished sentences, to graft another style upon his style, and to inflict the faults and responsibilities of another upon his glorious memory? Such profanation will not be committed.

Two chapters only of the second part, written probably as early as 1852, have been found, subjected apparently to so complete a revision, that Tocqueville himself would certainly not have disavowed them. It is the portion of the work which describes the state of France just before the " 18 Brumaire," and proves that though she had ceased to be republican, France still was revolutionary. It cannot be asserted that the author would not have retouched them, for he was always improving his compositions ; but these fragments may be considered as finished, and they can with confidence be offered as a curious and precious specimen of the entire work, which unfortunately will never appear. Except, indeed, this slender portion, it is resolved that nothing shall ever be published.

If another course were adopted, where should one stop? Ought one to endeavor to make up a third volume by applying to it the same labor as to the second, and to seek in Tocqueville's copious notes for the key to

that enigma, the secret of which perplexes his readers?
Who would dare to ransack such a sanctuary? How
would it be possible to deduce any clear and decided
opinion from the first essays and gropings of his independent mind, which long balanced the most opposite
notions; and was too candid to be in the least aware of
what it would be led to predict for the future from the
study of the present and past. As the chemist when he
begins the analysis of a body knows not what result to
expect.

The only safe assertion on this point is, that Tocqueville had faith in liberty, while he was showing what
perils it had to encounter; and believed, if not in its perpetual existence, yet in its amendment and partial recovery; and would have thrown down his pen, if he had
foreseen its extinction.

But if one were to allow one's self to be carried along
the slope, instead of determining to stop short, the publication would not end with the second and third parts of
Tocqueville's great work. It is impossible to look at his
numerous notes on the French Revolution, evidencing
his profound study of every theory nearly or distantly
connected with the subject, without being struck with the
value of his labors. It is an immense arsenal of ideas.
Many authors would find in one of his notes materials
for volumes. They are all in his handwriting; for Tocqueville wanted the faculty of working with foreign help,
and made use of no materials but those which he himself
collected. He alone possessed the key to their meaning.
He had no respect for books that are made up of other
books, but went always to the original sources. In his
estimation the chief part of the work consisted in exploring these sources. When he had discovered them he

considered his work half done. In pursuing these researches, he allowed nothing to stop him; he followed them up everywhere, not only in France, but in foreign countries. He went to Germany for the materials of this first volume, and in 1857 to England to prepare the second. He admitted of no obstacle to a journey which he deemed essential to his task, not even the risk of his life, already in considerable danger, and to which any change of habits and climate might be fatal. All this may give some idea of what authorship was to him. For one volume that he published he wrote ten; and the notes he cast aside as intended only for himself, would have served many writers as text for the printer. His notices upon the economists, especially on Turgot; on the instructions from their constituents to the different members of the states-general; his observations on Germany, and on many German publicists; his notes on England, are so many finished compositions. But if he thought them unworthy, who should venture to publish them, and to offer as finished works what he considered merely as materials for his own use? Who would exhibit, in a prolix and diluted state, thoughts which he only showed when condensed, and which he would have employed his whole skill to compress? This reserve will not be confined to his writings upon the revolution and the empire; but will be extended to his other manuscripts.

Such a man as Tocqueville, who could not live without thinking, nor think without writing, left, of course, many papers upon various subjects. But, except a few short pieces mentioned above, which, as they are completely finished, may be published, not one has received his last touches.

The most considerable of his unfinished works is un-

doubtedly that which he had commenced on the " Establishment of the English in India." He had deeply studied
this important question, and collected a considerable number of documents relating to it. The book is divided
into three parts; the title of the first is, " Picture of the
Present State of British India." The whole of this first
part is written out, and would make about sixty pages of
print. The motto is as follows: " The Hindoo religion
is abominable; perhaps the only one that is worse than
none at all." The title of the second part — which is
not yet fully written, though the order of the thoughts
and distribution of subjects is settled, — is, " Effects of
the British rule upon the Hindoos." The third part is
entitled: " How the British power in India may be overturned."

More important or more interesting questions cannot
be imagined. But against yielding to the temptation of
publishing any part of this MS. one would be protected
by these words, written by Tocqueville himself on the
cover: " All this is of no value, unless I resume my intention of writing on these questions. About the year
1843 I thought of composing a book on this subject,
which is well worthy of the trouble. The distractions
of political life, and the immense research requisite for
such a work, have prevented me." That an author
should publish, unless as a means of adding to his fame,
Tocqueville could never understand, nor could he ever
tolerate book-making.

This explains why Tocqueville published so little,
though he wrote so much, as well as the perfection of
the few works which he brought out. It accounts, also,
for his extreme dislike to writing in newspapers, or even
in reviews, where the writer is forced to compress his

subject within a prescribed limit. Only on a few rare occasions did he depart from this rule.

Thus in 1836, the year after the publication of his first book, the eminent editor of the *London and Westminster Review*, Mr. John Stuart Mill, who has since written so many remarkable works, asked him for an article upon France. Tocqueville sent him a very striking paper on the " Social and Political State of France," which appeared in the number of the following April, 1836, translated by Mr. Mill himself.* Another time, at the earnest request of M. Aristide Guilbert, author of the *Histoire des Villes de France*, Tocqueville sent him an account of Cherbourg, published in 1847, in that interesting collection, and which is the best possible proof that there is no subject, however apparently trifling, that may not become great when handled by a superior mind. This article is a masterpiece; the little town almost immediately disappears to make way for the historical interests of its port, one of the grandest and most marvellous creations of this century.

On considering, therefore, the reserve evinced by Tocqueville in the publication of his works, one is forced to observe the same reticence with regard to his inedited MSS.

He has left, however, one very important manuscript, under the name of " Souvenirs," which will certainly one day be published, and will make up an octavo volume. These souvenirs, written at Tocqueville, and at Sorrento, in 1850 and 1851, relate chiefly to the revolution of 1848, and to the following year. They will form a most precious fragment of contemporary history, but the time

* Printed in this volume immediately after the " Fortnight in the Wilderness." — Tr.

for publishing them is not yet come ; the author solemnly desired that no part should appear during the life of any whom it might injure.

But among his unpublished works, is one, perhaps the most valuable, the immediate publication of which seems to us not only possible but indispensable; we mean his private letters. They were certainly not written for publication, but Tocqueville said nothing to forbid it. Nothing that falls from the pen of a distinguished man can long remain private property. Some of his letters have already been made public; other partial publications less guarded by discretion and good taste might follow, both in France and in England, if this sad dispersion were not prevented by a collected publication.

If we had to give an opinion on the literary merit of this correspondence, we should place it, if not above, at least on a level with whatever Tocqueville has written and published; but it is not the art and talent displayed which principally strikes us, nor what we wish the public to notice. A letter is much less an intellectual exercise than an ebullition of feeling, a token of friendship, a passage in one's life, a conversation in which both the heart and mind take part. A letter is not a study, but a part of the writer's personality that survives it, and prolongs its existence. A collection of letters is not a literary production : it consists of the recovered fragments of a life that is broken up, put together by the piety of the survivors, each of whom, according to the nature and degree of his affection, feels satisfaction in contemplating the remains of the friend whom he loved and admired.

It has been a hundred times said that the style is the man. This is hardly true of the style of a book in which the author observes himself, and exerts all his skill to exhibit himself as he wishes to appear; but it is nearer the truth with respect to letters, which are written as one speaks, and because one cannot speak. They sometimes show the intellect of the writer; they always reveal his heart and disposition.

Although in some parts of Tocqueville's correspondence he has hit upon a felicity of expression which no study could have improved; what will chiefly be observed in it is the immense space that friendship occupied in his life. His published works have made him known as an author; by his letters he will be known and loved as a man. They will also exhibit the author in a new light; for Tocqueville excelled as a letter-writer. Accordingly no letter from him, however short, was ever received with indifference. This explains why they all have been preserved, and are now forthcoming; and why none of the persons who have lent them to us have been willing to give them up altogether. On the contrary, so highly are they valued, that every one of the friends who have trusted us with these precious manuscripts, has earnestly entreated us to restore the originals.* We need not say that this wish will be faithfully fulfilled. The delicate feeling which prompted Tocqueville's friends to place all their letters in the hands of Madame de Tocqueville, in whom alone they recognize the right of authorizing their publication, will assuredly meet with general appreciation.

If several reasons did not oblige us to suppress, at least for the present, the greater part of this correspondence, it would be very voluminous. Tocqueville had many

---

* In expressing his desire for the return of Tocqueville's letters, Mr. Senior added: " My children and grandchildren will read them with pride."

friends. Convinced that friendship is a tender plant that withers without cultivation, he bestowed the greatest attention upon his correspondence. He wrote many letters, not because he was, but although he was, an author. Literary men in general write few. They seem to keep all their talent and all their thoughts for their books. To Tocqueville, letter-writing was a need; it widened the circle of his life. He kept up many of those relations which are almost friendships, and would have become real friendships, if they had begun a little earlier. He did much to keep them alive. The difficulty to men of eminence is not to obtain acquaintances, or even friends, but to keep them. Attentions, kindness, and sincere regard, will alone retain what success and renown attracted. He was, however, as attentive to his slighter as to his intimate ties; hence his numerous correspondences in France as well as in foreign countries.

The most ancient of all in date, as well as, perhaps, the most remarkable, is the correspondence he kept up with one of his cousins, his friend from a child, Count Louis de Kergorlay. It throws so much light on the character of Tocqueville, that it is as well to explain in a few words the circumstances during which it sprang up and was maintained for more than thirty years. Alexis de Tocqueville and Louis de Kergorlay present the phenomenon of two men, completely separated in politics, yet always united in the closest intimacy. Kergorlay, the day after aiding as an officer of artillery in the capture of Algiers, left the service rather than give in his adhesion to the government of July, to which Tocqueville submitted, without enthusiasm, it is true, but without reservation. So strong, indeed, was Kergorlay's hostility to the new dynasty, that he was implicated in the first endeavor to overthrow it; while Tocqueville, persisting in the opposite course, entered the representative Chamber, and there renewed his oath of allegiance. Kergorlay, again, retired into private life; and, notwithstanding his extraordinary merit and great abilities, was glad to remain in the shade. On the other hand, Tocqueville threw himself into the agitation and glare of public life; yet, although their fortunes were so opposite, the two friends remained always the same to each other, not only without mutual suspicion or bitterness, but without the slightest shade or coolness. Yet they were exposed to every sort of trial, of which not the least cruel was, when Louis de Kergorlay compromised, together with his venerable father, in the affair of the *Carlo Alberto*, was sent by the government which Tocqueville had joined before the *cour d'assizes* of Montbrison. Tocqueville rushed to support his friend and zealously defended him; not as one would generally defend a person under accusation, but as one would plead for a loved and honored friend, in a few touching words which we shall try to recover, that we may introduce them at the end of this volume.* The claims of affection satisfied, Tocqueville pursued his own political course.

In the nature of these two men, though generally so diverse, there were evidently mysterious affinities and secret sympathies not confined to their moral, but extended even to their intellectual qualities, though they were so different in their actions.

Tocqueville never wrote without submitting his MS. to Kergorlay. How often, when stopped in the midst of his work, out of heart, almost in despair, he sought his

---

* As this speech is not to be found in the original, I presume that M. de Beaumont failed in his endeavor.—Tr.

friend Louis, who with one word dispersed the cloud and set him forward on his path. It is scarcely possible to form an idea of the help afforded to Tocqueville by the vast and fertile understanding of Kergorlay. It was to him an inexhaustible mine, in which he dug continually without ever reaching the bottom.

Their disagreement in politics was, in fact, a principal cause of the interest and moral value of their correspondence. Tocqueville, aware that in his friend's mind there was one interdicted zone; that of feelings and opinions relating to practical politics, was forced, therefore, when he wrote, to confine himself within an elevated and generally philosophical region. The restraint was sometimes irksome both to his heart and head, but it oftener was a relief to his mind, which found in this correspondence an occasional refuge, whither it might escape, or rather rise, when it could shake off the trammels of political struggles and business. On the other hand, from the fact of contemporary politics occupying so large a space, much of the most remarkable correspondence of Tocqueville with other friends cannot be published. Such is especially the character of a great many letters addressed to MM. de Corcelle, Ampère, Count Molé, Dufaure, Lanjuinais, Freslon, Charles Rivet, M. and Madame de Circourt, M. Duvergier de Hauranne, &c. &c. We have been obliged to make a selection, and to choose sometimes, not the most interesting, but the most fit for publication. There are correspondences which, though charming, we have been forced almost entirely to suppress, as too political, or too confidential, — such as those which Tocqueville kept up with his relations, particularly with his brothers; and, if their kind indulgence will permit the assimilation, with the friend whom he treated as a brother, the author of this memoir, who possesses 300 letters, none of which could with propriety be published.

One correspondence of Tocqueville's, though under very different circumstances, resembles in some points his correspondence with Kergorlay, and deserves especial mention, because, while it adds another proof of the strength of his friendships, it perhaps reveals, more than any other, his whole heart, his true character, his real opinions and feelings. We allude to his letters to Eugène Stoffels.

Alexis de Tocqueville and Eugène Stoffels, whose intimacy began at the college of Metz, parted when they left it at the age of sixteen. Nothing seemed likely to bring them again together, — certainly not a similarity of position and a conformity of habits; for one lived in Paris on an independent fortune, and the other in the provinces on the salary of a small place in the public revenue; — nor even the sympathy which sometimes draws together two superior intellects; for Stoffels possessed distinguished but not first-rate talents. What, then, was the tie between them? A purer mind, and a more independent character than his never existed. When this struck Tocqueville, he gave to Stoffels his whole heart. Although intellectual superiority had an immense attraction for Tocqueville, moral worth attracted him still more powerfully. He never engaged in any serious undertaking without consulting Stoffels, or did anything of importance without informing him; and for the very reason that Stoffels lived far removed from politics and the bustle of the world, Tocqueville delighted in confiding to him his impressions, and in placing his stormy and complicated existence in contact with the simple and uniform life of his friend. To Kergorlay he went for intellectual aid; to Stoffels for moral support and sympathy. Stoffels was, perhaps, the man of all others whose esteem he most valued, and whose blame he most dreaded.

Though many illustrious and variously distinguished personages figure in Tocqueville's letters, great names, mixed up with great or small affairs, are not the things to be sought for by the reader of this correspondence. This is not a publication of pride or ostentation. He will find sometimes, amidst obscure and unknown names, thoughts and feelings expressed in graceful and captivating language. In choosing the letters, the substance, much more than the name of the correspondent, has been considered.

Tocqueville's letters to his English friends fill a considerable space in this collection; especially those to Mr. Senior, Mr. Reeve, Mrs. Grote, Mr. J. S. Mill, Lord Radnor, Sir Cornewall and Lady Theresa Lewis, Mrs. Austin, Lord Hatherton, Mr. W. Greg, Sir James Stephen, &c. &c. They would occupy a still larger space if, here again, we were not stopped by the proper names and political questions, for which, at present, publicity would be neither possible nor desirable. Some day this obstacle will cease; and, with a view to this eventuality, more or less remote, I may announce that all is in readiness for an ulterior and complete publication.

In England, Tocqueville loved and honored a free country; and he estimated individual merit at too high a rate to be indifferent to the particular and distinguishing qualities which make relations with Englishmen so safe, friendships so lasting, and engagements so sacred.*

* With two exceptions, M. de Beaumont mentions merely the names of M. de Tocqueville's French correspondents, obviously because he

The last, the shortest, and the fullest correspondence of Tocqueville, is that with Madame Swetchine, portions of which were published last year in the Count de Falloux's interesting memoir. Those who have read it, can comprehend the singular fascination exercised by Madame Swetchine, the attraction of her "salon," the charm of her talent and disposition, as well as the extraordinary influence that she acquired over all who came near her, an influence which Tocqueville was the less likely to escape, as Madame Swetchine must have exercised on such a man all her powers of captivation.

It will be observed that none of the letters of Tocqueville's correspondents are inserted in this collection. Of course it would frequently have been interesting to see the letters of the correspondents, as one always likes to see question and answer side by side. But such a line once entered upon, where could we stop? We have avoided it altogether, with the single exception of a letter from Count Molé, explanatory of a public act of Tocqueville's. There are some other letters which cannot be brought forward here, his letters to his wife. When one considers that on the rare occasions when he was separated from her, he never passed a single day without writing and giving her a full account of all that he did and felt, the value of such letters and the light that they would throw upon the heart and character of the writer, can easily be imagined. Latterly, Tocqueville wrote more letters than ever. After he was secluded from political action, he had more leisure. There is, too, a time

thought them too well known to the French public to require description. He has given a slight biographical notice of each of Tocqueville's English correspondents, which was probably necessary for the information of his French readers. But, as these notices contain nothing with which the English reader is not acquainted, it has not been thought advisable to translate them. — TR.

of life at which the world around seems to grow narrower, and one strives to enlarge its sphere. It is when, estimating better one's fellow-men, one reckons them not by number but by worth; and this makes the world appear small. Then, without regard to distance, one seeks everywhere for the rare qualities which one has learned to appreciate.

These were the reasons that induced Tocqueville to extend the circle not only of his acquaintances, but of his intimate friends.

It is remarkable that, amid the events which extinguished the personal importance of so many men, his had gone on increasing; and never had he occupied a higher position in the estimation of foreign countries, than after he had ceased to hold any official one in France. This will be proved by a single instance. It has already been stated that in the year 1857, Tocqueville went to collect materials for his second volume in England, where there is a unique and precious collection of documents relating to the French Revolution. Thanks to the personal respect entertained for him, he was authorized to search the public archives without restriction, and to look into all the confidential correspondence between the British government and its diplomatic agents. Anxious to give himself up entirely to his researches, Tocqueville endeavored whilst he was in London, to see no persons but those whose assistance was necessary to the attainment of his object. He could not, however, entirely escape the marks of respect of which he was the object, and that in a free country are so liberally bestowed upon men who have honorably quitted a distinguished post. Lord Lansdowne, Lord Stanhope, Lord Macaulay, Lord and Lady Granville, Lord and Lady Hatherton, Sir G. C. and Lady Theresa Lewis, as well as his old friends, Reeve, Senior, Grote, &c. &c., vied with each other in demonstrations of regard. Prince Albert desired to have an interview with Tocqueville, to express his high esteem. A last tribute, for which he was little prepared, awaited him. When about to embark, he was informed that a vessel belonging to the British government had been placed at his disposal, to take him to any French port he might choose. The order had been given by the first Lord of the Admiralty, Sir Charles Wood, who thought that England owed this act of courtesy to her illustrious and honored guest; a homage as honorable to the offerer as to the receiver, and which was not the mere act of a minister, but that of a whole nation whose approbation must have been securely reckoned upon. It was universally applauded in England, different as it was from those public honors which, in other countries, are exclusively reserved for official personages. Though he had a lively sense of its value, Tocqueville was not dazzled by so great an honor, as is shown by his simple relation of the circumstance.

" I have been in England," * (he wrote on the 25th July, 1857), " where I received so many and such striking proofs of consideration, that I was almost as much embarrassed as gratified. The whole political world overwhelmed me with favors and attentions. . . .

" Last of all, Sir Charles Wood, hearing that I lived near Cherbourg, and was returning thither, placed at my disposal a little steamer, which carried me straight from Portsmouth to Cherbourg, last Tuesday, to the great astonishment of the natives of the latter place, who, waiting in the hope of seeing at least a prince land from the vessel, saw only your humble servant."

* Letter to M. de Beaumont.

CHAPTER VI.

CANNES.

SUDDENLY the evil which was to hurry Tocqueville to his grave showed itself in its worst and most alarming symptom. In the month of June, 1858, he broke a blood-vessel.

Although he had before received some slight warnings of the same kind, but not to the same extent, he had never understood them. Nothing, in fact, could be more contrary to what he knew of his own constitution. It had always been weak and delicate, and there had long been symptoms of some organic disease. Till now, everything had led him to believe that the diseased organ was not the chest; and those who knew him most intimately thought the same.

On his long journeys, especially when he was in America, he had sometimes suffered, but never in the chest, which appeared to be, perhaps, the soundest part of his body. His travelling companion had been able, on several occasions, to make the most satisfactory observations on this point. When, in exploring the forests and the wildernesses of the new world, they had to climb steep ascents, Tocqueville always reached the top first, without appearing to be out of breath. When, on returning from the bay of Saginaw, they were forced to ride more than forty miles without stopping, through the difficult paths of the virgin forest, or the wild prairies, Tocqueville showed no signs of fatigue or exhaustion. Sometimes, on these adventurous marches, they were brought to a sudden halt by a wide and deep stream ; on such occasions Tocqueville swam across it. Once he did so on Lake Huron, near Michilimackinac, in a latitude where, whatever be the season, the water is always icy cold when not frozen, and he never appeared the worse. In 1841, ten years later, when travelling in Africa, he fell ill in the camp of Eddis, on the road between Stora and Constantine, even then his lungs did not appear to be disordered ; for on the day before he ascended the Pic de Bougie, while most of his companions stopped half-way.

In 1850, however, soon after he gave up office, his friends were alarmed by serious symptoms ; the physicians did not even then discover that there was any formed disease of the lungs ; but only a dangerous accident which, if it did not return, might leave no trace ; and it did not return. A winter at Sorrento, and another in Touraine, seemed to have arrested the evil ; but much more was needed. To have saved his precious life he should have gone not for one winter, but for years, to a southern climate. Above all he ought, for an indefinite period, to have abandoned the, to him, destructive climate of Normandy. Madame de Tocqueville wished, and repeatedly entreated him to do so, but he could not make up his mind to this ; and it is easy to understand his reluctance to leave the country that he had loved so dearly, for one without any of his own interests, far from his friends, and from his books, and from the intellectual activity which to him was life itself. Such an exile would have been an almost certain sentence of death ; and, perhaps, more speedy than that with which he was threatened.

Although what happened in June, 1858, left no room
for any illusions, Tocqueville still harbored them. He,
however, submitted to the advice of his doctors to proceed to Provence; and after having, in spite of the ur-
gency of the case, spent three or four months in making
a provision of books, notes, and materials, for his work,
which he hoped to finish during his convalescence, he at
last left Normandy for Cannes, where he arrived in the
beginning of November, 1858.

Must we here record the sad time at Cannes, the long
and painful journey thither, the attacks which recurred
daily with increasing violence, in spite of which Tocqueville did not despair?   Even if we wished we could not.
How, indeed, describe that existence still so animated,
that intelligence retaining all its strength, that imagination still so brilliant and fertile, that fulness of life, separated but by a few days from the instant of final extinction!

When all hope of recovery was lost, Tocqueville still
hoped; and the objects by which he was surrounded conspired to keep up the deception.

The season was commencing when under the sky of
Provence nature seems to have a new birth. The little
villa to which Tocqueville had retired, is situated about
a mile and a half above Cannes, in the midst of a wood
of orange and lemon trees. Imagination can paint nothing
more enchanting than this spot, set in a frame of mountains and sea; nothing more intoxicating than the perfume yielded by the scented woods, and even by the
ground itself. Nothing can be more splendid than the
first awaking of nature from its slumber. In those be-
nign climates, and at the moment when the weakest and
most insignificant creatures return to existence, it is the

more sad to witness the gradual extinction of life in the grandest of all — a man uniting a great mind with a noble heart. It seems also impossible when all around is bursting into new life for the most desponding invalid to give up all hope of recovery.

His life, however, ebbed ; and rapidly, in spite of every care and devotion. Two first-rate physicians, Dr. Sève of Cannes, and a former colleague, Dr. Maure of Grasse, visited him continually. Two sisters of charity, sister Valérie and sister Gertrude, were about him night and day. That other life-long sister of charity, Madame de Tocqueville, never left him. Those who nursed him could not help sharing his hopes, and often under that pure sky, mournful fancies gave way to less sorrowful expectations.

At a few steps from the villa there extends an avenue of palms and cypresses, whence, on one side, the horizon is bounded by the lowest chain of the Alps, on the other by the Bay of Cannes, Gulf Juan, and the islands of St. Marguerite. Though the sea is seen from thence, its breezes are scarcely felt, for they arrive loaded with the perfume of flowers, and tempered by the warmth of the atmosphere. It was here that, leaning on the arm of a sister of charity, the poor invalid came every day to breathe the soft air, to contemplate the clear sky, and to enjoy the reviving rays of the sun. Alexis de Tocqueville walking slowly and silently in this little cypress avenue, his feeble body and pale countenance, with its deep sad expression, the true reflection of his present thoughts and of his mind, the simple ingenuous face of the poor sister who supported him, composed a scene which will long be fixed in the memory of all who once beheld it.

I have already said that Tocqueville hoped ; and how could he avoid the return of hope, when all around him was returning to life ? He persevered in his usual habits, his projects, and his writings. He read and was read to ; he wrote a great many letters, and devoured those which he received in great numbers. There was not one of his friends who did not receive, at least, one letter from him during the last month of his life. His thoughts dwelt constantly on public affairs. It was the eve of the Italian war. Some distinguished foreigners, then at Cannes, among others, the late Baron Bunsen, and Lord Brougham, sent to him regularly their despatches, in which he took intense interest. The chief object of his meditation, and to which all his reading was directed, was the continuation of his book on the revolution. The last book that he read was the *Memoirs of Count Miot de Mélitot*, which he highly prized. Although his faculties preserved all their activity, his mind seemed to become calmer every day. He appeared to grow gentler, kinder, more religious, more composed, and more resigned.

Yet, as if his own illness were not a sufficient calamity, another was added. Madame de Tocqueville, worn out by fatigue, and still more by grief, herself fell ill. Among other disorders, she was attacked by a complaint of the eyes, for which she was ordered to remain constantly in complete darkness. Such, however, was the tender love of Tocqueville for his wife, and so impossible was it for him to live without her and away from her, that, as she could no longer sit by his bed of suffering, he succeeded in dragging himself to hers. But the deep gloom of her room increased his illness, for daylight was as essential to him as darkness to her ; and, yielding to a sort of physical instinct, he escaped to the sunshine, which alone revived him. It was a sad fate for two beings so necessary to each other to be able no longer to live together or apart. In fact, in a few minutes, Tocqueville returned to his wife's bedside, and said — " Dear Marie, the sunshine ceases to do me good, if, to enjoy it, I must give up seeing you."

On another occasion, in a moment of despondency, for which there was only too much cause, the poor invalid acknowledged that he had come south too late, and feelingly owned to his wife his fault in not having followed her advice.

Amidst these heart-rending scenes, the disorder went on increasing, and every day became more threatening. The return of warm weather had done him, on the whole, more harm than good. He had felt, indeed, the stimulating influence which at that season pervades all nature, but it had stimulated only the disease.

His rapid loss of strength and flesh was evident to every one but to the patient himself, whose illusions seemed to increase with the imminence of the danger. At the end of March, Dr. Maure had lost all hope. Dr. Sève, though also very desponding, thought that he might live through the spring and summer, and reach the autumn. But the icy winds that in spring come down from the mountains, and from which the Bay of Cannes is not completely sheltered, blew so violently for several days that the catastrophe could be predicted; and in the evening of the 16th of April, 1859, Alexis de Tocqueville fell into a syncope of a few seconds, and expired. He was only fifty-four years old. He left no children.

At this last moment he had the consolation of being surrounded by his nearest relatives, to whom he had always been tenderly attached. His eldest brother, Count Hippolyte de Tocqueville, who had been with him ever since his arrival in Provence, till recently summoned by urgent business to Normandy; his second brother, Viscount Edward, his sister-in-law, the Viscountess de Tocqueville, and his nephew, Count Hubert, had hastened to Cannes at the first notice. His oldest friend from childhood, whose attachment had been so constant, so faithful, and so serviceable, Louis de Kergorlay, was at his death-bed. Need we say that she too was there, the gentle and worthy partner of his whole life, for whom was about to commence an existence more painful than death; she was there to receive and treasure in her heart his last breath, and his last look. Deceived by the illusions which the invalid's letters had kept up to the last, and detained in Rome by a melancholy duty, another of his dear and devoted friends, Jean Jacques Ampère, was on his way to Cannes, looking forward without immediate anxiety to the happiness of passing some time with the friend whom he wished so much to see again. On landing at Marseilles he heard the terrible news, and had the inexpressible affliction of reaching Cannes only in time to be present at the funeral. There is one more friend who has not been mentioned, whom Tocqueville yet loved well enough to send for a month before the fatal day; it is he who, hastening to obey the summons, witnessed the heart-rending scenes which he now describes.

Tocqueville passed peacefully away without any of the cruel pangs often caused by the immediate approach of death; and at the same time with the mental tranquillity of a man prepared for it, and for whom the close of existence has neither terrors nor threats. What better preparation can there be for death than a whole life spent in well-doing?

His death was that of a Christian, as had been his life. Conversion has been wrongly spoken of. He had no need of conversion, because he had never been in the slightest degree irreligious.

Tocqueville's mind was always much disturbed by doubt. It was an inseparable part of his nature. But in the midst of his greatest perplexities he never ceased to be sincerely Christian. This sentiment amounted in him to a passion, and was even a part of his political creed; for he believed that there could be no liberty without morality, and no morality without religion. Christianity and civilization were to him convertible terms. He believed firmly that, for the good of mankind, it was most desirable to see religious faith intimately united with the love of liberty; and it always deeply pained him to find them separated. Undoubtedly he would not have hesitated to put any force or restraint upon himself for the sake of showing openly his attachment to religion, and his respect for her ordinances, rather than, by his example, place arms in the hands of those who attack the doctrines of Christianity in order to escape from its morality. But in humbling himself before a minister of peace and of mercy,* he followed only the impulse of his conscience; and a more ample and particular confession than the priest's enlightened piety exacted from him would have been no more wounding to his pride than repentance was to his heart.

Tocqueville had expressed a desire that his remains should be deposited in the parish cemetery of Tocqueville. This desire was held sacred. His mortal remains were

---

* The venerable Curé of Cannes.

transported thither in pious fulfilment of it, by his brother Hippolyte and his nephew Hubert. We have passed in silence over all the religious honors paid to the memory of Tocqueville. One ceremony, however, ought perhaps to be described; we mean that which the little parish of Tocqueville witnessed when the funeral procession first reached its precincts, and proceeded towards the cemetery. There were to be seen only the sincere proofs of real grief; the mourning of two excellent brothers, that of many absent friends, represented by two who were worthy of the privilege (Corcelle and Ampère),* the tears of a crowd of peasants who had assembled of their own accord to lavish their blessings on the great man, who in their eyes was only the good man. Last of all, the deep and solemn grief, of which we hardly dare to speak, that occupied the deserted château, and towards which every one's thoughts were directed. In this retired and peaceful spot, Tocqueville had ordered that the most simple emblem of his faith, a wooden cross, should mark the resting-place of his remains. But if it be true that genius and virtue constitute true glory, we may say that the lowly cemetery of the little village of Tocqueville contains the remains of a great man. On hearing of his death, the Duke de Broglie said, " France produces no more such men." This is the opinion of France; it will be that of Europe. Tocqueville's fame was already very high, and very widely spread; we venture to predict that it will every day become more exalted and more extended. We have tried to paint the author, the philosopher, and the statesman; but who can paint the

---

*. On leaving Cannes, where a coffin was all that he found, Ampère had the melancholy satisfaction of accompanying Madame de Tocqueville to Paris; he resolved also to have that of attending the funeral.

man himself, his heart, his grace, his poetical imagination, and at the same time his good sense; that heart so
tender, that reason so firm, that judgment so keen and
so sure, that intellect so clear and so deep, never either
commonplace or eccentric, always original and sensible;
in a word, all the qualities that made him so superior
and distinguished above other men? Tocqueville not
only possessed great talents, but every variety of talent.
His conversation was as brilliant as his compositions.
He was as admirable as a narrator as he was as a writer.
He possessed another talent which is even more rare,
that of being a good listener as well as a talker. Gifted
with activity indefatigable, and almost morbid, he disposed of his time with admirable method. He found
time for everything, and never omitted a moral or a social
duty. It has already been said that he had many friends;
he had the additional happiness of never losing one, and
also that of having such a fund of affection to bestow
upon them, that none of his friends ever complained of
his own share on seeing that of others. His friendships
were as well chosen as they were sincere, and perhaps
there never was a more striking example than he afforded of the charm which intelligence adds to virtue.

Excellent as he was, he was always endeavoring to
become better; and he certainly drew nearer every day
to the moral perfection which seemed to him the only
aim worthy of man. The great problem of the destiny
of man impressed him with daily-increasing awe and
reverence; more and more piety, and gratitude for the
Divine blessings, entered every day into his actions and
feelings. He felt a greater respect for human life and
for human rights, and even for those of all created beings.
He thus reached a higher, purer, and more refined hu-

manity. He regarded rank less, and personal merit more. He became still more patient, more resigned, more industrious, more watchful to lose nothing of the life which he loved so much, and which he had a right to cherish, since he made such a noble use of it. Lastly, to his honor be it said, that, in a selfish age, his only aim was the pursuit of truths useful to his fellow-creatures, and his sole ambition to augment their welfare and their dignity.

To this rare ambition he will owe a fame which will never die; for the names of those who honor and elevate our race are registered by mankind.

The story of his life seems to be summed up in a reflection found among his papers: —

"Life is neither a pleasure nor a pain, but a serious business, which it is our duty to carry through and to terminate with honor."

UNPUBLISHED WORKS

OF ALEXIS DE TOCQUEVILLE.

EXTRACTS FROM THE TOUR IN SICILY.

[Written in 1827.]

THE MS. of the tour in Sicily makes a small quarto volume of 350 pages. To give the reader a notion of this first literary performance of Tocqueville, we furnish at random a few extracts taken word for word from the MS., without introducing any reflections or comments.

Tocqueville left Naples with his brother Edward in the beginning of March, 1827. He had scarcely set sail when he encountered a violent storm.

"The ship," he says, "in which we embarked, was a little brigantine of seventy-five tons. . . . . We sailed on slowly, with the magnificent Bay of Naples before our eyes, and the receding stir of life in that populous city still sounding in our ears. We passed along the shore of Herculaneum. Soon we descried the hill which conceals Pompeii. Night had come on when we neared the cliffs of Capri. On waking the next morning, we had still those precipitous rocks in view, and they continued so all day; they seemed to pursue us like some dreadful remembrance.

" Capri resembles the nest of a bird of prey; it is the fitting abode for a tyrant. Thither it was that Tiberius

drew in his victims from all parts of the Roman empire;
but thence also (and there is some consolation in the
thought), oppressed by the infirmities of a disgraceful
old age, completely disabused even as to the enjoyments
which he had hoped to find in the sight of human sufferings, and disgusted with his monstrous pleasures, he at
length allowed the truth to escape from the bottom of his
cruel heart.　From Capri is dated his letter to the senate,
in which he says : — ' Why do I write to you, conscript
fathers?　What have I to tell you?　May the gods cause
me to waste away more miserably even than they now
do, if I know ! '

"Towards evening, the calm which had stopped us
was succeeded by a west wind, and we were forced to
tack.　At morning we were out of sight of land.　All
day we struggled against a foul wind.　The sea began
gradually to swell.　The sun had just set; I was sitting
in the cabin, with my head resting on my hand, observing the horizon, which from time to time was covered by
a black cloud.　The white foam of the waves stood out
in the distance against this dark background.　I saw that
a storm was coming, though I did not think it was so
close at hand.　Soon we began to pitch deeply, and the
spray broke over the deck in every direction.　Lightning rent the sky, and distant, hollow thunder announced
the storm.　I have often enjoyed watching the approach
of a thunder-storm in the night.　There is to me something sublime and attractive in the preceding calm, — in
the sort of solemn expectation pervading the whole creation at the instant of the impending crisis; but whoever
has not beheld a similar scene on the open sea, has not
witnessed the most awful sight in nature.

"At the first clap of thunder for one moment the ship

was in agitation. The captain's voice was heard from the poop, and the monotonous cry of the sailors announced a new manœuvre. The wind rose with frightful suddenness. The thunder came nearer — every flash for one moment illuminated the whole sky, and immediately afterwards we were plunged in perfect darkness. I could have conceived nothing like the violent commotion of the sea. It resembled the seething of a huge caldron. I shall all my life remember the deep impression I felt when, in an instant of calm, I heard near me a low sound of voices repeating verses of a Psalm. I looked whence the voices came, and I found that it was from under a sail, where ten or twelve poor passengers had found shelter. Is there any philosopher so convinced of his own theories as not to have been tempted to do the like at the sight of this terrible display of Almighty power?

" The storm was now almost over our heads. Several times we had seen the bolt fall into the sea not far from us; every moment we feared to be capsized. Suddenly a sea caught the ship on her side, and threw her on her beam ends. The wave tore up the benches and poured into the cabins; frightful cries arose on every side, and a dog that had hid itself among some barrels howled the most dismal accompaniment. The alarm was sharp, but lasted only for a minute; the vessel righted herself.

" Torrents of rain greatly diminished the danger of the storm; and although the sea still ran high, we all thought that we might venture to retire to rest in spite of the flood by which we were inundated. The night must have appeared long to every one. As for us, when after two hours of a sleep, at every instant interrupted by the violent motions of the ship, and by the whistling of the wind in the rigging, we woke up thoroughly, we felt that the sea was far from having gone down. As the sun rose, however, with dazzling brightness, I thought that all danger was over, and, in high spirits, I put my head out of our cabin; the sailors, some hanging to the rigging, and others leaning against the masts, seemed all to be absorbed in the contemplation of one object. Anxiety was painted on every face, and the rigidity of their looks was more terrifying than the uproar of the night. I then examined the sky; on the west a violent wind seemed to be carrying over our heads a huge cloud, charged with rain, and I saw clearly that another storm was at hand. I then tried to discover what was the distant object which so struck the eyes of our crew; at length I saw rise up, through the mist, indistinct shapes of high mountains, extending from north to south, and barring our course; whilst the storm, which was beginning, and the fury of the waves increasing every moment, were driving us in that direction. I crawled along the deck, for no living creature could have moved on foot without being instantly washed overboard, and holding on by one thing after another, at last I reached the wheel of the rudder, which the captain himself held; I asked him if he thought there was danger.

"The man fixed his fierce eye on me, and roughly answered *Credo.cosi*, 'I think so;' and would not say another word. As I was returning to the cabin an old sailor caught me by the sleeve, and grinding his teeth, said to me, 'It was your hurry to leave that made us quit the port. You will soon see what will be the consequence to you and all of us.' The night before I had

seen these very men full of courage and hope springing
from one cable to another, and though between fire and
water, crying out as they passed, 'It is nothing, gentlemen ; only a squall,' *E niente signori, una burasca.*
But this time, I own, I thought that all was over with us.
I went back to the cabin ; I informed Edward of the state
of affairs, adding that we must be ready to snatch the
first chance of escape, though I then saw none. At that
instant a sailor came to beg a dole for the souls in purga-
tory. We then remembered the religion we were born
in, and to which our earliest thoughts had been directed ;
we said a short prayer, and sat down at the door of our
cabin. I folded my arms and thought over the few years
of my past life. I frankly own that, at that moment,
when I thought myself on the eve of appearing before
the supreme Judge, the object of human life seemed to
me to be quite different from what I had always considered it. The pursuits, which till then I had esteemed the
most important, now seemed to be infinitely trifling; whilst
the giant Eternity, enlarging every instant, hid behind him
all other objects. I then bitterly lamented that I was
not armed with a conscience prepared for every event ; I
felt that such a help would have been of more avail
than human courage against a danger that I could neither struggle with nor boldly face. But the hardest
part was when I came to think of those whom we were
leaving behind in this world. When I pictured to myself
the moment when the public news of the catastrophe
would reach their ears, I felt tears rise to my eyes, and
I instantly turned my thoughts to something else that I
might not lose the strength which I believed that I was
on the point of needing. The cloud burst over us with
great violence ; the waves became prodigious ; in a few

minutes we came in sight of several islands. I then learnt that in the night the storm had thrown us forty leagues out of our course into the midst of the Lipari Islands.

The ship, though freighted for Palermo, could not make it, on account of the contrary winds; but the little port of Olivieri hove in sight.

"It will be easily believed," continues Tocqueville, "that we were terribly impatient to quit the wooden walls within which we had spent such miserable hours. But, in this country, where the police regulations against travellers are stringent in proportion to their laxity against thieves, all locomotion seemed to be studiously impeded. We were ordered to stay in the ship till the next day, at noon, at which hour it would be the pleasure of the custom-house officers to pay us a visit.

"On the 12th of March, after their search, we landed at last, on a little beach close to us. We jumped out on the grass, shouting joyfully, 'At last, Sicily, we have you!'

"We immediately began to scamper over the surrounding country. A more enchanting scene was never presented to poor creatures who still fancied they felt the rolling of the vessel under their feet. We did not see the coast edged with those long strips of barren sand which sadden the gaze on the borders of the ocean, and indeed harmonize so well with the misty skies of its coasts. Here the waves washed the turf. Scarce thirty paces from the shore we saw enormous aloes, and long rows of Indian figs, and shrubs in bloom. We had left winter behind in Italy. Here spring, with all its bright colors and sweet odors, met our view. Two musket-shots off rose a village amidst the olive and fig trees. On

a green hill opposite were the ruins of a castle. Then
the valley, covered with flowers and verdure, mounted
rapidly, and assumed a wide triangular figure towards the
south. Thus Sicily first presented itself to our view,
from the coast of Olivieri. . . . . Then we first learnt
that neither the beauty nor the natural wealth of a country constitutes the well-being of its inhabitants. The
first thing that struck us was the total absence of glass
windows.

" . . . . On the 13th of March, before daybreak, we set
off. The caravan proceeded in this order : — A soldier,
carrying a musket, with a dagger in his sash, and a
cotton cap on his head, opened the march, mounted on
a powerful horse. . . . . After him we came in single
file ; some on horseback, and others rather uncomfortably
perched on parts of the baggage. Three young peasants,
barefooted, with the copper hue of Moors, ran continually from one end to the other urging on our mules ;
now and then uttering the wild cry which is peculiar to
Sicily, and every instant repeating their favorite curse,
Kasso. . . . ."

The troop proceeded in this way over part of the
island, and reached Palermo.

" . . . . The first object that strikes the eye on approaching the town is the Monte Pellegrino, whose
square and isolated mass shelters Palermo from the
north-westerly winds, and makes the sirocco still more
oppressive. Fifteen years ago the people believed, it is
said, that if Napoleon made himself master of Sicily,
he would cause this mountain to be thrown into the sea.
Nothing, perhaps, can better paint the kind of supernatural power which that man was able to acquire over the
minds of his contemporaries.

" . . . . On the 17th of March we left Palermo. . . .
After going on for two hours through these lonely scenes,
the guide signed to us to look at something a long way
off on the top of a hill. We were amazed at seeing a
Greek temple, standing upright and alone, and in the
most complete preservation. It was Segestum. Although since our arrival in Italy we had become accustomed to the sight of ruins of every age, and of every
description, and had been enabled by their terrible example to appreciate the fragility of all human works, till
now it had not been our fate to meet with (as it were)
the corpse of a dead city in the midst of a desert. We
had never been so thoroughly and so deeply impressed.
We stood as if fixed to the spot ; we tried to group
round these splendid remains of ancient magnificence
other temples, palaces, and porticoes. We wished that
we could have restored to the soil the fertility that made
Segestum so powerful from its foundation ; and then we
rejoiced in the absence of petty modern houses in the
neighborhood of this antique colossus.

" . . . We soon reached the steep banks of a torrent.
It is the Xanthus ; farther on flows the Simoïs. Why
do these Trojan names — the ruins of this Trojan town
— and, in general, the relics of this classical antiquity —
interest us more than the vestiges of more modern times,
even than events which nearly concern us ?

" . . . . After quitting Selinonte, we went sometimes
over tracts of sand, sometimes across valleys without
trees or inhabitants. . . .

" It may be said, though at first it seems hardly credible, that in Sicily there are no villages, but only towns,
and these very numerous. One is astonished, after travelling for twenty or thirty miles in almost a desert, sud-

denly to come upon a town of 20,000 inhabitants, for
which one has been prepared by no high-roads nor distant
sound. Here is to be found the little that exists of industry and comfort, as in a paralytic body the heat retires
gradually towards the heart. It is not impossible to assign a cause for this irregular state of things. The only
great landed proprietors in Sicily are the nobles, and
especially the ecclesiastical bodies; these two classes are
far from any thought of improvement, and have long
been used to the amount of rents paid to them. The
nobles squander theirs in Palermo or Naples, without
thinking of their Sicilian property, except to sign the
receipt they send thither. We were told that there are
many who have never even been to their estates. As for
the monks, a race naturally given up to routine, they
spend their usual income quietly, without caring to increase it. Meanwhile the people, having little or no
interest in the soil, and no market for the produce, gradually leave the country. It is known how few inhabitants are enough to cultivate badly an immense extent
of land. The environs of Rome are an evidence of
this.

" The visitor who should confine himself to the coast of
Sicily, might easily believe her to be rich and flourishing, though there is not a more wretched country in' the
world ; he would consider it populous whilst the fields
are deserted, and will remain so till the subdivision of
property and an outlet for produce, give the people a
sufficient interest in the soil to call them back. . . . ."

After visiting Sciacca and Siculiano, the travellers proceeded towards Girgenti . . . . . " . . . . . From this
point is seen the immense enclosure, formed by the walls
of Girgenti (Agrigentum). We estimated it at not less

than from twelve to fifteen miles round. Almost all the remains of antiquity are ranged along the natural wall which overlooks the sea. First, we saw the Temple of Juno Lucina, of which the frieze and several columns have fallen. We then went on to the Temple of Concord. I have never seen anything in such extraordinary preservation. Nothing is wanting: pediment, friezes, and interior, all have been spared by time. It has done more, it has given the whole an admirable tint; to us who gaze upon this temple after a lapse of about 2,500 years, it probably is a finer object than it presented to its builders. Both these temples resemble exactly that of Segestum, except that they are smaller; the columns have the same proportions, the lines the same simplicity, the accessories the same arrangement.

" It is remarkable that the Greeks, whose imagination was so versatile, should never have thought of varying in any manner the architectural system they had once adopted. I may be wrong; but this seems to me to show such a steadfast conviction of the really great and beautiful, as could have belonged only to a people so extraordinarily gifted with general artistic capacities.

" On the same line with these temples, but farther on, are the remains of that of Jupiter Olympius. The most remarkable feature of these remains is, that they must have belonged to a building larger than any that has been left us by the ancients. In general, the Greeks, and even the Romans, who had so much grandeur in their genius, and in their conduct of worldly affairs, yet in art never fell into a taste for the gigantic. They considered, and with truth, that it is more difficult to produce the very fine than the very big; and almost impossible to produce at once the very fine, and the very big."

Our travellers proceeded from Girgenti to Catania,
across the fertile plain of the Lestrigones.

"When we reached Catania," continues Tocqueville,
"we determined to start that very evening for Nicolosi,
and attempt in the night the feat of ascending Etna. . . .
We started at four for Nicolosi. . . . . On leaving
the town, our path lay through a few cultivated fields;
and then we reached an old deposit of lava, still barren
and of horrid aspect. From thence is the best view of
Catania surrounded by groves. . . . . .

"Soon we left the lava, and found ourselves immediately in the midst of a kind of enchanted country which
anywhere would be striking; but in Sicily it is ravishing.
Orchard succeeds orchard, surrounding cottages and pretty
villages; no spot is lost; everywhere there is an appearance of prosperity and plenty. In most fields I observed
corn, vines, and fruit-trees growing and thriving together.
As I went on, I asked myself what was the cause of this
great local prosperity? It cannot be attributed only to
the richness of the soil, for the whole of Sicily is so fertile
as to require less cultivation than most countries. The
first reason for the phenomenon that occurred to me was
this: Etna being situated between two of the largest
towns in Sicily, Catania and Messina, finds on both sides
a market for its produce, which does not exist in the
centre, nor on the south coast. The second reason, which
I was slow in admitting, seemed to me finally to be more
conclusive. The land round Etna being subject to
frightful ravages, the nobles and the monks grew disgusted with it, and the people became the proprietors. It
is now subdivided almost without any limit. Each culti-
vator has an interest, however small, in the soil. This is
the only part of Sicily where the peasant is a proprietor.

" But whence comes it that this extreme division of property, which so many sensible people consider an evil in France, must be regarded as a blessing, in fact a great blessing, in Sicily? This will be easily understood. I quite acknowledge that in an enlightened country where the climate is favorable to labor, and every class desires to grow rich, as for instance in England, the extreme division of property may be hurtful to agriculture, and therefore to internal prosperity, because it deprives men who would have the will and the power to turn them to account of a great means of improvement, and even of employment; but on the other hand, when the object is to excite and awaken an unhappy people half paralyzed, to whom rest is a pleasure; where the higher classes are sunk into hereditary sloth and vice, I know of no better way than to parcel out the land. If then I were king of England, I should favor large properties, and if I were ruler of Sicily, I should encourage as much as possible small estates; but as I am neither the one nor the other, I hasten back to my journal. . . .

" It was dark when we reached Nicolosi; at eleven at night they knocked at our door to tell us to get ready. . .

" As soon as we were in the air, our first care was to examine the state of the weather. We were glad to find that the wind had fallen, and that we could see the stars, but there was no moon. Profound darkness surrounded us. However, we soon discovered that we were riding over vast tracts of volcanic ashes, in which the feet of our mules sank deep. Soon afterwards it seemed as if we were becoming entangled in the windings of a great stream of lava. At last we came upon the wooded region. . . .

" Here we fell into a deep silence. This nocturnal

march in the midst of one of the most ancient forests in the world; the strange effects of light produced by our lantern on the knotted trunks of the oaks; the fabulous traditions which seemed to be called up by all around us; even the rustling of the leaves under our feet; all transported us to an unreal world. . . .

"At last we reached the foot of the last cone of Etna. We distinguished the most minute details, and we thought that we were close to the crater. In this we were mistaken, as will presently be shown. We were another hour in gaining the points that we had thought so close to us; and an hour of the most fatiguing walking that I ever had in my life. First we clambered for about twenty minutes up an icy slope covered with irregularities, so sharp and slippery that we could scarcely keep our footing; then we reached the last peaks, formed by successive falls of ashes, and consequently very steep. On this shifting ground, which inclines as rapidly as a roof, one cannot take a step without sinking in deeply, and often slipping back above six feet. I had already experienced the unpleasantness of such an ascent in my visit to Mount Vesuvius. But here it was much worse; to the difficulty of advancing on such a road was joined that of breathing at such a height; and each of these obstacles was increased by the other. We then found ourselves at about 11,000 feet above Catania. The air was rare and yet not light. Volcanic emanations filled it with sulphurous vapors. Every ten or fifteen steps we were obliged to stop. We then threw ourselves on the ashes, and for a few seconds we felt the most extraordinary palpitations of the heart. My head felt as if it were screwed in a tight iron cap. Edward owned to me that he did not feel certain of reaching the summit.

" We were making one of these forced halts when the guide, clapping his hands, exclaimed, in a tone which I seem still to hear, ' *Il sole! Il sole!* ' (the sun). We turned instantly towards the east; clouds covered the sky, yet the sun's disk, which was like a shield of red-hot iron, pierced through every obstacle, and showed itself half above the Ionian sea. Red and violet tints were diffused over the waves, and gave to the mountains of Calabria, opposite to us, a blood-red and violet hue. It was a sight such as can be beheld but once in a life-time; an aspect of nature in stern and awful beauty that penetrates and crushes you with a sense of your own insignificance. This grandeur was mingled with something of singular sadness and mournfulness. The immense star gave out only a dubious light. He seemed to drag himself rather than mount to the upper sky. Even so, said we to each other, will he, no doubt, rise on the last day.

" This sight restored our failing strength. We made tremendous efforts, and in a few seconds reached the edge of the crater. It was with a sort of terror that we looked into it. . . . . A vapor, white as snow, whirled and tumbled with unceasing noise in the depth which it concealed; it rose to the edge of the enormous basin, and then stopped, sank, and rose again; only a small quantity escaped, but that was enough to form a cloud which covered a quarter of the sky, and in which we were, against our will, often enveloped.

" The sun had scarcely cleared the waves of the sea when he hid himself in a bank of clouds, from which he soon emerged in splendor.

" The sea extended all round us, and Sicily narrowed to a point before our eyes. Etna projected its shadow as far as the environs of Trapani, and covered nearly the whole island with its immense cone. But the shadow was not at rest; like a living creature it appeared in perpetual motion. From minute to minute it contracted, and as it retreated whole provinces came in view. The island seemed to us to be rather rugged than mountainous. In the midst of its numberless hills we saw a blue line wind about — that was a river; a small white plate denoted a lake; something shining in the sun was a town. As for the poor human creatures, they could only have been perceived by the eye of Him who formed with the same ease an insect and Mount Etna.

"Here then, at last, we said, is Sicily, the object of our journey, the topic of our conversation for so many months; here is·the whole country spread out beneath our feet. By turning round we can travel all over it in an instant; our eyes can pierce into every nook; scarcely any part escapes us, and yet it is far from reaching the horizon. We had just come from Italy; we had trodden on the ashes of the greatest men that ever lived, and inhaled the dust of their monuments; we were full of the grandeurs of history. But here something of another kind addressed the imagination: every object that struck us, the crowd of thoughts that rushed into our minds, carried us back to primitive times. We came close to the earliest ages of the world, those ages of simplicity and innocence, before men were saddened by the remembrance of the past, or terrified by the uncertainty of the future; when satisfied with present happiness, and confident of its duration, they gathered the fruits freely bestowed by the earth, and almost as pure as the gods themselves, met everywhere with the footsteps of their deities, and lived, as it were, among them. It is here that fable shows us the first men. This is the home of the divinities of Grecian mythology. Near this spot Pluto tore Proserpine from her mother's arms; in the wood we had just passed through, Ceres halted in her rapid pursuit, and, tired with her fruitless search, seated herself on a rock ; and, though a goddess, wept, say the Greeks, because she was a mother. Apollo tended his flocks in these valleys; these groves, which reach to the coast, echoed to Pan's flute; nymphs strayed beneath their shade, and inhaled their perfume. Here Galatæa fled from Polypheme ; and Acis, on the eve of falling under his rival's strokes, still charmed these shores, and left to them his name. The lake of Hercules, and the rocks of the Cyclops, are visible in the distance.

"Land of gods and heroes! Poor · Sicily, what has become of thy brilliant chimeras ? . . . ."

A few days afterwards, Tocqueville left Sicily to visit the Lipari Islands, and chiefly the volcano of Stromboli. He explores and describes it; but when wishing to return to Sicily, he is detained by a contrary wind. This impediment lasts several days, and in this desert spot, to which he is chained without knowing how long his captivity may continue, his mind receives a variety of impressions, which he thus describes : —

"There was in our position on this burning rock, surrounded by the sea, and cut off from the whole world, a feeling of desertion and isolation which fell like a dead weight on our imagination.

" When we had in some degree recovered from this impression, we tried to employ the leisure, of which we had more than of anything else, and we should have then been glad to give away the time which one often would willingly buy so dear. . . . .

" One day I was sitting on the sands, with my head on my hands, looking out on the sea, and turning over carelessly in my mind the saddest thoughts. I had long been looking at a boat coming in ; it annoyed me, for it was full of people singing at the top of their voices as they drew near. It was a poor fisherman's family, husband, wife, and children ; it comprehended at least three generations. They all rowed, and the boat soon touched the land. The father and the elder ones jumped into the water, and dragged the boat upon the beach. Just then I saw come out of one of the huts on the coast a half-naked child, about two or three years old ; he hurried along, crawling on all fours, and shouting for joy.

" This baby became the object of general attention. As soon as a middle-aged woman who had just stepped out of the boat caught sight of him, she ran to embrace him, and raising him in her arms, covered him with kisses, and said to him a thousand things which I could not understand. He was soon surrounded by all the party, each had something to say to him ; he was passed from one to the other ; the men set their fish before him, and made him touch the scales ; the children all brought him some trifle from their recent expedition, and even the little ones of all took pains to put bracelets of shells on his arm, and then ran away quite delighted. He was evidently the last-born of the family.

" Till now I had never understood the misery of banishment, and the reality of those instincts which, however far one may be from one's country, draw one towards it in spite of obstacles and dangers.

" The recollection of France and of all that is comprehended in that one word, pounced upon me as its prey. The longing that I had to see her again was so

vehement, as to be far beyond any wish that I had ever
formed for anything, and I know not what sacrifice I
would not have made to find myself instantly on her
shores.

" The happiness of living in one's own country, like all
other happiness, is not felt while it is possessed. But let
exile or misfortune come upon you, and then leave memory to do its work. You will then learn to value things
aright; or rather you will learn nothing, for their value
depends on things no longer existing for you.

" In a foreign land there is an element of sadness often
mixed even with pleasure, and then many things, which
when at home you forgot to notice, many that use had
rendered indifferent, insipid, and even tiresome, recur to
your mind in banishment, not wearing the same look as
when they were present, but bright and vivid, and full
of charms which you only now perceive. They could
not make you happy, but they now have power enough
to make you miserable.

" I remember, before the period of which I am now
speaking, once thinking of the risk of imprisonment, for
which the experience of the last forty years has shown
that it was not absurd to prepare one's self beforehand; I
had succeeded in forming an almost agreeable idea of a
place which is in general so much dreaded. I fancied
that a man who was shut up with books, pens, and
paper, must find easy means of passing away the time
pleasantly enough. Besides, there is a multiplicity of
studies which the hurry of public life will not admit
of pursuing effectually. And then I wondered at the
numbers of people, who, from the years during which
they were imprisoned, ought to have written volumes,
yet have come out having done nothing at all.

"The days that we spent at Stromboli served to explain to me the phenomenon, and showed me my error. Although time was our greatest foe, we never could make up our minds to fight against it, by employing ourselves. Indeed, in the flattering picture that I had drawn of a prison, I had left out of the account the prevalent anxiety for the future, the indefinite duration of the present, and especially the want of a certain object. You cannot command the mind to work as you do a laborer to dig or delve. There must be a cause, a motive to set it in action; and the term of imprisonment may be lengthened, or it may end the next day. What is the use of beginning what one is not sure of finishing, a work which, perhaps, will never be useful or agreeable to one's self any more than to others? And then time crushes you by its slow progress; a long perspective of similar hours and days discourages you. It always requires an effort to begin. Why should this effort be made now rather than an hour hence, to-day rather than to-morrow? Who is there to urge you? Where is the exciting cause? Ennui, that overpowering kind of ennui which is not produced by idleness alone, but by the influence of a painful position, benumbs the faculties, makes the heart sink, extinguishes the imagination, and at last one dies, like a miser starved in the midst of his riches. . . . ."

However, just when the travellers had begun to think that they were to be forever chained by adverse fate to the rock of Stromboli, a favorable wind came to their rescue and enabled them to proceed.

In one part of his narrative, Tocqueville brings on the stage two persons more or less imaginary, — a Sicilian (Don Ambrosio) and a Neapolitan (Don Carlo); he draws their portraits, and records their conversations;

and in their dialogue gives the sum of his own opinions on Naples and Sicily. . . . "They were both," he says, "in the prime of life; but in other respects so different that they might seem to have been born on opposite shores of the ocean. . . ."

"The first impression produced by Don Ambrosio was that of a debased nature. He presented such a mixture of strength with weakness, of courage with cowardice, of pride with meanness, that the sight of him filled us with pity. Discontent and vexation were expressed in his countenance; yet his animated looks and occasional flashes of intelligence led us to conclude that mirth and joy would not have been strangers to him, had he dared to yield himself with confidence to their influence. I doubt whether his physiognomy would ever have been good, at whatever time Heaven had given him birth; but the long endurance to which he seemed to have been subjected had heaped up in his mind a load of indignation and resentment, which weighed on him the more that he appeared to see no hope of ever shaking it off.

"However unfavorable might be the impression produced by this man, the appearance of his companion was still more repulsive. Every feature, every movement, every word, announced that complacent corruption the worst and most hideous of all.

"Amid the degradation of the first, something of the dignity natural to man remained erect. It was absolutely wanting in the second; his look expressed at once presumption and weakness. In a word, he was a child, but a depraved child.

"There was one point of resemblance, however, between these two men. Both seemed to have acquired a long habit of duplicity; but in the Sicilian it was more like the bitter fruit of slavery and want; while the Neapolitan seemed to deceive simply because fraud was the shortest and easiest road to his ends.

"These two men, though so different, were born under the same sky, subjects of the same king, and under the same laws.

"Soon after we met them, Don Carlo (the Neapolitan) spoke first, and addressed his companion in a mocking tone : —

"'What is this, Don Ambrosio? either I greatly deceive myself, or we seem to be entering on a beaten track. If this vast plain were not untilled, we might almost begin to think ourselves in a civilized country.'

"The Sicilian did not answer, and the other went on : —

"'Own that we must be, as I am, under some stern necessity; or, like these strangers, possessed by an evil spirit of travelling, to abandon the enchanting skies of Naples, and come to lose ourselves in your deserts.'

"'Don Carlo,' answered the Sicilian, with a gloomy and constrained air, 'pray do not let us open such a subject, which naturally must be disagreeable to us both. You know that Sicily was not always what she now is. There was a time — remote, I own — when a single town of ours contained more inhabitants than the whole island does in these days of wretchedness and mourning. Then the Sicilians led the van of the human race. Our ships spread even to the shores of the ocean. Our arts, our imagination, and our manners, civilized our neighbors; the fertility of our soil, and the bravery of our soldiers, were celebrated throughout the world; gold ran in the streets of our fortunate cities' . . . .

"Here Don Ambrosio was interrupted by a burst of laughter from the Neapolitan: he bit his lip, and was silent.

"'Yes; there was some truth in what you say in the time of Dionysius the Tyrant,' replied his companion. . . . 'But why make so much noise about advantages which are yours no longer? Two or three thousand years ago, indeed, your plains were highly cultivated; now they are barren and deserted. Your towns were large and rich, but now they are small and mean. You used to cover the seas with vessels, but at present your harbors are silting up. Formerly you shone in arts and mental accomplishments; but at this day you are in want of the simple necessaries of life; and what country in the world is more ignorant than Sicily? Finally, you have no soldiers; you would be only too happy if you had hands enough to till your ground!'

"The storm that had long been gathering in the Sicilian's heart burst out at these last words.

"'It is too hard,' he cried, 'to hear the authors of our greatest misfortunes boast before our faces of the fruits of their atrocious machinations. Who is to blame for the unheard of calamities which oppress us? Whom are we to accuse of causing the gradual decay and final ruin of a whole nation? Whom, if not you? And it is you who to-day come to sport with our ruins, to joke in the midst of a desert which you have created, to insult a misery which is your own work! Since Sicily has fallen under your dominion, not by your own conquest, but by a conquest which another made for you, since treaties handed her over to your kingdom, have we ever found in you — I will not say fellow-citizens (although you ought always to have shown yourselves such), but masters who, looking to their own interest, should have sought for it in promoting ours? Without our sad example, would it be possible to imagine, that through a long course of years a whole nation could have been subjected to a system of oppression so disastrous at once to the subject and the prince as to make each useless to the other ?'

" ' Are you not yourselves,' quickly rejoined the Neapolitan, ' your own most cruel oppressors ? Did tyranny — if tyranny it be — ever find more despicable instruments fitted to her hand ? Are your public functionaries Neapolitans ? No — invariably Sicilians. They are Sicilians, none but Sicilians, who offer their necks to the yoke of Naples, and bless it, provided that they are allowed in turn to inflict it upon unhappy Sicily. They are Sicilians who occupy your tribunals and make a public sale of justice ! If our desire was to deprave you, you have certainly surpassed our hopes. Your aristocracy has surpassed its rulers ! I think that it may justly boast of being the most dissolute in Europe.'

" ' Our aristocracy,' replied Don Ambrosio, ' is no longer Sicilian. You deprived its members of all inter- est in public affairs long before you struck the last blow at our constitution. You have drawn them over in a body to Naples. There you have destroyed their primitive energy and national character ; you have plunged them into luxury, bastardized their principles, substituting courtly ambition for the desire of reputation, and the influence of court favor for that of merit and valor ' . . .

"Whilst Don Ambrosio was speaking, the Neapolitan's countenance grew darker and darker. It was evident

that the violence of the attack had succeeded in dis-
turbing even the apathy of his nature. As the Sicilian
pronounced his last sentence, Don Carlo gave him a look
which expressed with more energy than one would have
given him credit for,—insolence and the most insulting
contempt.

" He thus interrupted him :—

" ' Well,' cried he, with a bitter laugh ; ' as you find
our yoke so heavy, why do you delay to break it ? Why
not sound the tocsin in your fields ? What do you wait
for ? Assemble yourselves ! March ! But, no ; you
never will believe that oppression has reached its height;
and down to your last posterity you will put off vengeance to the morrow ; but, were you even bold enough
to raise the standard of revolt, how easily would Naples
smash your weak efforts ! Recollect, remember 1820.
Where are your ships, your troops ? Your youths
detest the profession of arms. There are no Sicilians
in our army. . . . .'

" ' That is true,' replied Don Ambrosio, in a hoarse
and constrained tone, ' all that is but too true ; what
would be the use of concealing it ? . . . . and yet we
were not born to be slaves. Our history proves it, and
no nation has ever given more terrible lessons to its
oppressors. Freedom is still fermenting in our inmost
souls. We are far from that lowest degradation in which
vengeance is lost sight of, and no different state of things
is even thought of. The energy of our national character is not extinguished ; its germ lives in every heart,
and alone may raise us from our abasement and restore
to us our ancient virtues. It is true that we do not defile
before you at your reviews ; but we never have been
seen to fly before the enemy's sword had left its sheath.

Is there a wretch so degraded as not to prefer tilling
the land of his ancestors to serving in your army?
Distorted by oppression, that hidden strength reveals
itself only by criminal acts; as for you, you have nothing but vices. By refusing justice to us, or still better,
by selling it to us, you have taught us to consider assas-
sination a right. Perhaps the time will come when
political interests will again be conflicting in Europe,
and kings will no longer feel obliged to support each
other. Some day, France or England will extend a
helping hand, and open her arms to us. Now we flatter
you, Neapolitans; but then, beware of being amongst us
singly!'

"Deep silence followed these words. The boldness
which a moment before had animated the looks of Don
Carlo, had vanished. He crossed over the way, went up
to the Sicilian, and said a few words to him in a low tone,
and with a caressing air. At this the other was struck
with surprise. But soon, estimating the imprudence of
his speech by the effect it produced on his companion, he
seemed alarmed in his turn. We saw him force a smile,
and turn what had escaped him into a joke. Thus these
two men, divided by hostile passions, joined in one common feeling — fear."

Tocqueville finished this narrative, of which we have
given here only a few morsels, with a thought which
deserves to be reported. In the simplest and most un-
assuming manner he touches the main-spring of human
existence, and by this one observation takes a place
among the men destined to give their lives, at a later
time, a value and a purpose.

"It will be perhaps thought strange," he says, "that we
could have endured such a way of life for so long, doing

so much, sleeping so little, and never taking a thorough rest. The only explanation that I can give of this phenomenon is this : we *willed* it, not feebly, or as, for instance, one wills in a sort of general way the good of one's neighbor, but firmly and resolutely. The aim, it is true, did not correspond with the effort, and it was a test, on our part, of strength and perseverance. But if the aim was trifling, we acted as if it had not been so, and we attained it. As for me, and with these words I will conclude this narrative, I ask of God but one favor. It is that He may grant me to find myself, on some future day, willing in the same manner something worth the exertion."

VISIT TO LAKE ONEIDA.

[Written in 1831.]

AT sunrise on the 8th of July, 1831, we left the little village called Fort Brewington, and turned our steps towards the northeast.

About a mile and a half from the house of our host, we took a path which opened into the forest, as the heat began to be troublesome. A close morning had succeeded to a stormy night. We were soon under shelter from the rays of the sun, and in the midst of one of those dense forests in the New World, whose gloomy and savage majesty seizes the imagination and fills the mind with a sort of religious awe. How can such a scene be described?

A thousand little rivulets, as yet unconfined by the hand of man, trickled and lost themselves in perfect freedom over a marshy ground, in which nature had scattered with incredible profusion the seeds of almost every plant, that either creeps along or rises above the ground.

Over our heads was a vast green vault. Beneath this thick veil and in the damp recesses of the woods, strange confusion meets the eye; a chaos of trees of all ages, leaves of every color, grasses, fruits, and flowers of a thousand sorts mingled and plaited together. For centuries has one generation of trees succeeded to another, and the ground is covered with their remains. Some seem to have been felled yesterday, others already half buried in the earth exhibit only a shell, others again reduced to dust serve as manure to their latest offshoots. Among them thousands of plants of different kinds struggle in their turn towards the light. They insinuate themselves between these motionless corpses, creep over their surface and under their withered bark, raise and scatter their dust. It is like a struggle between death and life. We sometimes came upon an immense tree uprooted by the winds, but in spite of its weight often unable to reach the ground through the crowded forest, the withered branches still hanging in the air.

A solemn silence reigned in this profound solitude. Scarcely a living creature was to be seen. Man was absent, and yet it was not a desert. On the contrary, nature exhibited a productive force unknown elsewhere. All was activity; the air appeared impregnated with an odor of vegetation; one seemed even to hear nature at work, and to see sap and life circulating through the ever-open channels.

We rode for many hours through this imposing solitude in a dim light, and hearing no sound but that made by our horses trampling over the leaves heaped up by many winters, or forcing their way through the dry branches which covered the ground. We kept silence; our minds filled by the grandeur and strangeness of the scene. At length we heard the first sounds of the axe, which proclaimed from afar the presence of an European. Prostrate trees, burnt and blackened trunks, some of the plants which serve as food for man sown confusedly among all sorts of rubbish, guided us to the abode of the pioneer. In the centre of a narrow circle, cleared by

fire and steel, rose the rough dwelling of the precursor
of civilization. It was an oasis in the midst of the desert. After talking for a few moments with the inhabitant
of this spot, we resumed our journey, and half an hour
afterwards reached a fisherman's hut, built on the shore
of the lake we came to see.

Lake Oneida stands in the midst of low hills, and of
still virgin forests. A belt of thick foliage surrounds it
on every side; its waters bathe the roots of the trees,
which are reflected on its calm, transparent face; a single
fisherman's cabin is the only dwelling on its shore. Not
a sail was to be seen on its whole expanse, nor even
smoke ascending from the woods: for the European,
though he has not yet taken possession of its shores, is
near enough to expel the populous and warlike tribe from
which the lake was named.

About a mile from where we stood were two oval-
shaped islands of equal length. These islands are covered
with trees so crowded that they hide the ground; they
look like two thickets floating quietly on the surface of
the lake.

No road passes near. In this region are no vast industrial establishments, nor spots celebrated for their
picturesque beauty. It was not, however, chance that
had led us towards this solitary lake. For it was the
end and aim of our journey.

Many years before, I had met with a book called
" Voyage au lac Oneida." The author related that a
young Frenchman and his wife, driven from their country
by the storms of our first revolution, sought an asylum in
one of the islands on the lake. There, separated from
the whole world, far from the tempests of Europe, and
cast off by the society in which they were born, they

lived for each other, and found mutual consolation in
their misfortune.

This book had left a deep and lasting impression on
my mind. Whether its effect on me were due to the
talent of the author, to the real charm of the incidents,
or to my youth, I cannot say; but the remembrance of
the French couple on the Lake Oneida was never effaced
from my memory. How often I had envied the peaceful
joys of their solitude! Domestic bliss, the charms of
conjugal union — even love — became mixed up in my
mind with the image of the solitary island which my
imagination had transformed into a new Eden. The
story interested my companion. We often talked of it,
and we every time ended by repeating, gayly or sadly —
"The only happiness in this world is on the Lake
Oneida."

When unexpected circumstances led us to America,
the recollection pressed upon us still more strongly. We
determined to visit the French pair, if they still lived, or
at least to explore their dwelling. So strong is the power
of imagination over the mind, that this wild spot, this
still and silent lake, these green islands, did not strike us
as new objects; we seemed to see again a place which
we had known in our youth.

We at once entered the fisherman's hut. The man
was in the forest; an old woman lived there alone; she
hobbled out to her door to greet us. "What is the name
of that green island about a mile off in the midst of the
lake?" said we. "It is called the Frenchman's island,"
she replied. "Do you know why that name was given
to it?" "I have been told that it was so called after a
Frenchman who, many years ago, came to live there."
"Was he alone?" "No: he brought with him a young

wife." "Do they still live there?" "One-and-twenty years ago when I settled in this place the French couple had left the island; I remember that I had the curiosity to go to see it. That island, which from hence looks so wild, was then a beautiful spot; the interior was carefully cultivated, the Frenchman's house was in the middle of an orchard surrounded by fruits and flowers, a great vine climbed up the walls and spread all round it, but the place was already falling to pieces for want of inhabitants." "What then had become of the French pair?" "The wife had died and the man abandoned the island, and no one knows what became of him." "Will you lend us the canoe moored at your door that we may cross over to the island?" "Willingly; but it is a long distance to row, and it is hard work for people who are not accustomed to it; and besides, what can you see to interest you in a place which has grown wild again?"

As instead of answering we made haste to push the canoe into the water, "I see what it is," she said, "you want to buy the island. The soil is good, and land is not yet dear in our country." We replied that we were travellers. "Then," said she, "you are no doubt related to the Frenchman, and he has desired you to visit his property?" "Not at all; we do not even know his name." The good woman shook her head incredulously, and handling our oars we proceeded rapidly to the Frenchman's island. During this little voyage we were silent. Our hearts were full of sad and tender feelings. The nearer we came the less could we understand that the island had ever been inhabited, so wild was its appearance. We fancied that we had been duped by a fable. At last we reached the shore, and creeping under the huge branches that hung over the lake, we pushed on farther. First we penetrated through a belt of venerable trees which seemed to defend the approach. Beyond this leafy fortification we suddenly came upon another scene. A thin growth of underwood and of young forest trees covered the interior of the island. In the woods, through which we had ridden that morning, we had often seen man struggling bodily with nature, and succeeding with difficulty in effacing its wild and fierce character, and subjecting it to his laws. Here we saw the forest re-asserting its supremacy, reconquering the desert, defying man, and rapidly obliterating the fleeting traces of his triumph.

It was easy to perceive that a diligent hand had once cleared the space in the middle of the island now filled by the young race of trees which I mentioned. No ancient trunks lay on the scattered remains. All bore the appearance of youth. We could see that the surrounding trees had thrown offshoots into the deserted fields, grass had grown over the spot which once yielded a harvest to the exile; briers and parasites had returned to the possession of their ancient domain. It was only at rare intervals that the trace of a fence, or the appearance of a field, was visible. We were an hour searching in vain among the trees and other brushwood which choked up the ground for some vestige of the forsaken dwelling. The rustic spot that the fisherman's wife had just described to us, the lawn, the flowers, the fruit, the products of civilization introduced by intelligent and tender care into the midst of a desert, all had disappeared with the beings who inhabited it. We were about to renounce our undertaking when we espied an apple-tree perishing of old age; this first put us in the right direction. Soon we discovered a plant, which we at first took for a convolvulus, climbing up the tall trees, winding round their slender trunks, or hanging like a green wreath from their branches; on further examination we found it to be a vine-stock. We then felt certain that we were on the very spot chosen, forty years ago, by our two unfortunate countrymen as their last asylum. But even by digging in the thick layer of leaves which covered the ground we could find only a few fragments falling into dust, and which will soon disappear. Of the remains of her who had not feared to exchange the pleasures of civilized life for a tomb in a desert island in the New World, we could not find a trace. Did the exile leave these precious relics in the desert; or did he remove them to the spot whither he went to end his own days? No one could tell us.

They who read these lines will perhaps not be able to conceive the feelings here described, and will deem them, perhaps, exaggerated or fanciful. Still I must say, that it was with hearts full of emotion and agitated with hope and fear, that it was with a kind of pious sentiment that we engaged in these minute researches, and followed the traces of the two beings whose name and family were unknown to us, of whose history we knew little, and whose only claim on us was their having experienced in this spot the joys and sorrows which touch every heart, because every heart contains the spring of them.

Here was an unfortunate being, bruised by his fellow-men, shut out and expelled from their society ; forced to renounce their intercourse, and to flee to the desert. One friend clung to him, followed him into solitude, came forward to dress his wounds, succeeded in healing his broken spirit, and in substituting for worldly pleasures the most powerful emotions of the heart. He is reconciled to his lot. He has forgotten revolution, politics, cities; his rank and his family. He at length breathes freely. But his wife dies. Death strikes her and spares him. How will he be able to endure the remaining years? Will he remain alone in the desert? Will he return to the society which has long forgotten him? He is no longer fit for solitude, nor for the world. He can live no longer alone, nor with other men; he is neither a savage nor a civilized man; he is a wreck, like those trees of the American forest that the wind has been strong enough to uproot, but not to prostrate. He is still erect, but he lives no longer.

We explored the island in every direction, examined every relic, and, impressed by the icy silence which now reigns in its woods, we returned to the mainland.

Not without regret I saw disappearing the high verdant bulwark which for so many years had shielded the two exiles against the bullet of the European, and the arrow of the savage, but could not protect their cottage from the invisible stroke of death.

A FORTNIGHT IN THE WILDERNESS.

[Written on board the steamboat *Superior*, August 1831.]

. ONE of the things we were most curious about on
arriving in America, was to visit the extreme limits of
European civilization; and, if we had time, even some
of the Indian tribes which have preferred flying to the
wildest deserts to accommodating themselves to what the
white man calls the enjoyments of social life. But to
reach the desert has become more difficult than might be
supposed. After we left New York, and advanced towards the north-east, our destination seemed to flee before
us. We traversed places celebrated in Indian history;
we reached valleys named by them; we crossed streams
still called by the names of their tribes; but everywhere
the wigwam had given way to the house — the forest had
fallen — where there had been solitude there was now
life. Still we seemed to be treading in the steps of the
aborigines. Ten years ago (we were told) they were
here; five years ago, they were there; two years ago,
there. "Where you see the finest church in the village,"
some one said to us, "I cut down the first tree in the
forest." "Here," said another, "was held the great
council of the Iroquois confederation." "And what has
become of the Indians?" I asked. "The Indians," replied our host, "are gone I know not whither, beyond

the great lakes; the race is becoming extinct; they are not made for civilization — it kills them."

Man becomes accustomed to everything, — to death on the battle-field, to death in the hospital, to kill and to suffer.   Use familiarizes all scenes.   An ancient people, the first and legitimate masters of the American continent, melts away every day from the earth, as snow before the sun, and disappears.   Another race rises up in its place with still more astonishing rapidity; before this race the forests fall, the marshes dry up; vast rivers, and lakes extensive as seas, in vain oppose its triumph and progress.   Deserts become villages — villages towns.   The American who daily witnesses these marvels sees nothing surprising in them.   This wonderful destruction, and still more astonishing progress, seem to him to be the ordinary course of events.   He considers them as laws of nature.

It is thus that, always on the search for savages and deserts, we travelled over the 360 miles between New York and Buffalo.

A large body of Indians collected at Buffalo, to receive payment for the land which they have given up to the United States, was the first object that struck us. I do not think that I ever was more completely disappointed than by the appearance of these Indians.   I was full of recollections of Chateaubriand and of Cooper, and I expected, in the countenances of these aborigines of America, to discover some traces of the lofty virtues engendered by the spirit of liberty.   I thought to see men whose bodies, developed by war and the chase, lost nothing by the absence of covering.   My astonishment may be estimated, on comparing these anticipations with the following description.

These Indians were short; their limbs, so far as could be seen under their clothes, were meagre; their skins, instead of being, as is generally supposed, a red copper color, were dark, almost like those of mulattoes. Their black and shining hair fell straight down their necks and shoulders. Their mouths were in general immoderately large. The mean and malicious expression of their countenances showed the depth of depravity which a long abuse of the benefits of civilization alone can give. One would have taken them for men from the dregs of our great European towns; and yet they were savages. With the vices which they had caught from us was mixed a rude barbarism, which made them a hundred times more revolting. These Indians were unarmed; they wore European clothes, but put on in a different way from ours. It was evident that they were unaccustomed to them, and that they felt imprisoned in their folds. To the ornaments of Europe they joined barbarous finery, feathers, enormous ear-rings, and necklaces of shells. Their movements were quick and irregular; their voices sharp and discordant, their looks wild and restless. At first sight they might have been taken for wild animals, tamed to resemble men, but still brutal. These feeble and degraded creatures belonged, however, to one of the most celebrated tribes of ancient America. We had before us, and it is a sad fact, the last remains of the famous confederation of the Iroquois, whose manly sense was as renowned as their courage, and who long held the balance between the two greatest European nations.

Still it would be wrong to judge of the Indian race from this imperfect specimen; the cuttings of a wild tree which has grown up in the mud of our towns.

We ourselves made this mistake, and afterwards had to correct it.

In the evening we walked out of the town, and at a short distance from the last houses, we saw an Indian lying by the side of the road. He was young. He lay still, and we thought him dead. Some stifled sighs which escaped with difficulty from his chest, proved to us that he still lived, and was struggling against the fatal drunkenness produced by brandy. The sun had already set; the ground was growing damper and damper; it was clear that, without help, he would die on the spot. The Indians were leaving Buffalo for their villages; from time to time a group of them passed close to us. As they passed they brutally turned over the body of their countryman to see who it was, and walked on without attending to what we said. Most of them were themselves drunk. At length came an Indian girl who seemed to approach with some interest. I thought that she was the wife or the sister of the dying man. She looked at him attentively, called him aloud by his name, felt his heart, and having ascertained that he was alive, tried to rouse him from his lethargy. But as her efforts were fruitless, we saw her become enraged with the inanimate body that lay before her. She struck him on the head, pulled about his face, and trampled on him. With these brutal acts she mixed wild inarticulate cries, which I seem to have still in my ears. We thought at last that we ought to interfere, and we ordered her away. She obeyed; but we heard her burst into a fit of savage laughter as she went off.

When we returned to the town we talked to several people of the young Indian. We spoke of his imminent danger; we offered to pay his expenses in an inn. It was

useless. We could persuade no one to care about him.
Some said: "These men are accustomed to drink to
excess, and to sleep on the ground ; and they do not
die of such accidents." Others owned that the Indian
probably would die ; but evidently there rose to their
lips the half-expressed thought : What is the life of an
Indian? Such was the general feeling. In this society,
so proud of its morality and philanthropy, one meets
with complete insensibility, with a cold, uncompassionat-
ing egotism, when the aborigines are in question. The
inhabitants of the United States do not hunt the Indians
with cries and horns as the Spaniards used to do in
Mexico. But an unpitying instinct inspires here as
elsewhere the European race.

How often in the course of our travels we met with
honest citizens, who said to us, as they sat quietly in the
evening at their firesides, " every day the number of the
Indians is diminishing; it is not that we often make war
upon them, but the brándy which we sell to them at a
low price, carries off every year more than our arms
could destroy. This western world belongs to us," they
added ; " God, by refusing to these first inhabitants the
power of civilization, has predestined them to destruction.
The true owners of this continent are those who know
how to turn its resources to account."

Satisfied by this reasoning, the American goes to
church to hear a minister of the gospel repeat to him
that all men are brothers, and that the Almighty, who
made them all on the same model, has imposed on all
the duty of helping each other.

On the 19th of July, at 10, A. M. we embarked on
the Ohio steamboat, steering towards Detroit ; a strong
breeze blew from the north-east, and gave to the waters

of Lake Erie the appearance of ocean waves. On the right stretched a boundless horizon; on the left we hugged the southern shores of the lake, and sometimes ran so near as to be within earshot. These shores are flat, and unlike those of all the European lakes that I have seen. Nor do they resemble the shores of the sea ; immense forests overshadow them, and surround the lake with a thick belt rarely broken. Yet sometimes the aspect of the country changes altogether. At the end of a wood rises an elegant spire, among white houses exquisitely clean, and shops. Two steps farther the primitive, apparently impervious, forest reasserts its empire, and again throws its shadow on the lake.

Those who have travelled in the United States will find in this a picture of American society. All is abrupt and unforeseen. Extreme civilization and unassisted nature are side by side in a manner scarcely to be imagined in France. Like every one else, travellers have their illusions. I had seen in Europe that the more or less retirement of a province or of a town, its wealth or its poverty, and its greater or less extent, exercised an immense influence over the ideas, the manners, the whole civilization of its inhabitants, and often made a difference of many centuries between portions of a single country.

I had thought that this rule would apply, and in an even wider sense, to the New World, and that a country peopled gradually and imperfectly, must present every condition of existence, must exhibit society in all its stages, and, as it were, of every different age. I supposed America to be the country in which every phase which the social scale makes man undergo, could be studied; and in which might be seen all the links of a huge chain, reaching from the opulent patrician of the town, to the savage of the wilderness. There, in short, within a few degrees of longitude, I expected to find, as in a frame, the whole story of the human race.

There is no truth in this picture. Of all countries, America is the least fitted to present the scenes that I sought. In America, more even than in Europe, there is but one society, whether rich or poor, high or low, commercial or agricultural; it is everywhere composed of the same elements. It has all been raised or reduced to the same level of civilization. The man whom you left in the streets of New York you find again in the solitude of the Far West; the same dress, the same tone of mind, the same language, the same habits, the same amusements. No rustic simplicity, nothing character- istic of the wilderness, nothing even like our villages. This peculiarity may be easily explained. The portions of territory first and most fully peopled have reached a high degree of civilization. Education has been prodi- gally bestowed; the spirit of equality has tinged with singular uniformity the domestic habits. Now, it is re- markable that the men thus educated are those who every year migrate to the desert. In Europe a man lives and dies where he was born. In America you do not see the representatives of a race grown and multiplied in retire- ment, having long lived unknown to the world, and left to its own efforts. The inhabitants of an isolated region arrived yesterday, bringing with them the habits, ideas, and wants of civilization. They adopt only so much of savage life as is absolutely forced upon them; hence you see the strangest contrasts. You step from the wilder- ness into the streets of a city, from the wildest scenes to the most smiling pictures of civilized life. If night does

not surprise you and force you to sleep under a tree,
you may reach a village where you will find everything;
even French fashions, and caricatures from Paris. The
shops of Buffalo or Detroit are as well supplied with all
these things as those of New York. The looms of Ly-
ons work for both alike. You leave the high road, you
plunge into paths scarcely marked out; you come at
length upon a ploughed field, a hut built of rough logs,
lighted by a single narrow window; you think that you
have at last reached the abode of an American peasant:
you are wrong. You enter this hut which looks the
abode of misery; the master is dressed as you are; his
language is that of the towns. On his rude table are
books and newspapers; he takes you hurriedly aside to
be informed of what is going on in Europe, and asks you
what has most struck you in his country. He will trace
on paper for you the plan of a campaign in Belgium,*
and will teach you gravely what remains to be done for
the prosperity of France. You might take him for a
rich proprietor, come to spend a few nights in a shooting-
box. And, in fact, the log-hut is only a halting-place for
the American, a temporary submission to necessity. As
soon as the surrounding fields are thoroughly cultivated,
and their owner has time to occupy himself with super-
fluities, a more spacious and suitable dwelling will succeed the log-hut, and become the home of a large family
of children, who, in their turn, will some day build themselves a dwelling in the wilderness.

To return to our journey. All day we steamed slowly
in sight of the coast of Pennsylvania, and afterwards of
that of Ohio. We stopped for a minute at " Presqu' Ile,"
now called Erie. In the evening, the weather having

* The French were then creating the kingdom of Belgium.

become fair, we crossed quickly the middle of the lake towards Detroit. On the following morning we sighted the little island called "Middle Sister," near to which Commodore Perry gained, in 1813, a celebrated naval victory over the English.

Soon after the flat shores of Canada seemed to approach rapidly; and we saw opening before us the channel of Detroit, and in the distance the walls of Fort Malden. Founded by the French, this town still bears numerous marks of its origin. The houses are built and situated like those of a French village, and in the centre rises a Catholic spire, surmounted by a cock. It might be a hamlet near Caen or Evreux. Whilst we were contemplating, not without emotion, its resemblance to France, a strange object attracted us. On the beach at our right was a Highlander on guard, in full uniform. He wore the dress that Waterloo has made famous; the plumed bonnet, the kilt, all was there; his arms and accoutrements glittered in the sun. On our left, as a contrast, two naked Indians, with painted bodies, and rings in their noses, appeared at the same instant on the opposite bank. They embarked in a little canoe, with a blanket for a sail, committing themselves to the wind and the current. They shot in this frail vessel towards our ship, sailed rapidly round us, and then proceeded quietly to fish before the British soldier, who, still standing motionless in his shining uniform, seemed to represent the gorgeous civilization and the military force of Europe.

We reached Detroit at three o'clock. It is a little town of between 2,000 and 3,000 inhabitants, founded by the Jesuits in the midst of the forest, in 1710, and still containing many French families.

We had crossed the State of New York, and steamed

400 miles on Lake Erie; we now were on the frontier of civilization. Still we did not know what course to take. Information was not obtained so easily as might have been expected. To cross almost impenetrable forests; to swim deep rivers; to encounter pestilential marshes; to sleep exposed to the damp air of the woods; — these are efforts which an American easily conceives, if a dollar is to be gained by them — that is the point. But that a man should take such journeys from curiosity, he cannot understand. Besides, dwelling in a wilderness, he prizes only man's work. He sends you to visit a road, a bridge, a pretty village; but that you should admire large trees, or wild scenery, is to him incomprehensible. We could make no one understand us.

"You want to see forests," said our hosts to us with a smile: "go straight on — you will find them to your heart's content. There are fortunately in this neighborhood new roads and well-cleared paths. As for Indians, you will see more than enough of them in our squares and our streets. You need not go far for that. Those whom you see amongst us are beginning at any rate to be civilized. They look less savage." We soon felt that it would be impossible to obtain the truth from them in a straightforward manner, and that we must manœuvre.

We therefore went to the United States' Agent for the sale of wild land, of which there is much in the district of Michigan. We presented ourselves to him as persons who, without having quite made up our minds to establish ourselves in the country, were interested to know the price and situation of the Government lands.

Major Biddle, the officer, now understood perfectly what we wanted, and entered into a number of details, to which we eagerly listened. "This part," he said, (showing us on the map the river of St. Joseph, which, after many windings, discharges itself into Lake Michigan), "seems to me to be the best suited to your purpose. The land is good, and large villages are already founded there; the road is so well kept up that public conveyances run every day." Well, we said to ourselves, now we know where not to go, unless we intend to travel post over the wilderness.

We thanked Major Biddle for his advice, and asked him, with an air of indifference bordering on contempt, towards which side of the district the current of emigration had, up to the present time, least tended. "This way," he said, without attaching more importance to his answer than we had seemed to do to our question, "towards the north-west. About Pontiac and its neighborhood, some pretty fair establishments have lately been commenced. But you must not think of fixing yourselves farther off; the country is covered by an almost impenetrable forest, which extends uninterruptedly towards the north-west, full of nothing but wild beasts and Indians. The United States propose to open a way through it immediately; but the road is only just begun, and stops at Pontiac. I repeat, that there is nothing to be thought of in that quarter."

We again thanked Major Biddle for his good advice, and determined to take it in a contrary sense. We were beside ourselves with joy at the prospect of at length finding a place which the torrent of European civilization had not yet invaded.

On the next day (the 23d of July) we hired two horses; as we intended to keep them about ten days, we wished to leave a certain sum with the owner, but he refused to take it, saying that we should pay on our

return; he was not uneasy. Michigan is surrounded on
all sides with lakes and woods. He turned us as it were
into a sort of riding-school, the door of which he held.
Having bought a compass, and some provisions, we set
off with our guns over our shoulders, and our hearts as
light as if we had been two school-boys going home for
the holidays.

Our hosts at Detroit were right in telling us that we
need not go far to see woods, for a mile from the town
the road enters the forest, and never leaves it. The
ground is perfectly flat, and often marshy. Now and
then we met with newly-cleared lands. As these settlements are all exactly alike, whether they be on the outskirts of Michigan or of New York, I shall try to describe
them once for all.

The little bell which the pioneer takes care to hang
round the necks of his cattle, that he may find them in
the dense forest, announces from a great distance the
approach to the clearing. Soon you hear the stroke of
the axe; as you proceed traces of destruction prove the
presence of man. Lopped branches cover the road;
trunks half calcined by fire, or maimed by steel, are still
standing in the path. You go on, and reach a wood,
which seems to have been struck with sudden death.
Even in the middle of summer the withered branches
look wintry. On nearer examination a deep gash is discovered round the bark of each tree, which, preventing
the circulation of sap, quickly kills it. This is generally
the planter's first measure. As he cannot in the first
year cut down all the trees on his new property, he kills
them to prevent their leaves overshadowing the Indian
corn which he has sowed under their branches.

Next to this incomplete attempt at a field, the first

step of civilization in the wilderness, you come suddenly upon the owner's dwelling. It stands in a plot more carefully cleared than the rest, but in which man still sustains an unequal struggle with nature. Here the trees have been cut down but not uprooted, and they still encumber with their stumps the ground that they formerly shaded; round these withered remnants, corn, oak saplings, plants, and weeds of every kind spring pell-mell, and grow side by side in the stubborn and half-wild soil. In the centre of this strong and diversified vegetation, stands the planter's log-house. Like the field round it, this rustic dwelling is evidently a new and hasty work. Its length seldom exceeds thirty feet; its width twenty, and height fifteen.* The walls as well as the roof are composed of half-hewn trees; the interstices are filled up with moss and mud. As the traveller advances the scene becomes more animated; at the sound of his steps a group of children who had been rolling in the dirt jump up hastily, and fly towards the paternal roof, frightened at the sight of man; whilst two great half-wild dogs, with ears erect, and lengthened nose, come out of the hut, and growling, cover the retreat of their young masters.

At this moment the pioneer himself appears at his door. He casts a scrutinizing glance on the new-comer, bids his dogs go in, and himself sets immediately the example without exhibiting either uneasiness or curiosity.

On entering the log-house the European looks around with wonder. In general there is but one window, before

* These are English measures, differing a little from the French; but I have used them, as they are the measures which the Americans must have employed when talking to M. de Tocqueville. — Tr.

which sometimes hangs a muslin curtain; for here, in
the absence of necessaries, you often meet with super-
fluities.   On the hearth, made of hardened earth, a fire·
of resinous wood lights up the interior better than the
sun.   Over the rustic chimney are hung trophies of
war or of the chase; a long rifle, a doeskin and eagles'
feathers.   On the right hangs a map of the United
States, perpetually shaken by the wind which blows
through the interstices of the wall.   On a rough shelf
near it are placed a few odd volumes, among them a
Bible, the leaves and binding of which have been spoilt
by the devotion of two generations, a Prayer-book, and
sometimes one of Milton's poems, or Shakspeare's plays.
With their backs to the wall are placed some rude seats,
the product of the owner's industry; chests instead of
wardrobes, agricultural tools, and specimens of the crop.
In the middle of the room is an unsteady table, the legs
of which, still covered with leaves, seem to have grown
where they stand.   Round this table the family assemble
for their meals; on it is left an English china teapot,
spoons, generally of wood, a few cracked cups, and some
newspapers.

The appearance of the master of this dwelling is as
remarkable as his abode.   His sharp muscles and slender limbs, show him at the first glance to be a native of
New England; his make indicates that he was not born
in the desert.   His first years were passed in the heart
of an intellectual and cultivated society.   Choice impelled him to the toilsome and savage life for which
he did not seem intended.   But if his physical strength
seems unequal to his undertaking; on his features,
furrowed by care, is seated an expression of practical
intelligence, and of cold and persevering energy.   His

step is slow and measured, his speech deliberate, and his appearance austere. Habit, and still more pride, have given to his countenance a stoical rigidity, which was belied by his conduct. The pioneer despises (it is true) all that most violently agitates the hearts of men; his fortune or his life will never hang on the turn of a die, or the smiles of a woman; but to obtain competence he has braved exile, solitude, and the numberless ills of savage life; he has slept on the bare earth, he has exposed himself to the fever of the woods, and the Indian's tomahawk. Many years ago he took the first step. He has never gone back; perhaps twenty years hence he will still be going on without desponding or complaining. Can a man capable of such sacrifices be cold and insensible? Is he not influenced by a passion, not of the heart but of the brain, ardent, persevering, and indomitable?

His whole energies concentrated in the desire to make his fortune, the emigrant at length succeeds in making for himself an entirely independent existence, into which even his domestic affections are absorbed. He may be said to look on his wife and children only as detached parts of himself. Deprived of habitual intercourse with his equals, he has learnt to take pleasure in solitude. When you appear at the door of his lonely dwelling, the pioneer steps forward to meet you; he holds out his hand in compliance with custom, but his countenance expresses neither kindness nor joy. He speaks only to question you, to gratify his intelligence, not his heart; and as soon as he has obtained from you the news that he wanted to hear he relapses into silence. One would take him for a man who, having been all day wearied by applicants and by the noise of the world, has retired home at night to rest. If you question him in turn, he will give you in a clear manner all the information you require; he will even provide for your wants, and will watch over your safety as long as you are under his roof; but, in all that he does there is so much constraint and dryness; you perceive in him such utter indifference as to the result of your undertakings, that your gratitude cools. Still the settler is hospitable in his own way, but there is nothing genial in his hospitality, because, while he exercises it, he seems to submit to one of the painful necessities of the wilderness; it is to him a duty of his position, not a pleasure. This unknown person is the representative of the race to which belongs the future of the New World; a restless, speculating, adventurous race, that performs coldly feats which are usually the result of passionate enthusiasm; a nation of conquerors, who endure savage life without feeling its peculiar charms, value in civilized life only its material comforts and advantages, and bury themselves in the wilds of America, provided only with an axe and a file of newspapers! A mighty race which, as is the case with all great nations, is governed by one idea, and directs its sole efforts to the acquisition of wealth with a perseverance and contempt for life which might be called heroic, if such a term could be applied to any but virtuous efforts. A migratory race, which neither rivers nor lakes can stop, before which the forest falls and the prairie becomes covered with foliage, and which, having reached the Pacific Ocean, will retrace its steps to disturb and to destroy the social communities which it will have formed and left behind. In describing the settler, one cannot forget the partner of his sufferings and perils. Look at the young woman who is sitting on the other side of the fire with her youngest child in her lap, superintending the preparations for supper. Like the emigrant, this woman is in the prime of life; she also recollects an early youth of comfort. The remains of taste are still to be observed in her dress. But time has pressed hardly upon her: in her faded features and attenuated limbs it is easy to see that life has to her been a heavy burden. And, indeed, this fragile creature has already been exposed to incredible suffering. At the very threshold of life she had to tear herself from the tender care of her mother, from the sweet fraternal ties that a young girl can never leave without tears, even when she quits her home to share the luxurious dwelling of a young husband. The wife of the settler, torn at once and forever from the cradle of her childhood, had to exchange the charms of society and of the domestic circle for the solitude of the forest. Her marriage-bed was placed on the bare ground of the desert. To devote herself to austere duties, to submit to unknown privations, to enter upon an existence for which she was not fitted; such has been the employment of her best years; such have been the delights of her married life. Destitution, suffering, and lassitude have weakened her delicate frame, but have not dismayed her courage. While deep sadness is painted on her chiselled features, it is easy to descry religious resignation, peace, and a simple, quiet fortitude, enabling her to meet all the ills of life without fearing or defying them.

Round this woman crowd the half-clothed children, glowing with health, careless of the morrow, true children of the wilderness. Their mother turns on them from time to time a mingled look of sadness and of joy. Judg-

ing from their strength and her weakness, it would seem
as if she had exhausted herself in giving them life, and
without regretting the cost. The log-house consists of a
single room, which shelters the whole family at night;
it is a little world, an ark of civilization in the midst of
a green ocean. A few steps off the everlasting forest
extends its shades, and solitude again reigns.

We did not reach Pontiac till after sunset. Twenty
very neat and pretty houses, forming so many well-
provided shops, a transparent brook, a clearing of about
a square half-mile surrounded by the boundless forest:
this is an exact picture of Pontiac, which in twenty years
hence may be a city. The sight of this place recalled to
me what M. Gallatin had said to me a month before in
New York: "There are no villages in America, at least,
in your meaning of the word. The houses of the cultiva-
tors are scattered all over the fields. The inhabitants con-
gregate only in order to set up a sort of market to supply
the surrounding population. In these so called villages
you find none but lawyers, printers, and shopkeepers."

We were taken to the best inn in Pontiac (for there
are two), and as usual we were introduced into the bar-
room; here all, from the most opulent to the humblest
shopkeeper, assemble to smoke, think, and talk politics
on the footing of the most perfect equality. The owner
of the house, or rather the landlord, was, I must not say
a burly peasant, for there are no peasants in America,
but at any rate a very stout gentleman, whose face had
about as much of frankness and simplicity as that of a
Norman horse-dealer. This man, for fear of intimidating
you, never looked you in the face when he spoke, but
waited till you were engaged in talking with some one
else to consider you at his leisure; he was a deep politi-

cian, and, according to American habits, a pitiless querist.
They all looked at us at first with surprise; our travelling
dress and our guns proved that we were not traders, and
travelling for curiosity was a thing never heard of.   In
order to avoid explanations, we declared at starting, that
we came to buy land.   The word had scarcely escaped
us, when we discovered that in trying to avoid one evil,
we had incurred another still more formidable.

They ceased, indeed, to treat us like extraordinary
animals, but each wanted to bargain with us.   To get rid
of them and their farms, we told our host that before de-
ciding on anything we wished to obtain from him useful
information on the price of land, and the course of cultivation.   He instantly took us into another apartment,
spread out with due solemnity a map of Michigan on the
oaken table in the middle of the room, and placing the
candle before us, waited in silence for our inquiries.
Though the reader has no intention of settling in an
American wilderness, he may perhaps be curious to know
how the thousands of Europeans and Americans who
every year seek a home in this country, set about it.   I
shall therefore transcribe the information afforded by our
host in Pontiac.   We often afterwards had occasion to
verify its accuracy.

"This country is not like France," said our host, after
listening quietly to all our questions, and snuffing the
candle.   "With you labor is cheap, and land is dear.
Here the price of land is nothing, but hands cannot be
bought; I tell you this to show you that to settle in
America as well as in Europe, one must have capital,
only it must be differently employed.   For my part, I
should not advise any one to seek his fortune in our
wilds, unless he has 150 or 200 dollars at his disposal.

In Michigan, an acre never costs more than four or five shillings, when the land is waste. This is about the price of a day's work. In one day, therefore, a laborer may earn enough to purchase an acre. But the purchase made, the difficulty begins. This is the way in which we generally try to get over it.

"The settler betakes himself to his newly-acquired property with some cattle, a salted pig, two barrels of meal, and some tea. If there happens to be a hut near, he goes to it, and receives temporary hospitality. If not, he pitches his tent in the middle of the wood which is to be his field. His first care is to cut down the nearest trees; with them he quickly builds the rude log-house which you must have seen. With us, the keep of cattle costs nothing. The emigrant fastens an iron bell to their necks, and turns them into the forest. Animals thus left to themselves seldom stray far from the dwelling.

"The greatest expense is the clearing. If the pioneer brings with him a family able to help him in his first labors, the task is easy. But this is seldom the case. The emigrant is generally young, and if he has children they are small. He is therefore obliged either himself to supply all the wants of his family, or to hire the services of his neighbors. It costs from four to five dollars to clear an acre. The ground once prepared, the new owner lays out an acre in potatoes and the rest in wheat and maize. Maize is a providential gift in the wilderness; it grows in our marshes, and flourishes under the shade of the forest better than when exposed to the rays of the sun. Maize saves the emigrant's family from perishing, when poverty, sickness, or neglect has hindered his reclaiming sufficient land in the first year. The great difficulty is to get over the years which immediately succeed the first clearing. Afterwards comes competence, and later wealth."

So spake our host. We listened to these simple details with almost as much interest as if we intended to profit by them ourselves. And when he had done, we said to him : " The soil of these forests left to themselves is generally marshy and unwholesome; has the settler who braves the misery of solitude no cause to fear for his life ? " " Cultivation, at first, is always a dangerous undertaking," replied the American, "and there is scarcely an instance of a pioneer and his family escaping, during the first year, the forest fever; sometimes while travelling in the autumn you find all the occupants of a hut attacked by fever, from the emigrant himself down to his youngest child." " And what becomes of these poor creatures when thus struck by Providence ? " " They resign themselves and hope for better times." " But have they no prospect of help from their neighbors ? " " Scarcely any." " Can they not at any rate procure the aid of medicine ? " " The nearest doctor often lives sixty miles off. They do as the Indians do, they die or get well as it pleases God."

We resumed : " Do the ministrations of religion ever reach them ? " " Very seldom. As yet we have not been able to set up public worship in our forest. Almost every summer, indeed, some Methodist ministers come to visit the new settlements. The news of their arrival spreads rapidly from dwelling to dwelling : it is the great event of the day. At the time fixed, the emigrant, with his wife and children, makes his way through the scarcely cleared paths in the forest towards the place of meeting. Settlers flock from fifty miles round. The congregation have no church to assemble in, they meet in the open air under the arches of the forest. A pulpit of rough logs, great trees cut down to serve as seats, such are the fittings of this rustic temple. The pioneers encamp with their families in the surrounding woods. Here for three days and nights, the people scarcely intermit their devotional exercises. You should see the fervent prayers and the deep attention of these men to the solemn words of the preacher. In the wilderness men are seized with a hunger for religion."

"One more question: among us it is generally thought that European emigration mainly peoples the deserts of America; how is it then that since we have been travelling in your forests we have not happened to meet a single European?" At these words, a smile of proud satisfaction spread over the countenance of our host.

"None but Americans," replied he solemnly, "are brave enough to submit to such privations, and are willing to pay such a price for competence. The European emigrant stops in the large towns of the seaboard, or in the surrounding districts. There he becomes a mechanic, a laborer, or a servant. He leads an easier life than in Europe, and appears content that his children should follow his example. The American takes possession of the land, and tries to create out of it a great social position."

After pronouncing the last words, our host was silent. He let an immense column of smoke escape from his mouth, and seemed prepared to listen to what we had to tell him about our plans.

We first thanked him for his valuable information and wise counsels, assured him that some day we should profit by them, and added, " Before fixing in your country, my dear landlord, we intend to visit Saginaw, and we wish to consult you on this point." At the name of Saginaw, a remarkable change came over his features. It seemed as if he had been suddenly snatched from real life and transported to a land of wonders. His eyes dilated, his mouth fell open, and the most complete astonishment pervaded his countenance.

"You want to go to Saginaw!" exclaimed he; "to Saginaw Bay! Two foreign gentlemen, two rational men, want to go to Saginaw Bay! It is scarcely credible." "And why not?" we replied. "But are you well aware," continued our host, "what you undertake? Do you know that Saginaw is the last inhabited spot towards the Pacific; that between this place and Saginaw lies an uncleared wilderness? Do you know. that the forest is full of Indians and mosquitoes; that you must sleep at least for one night under the damp trees? Have you thought about the fever? Will you be able to get on in the wilderness, and to find your way in the labyrinth of our forests?"

After this tirade, he paused, in order to judge of the effect which he had produced. We replied: "All that may be true, but we start to-morrow for Saginaw Bay."

Our host reflected for an instant, shrugged his shoulders, and said slowly and positively, "Some paramount interest alone can induce two strangers to take such a step. No· doubt you have a mistaken idea, that it is an advantage to fix as far as possible from any competition?"

We do not answer.

He continues: "Perhaps you are sent by the Canadian Fur Company to establish relations with the Indian tribes on the frontier?"

We maintain our silence.

Our host had come to an end of his conjectures, and

he said no more; but he continued to muse on the strangeness of our scheme.

"Have you never been in Saginaw?" we resumed. "I," he answered, "I have been so unlucky as to go thither five or six times, but I had a motive for doing it, and you do not appear to have any." "But you forget, my worthy host, that we do not ask you if we had better go to Saginaw, but only how we can get there most easily."

Brought back thus to the matter in hand, our American recovered his presence of mind and the precision of his ideas. He explained to us in a few words and with excellent practical good sense how we should set about our journey through the wilderness, entered into the minutest details, and provided for every possible contingency. At the end of his recommendations he paused once more, to see if at length we should unfold the mystery of our journey, and perceiving that neither of us had anything more to say, he took the candle, showed us a bedroom, and after giving us a truly democratic shake of the hand, went to finish his evening in the common room.

On the next day we rose with the dawn, and prepared to start. Our host was soon stirring: the night had not revealed to him the motives of our extraordinary conduct. As, however, we appeared quite determined to despise his advice, he dared not return to the charge; but he kept constantly at our side, and now and then reflected, in an under-tone: — "I do not well make out what can take two strangers to Saginaw." . . . till at last I said to him, as I put my foot into the stirrup, — "We have many reasons for going thither, my dear landlord!"

He stopped short at these words, and, looking me in

the face for the first time, seemed prepared to receive the revelation of the great mystery. But I, quietly mounting my horse, gave him no other solution than a friendly wave of the hand, after which I trotted off as fast as I could.

We had been advised to apply to a Mr. Williams, who, as he had long dealt with the Chippeway Indians, and had a son established at Saginaw, might give us useful information. After riding some miles in the forest, just as we fancied that we had missed our friend's house, we saw an old man working in a little garden. We spoke to him, and found that he was Mr. Williams.

He received us with much kindness, and gave us a letter to his son. We asked him if we had anything to fear from the Indian tribes through whose territories we were about to pass. Mr. Williams rejected this idea with a sort of indignation. " No, no," he said, " you may proceed without fear. For my part, I sleep more fearlessly among Indians than among white people."

I note this, as the first favorable impression given to me of the Indians since my arrival in America. In the thickly-peopled districts, they are always spoken of with a mixture of fear and contempt; and I think that in those places they deserve both. A few pages back may be seen what I myself thought of them when I met the first specimens at Buffalo. If the reader, however, will go on with this journal, and follow me among the European settlers on the frontier, as well as among the Indian tribes, he will form a higher, and at the same time a juster idea of the aborigines of America.

After we left Mr. Williams, we pursued our road through the woods. From time to time a little lake (this district is full of them) shines like a white table-cloth under the green branches.   The charm of these lonely spots, as yet untenanted by man, and where peace and silence reign undisturbed, can hardly be imagined.

I have often climbed the wild and solitary passes of the Alps, where Nature refuses to obey the hand of man, and, displaying all her terrors, fills the mind with an exciting and overwhelming sensation of greatness. The solitude here is equally deep, but the emotions it excites are different.   In this flowery wilderness, where, as in Milton's Paradise, all seems prepared for the reception of man, the feelings produced are tranquil admiration, a soft melancholy, a vague aversion to civilized life, and a sort of savage instinct which causes you to regret that soon this enchanting solitude will be no more. Already, indeed, the white man is approaching through the surrounding woods ; in a few years he will have felled the trees now reflected in the limpid waters of the lake, and will have driven to other wilds the animals that feed on its banks.

Still travelling on, we reached a country of a different aspect.   The ground was no longer flat, but thrown into hills and valleys.   Nothing can be wilder than the appearance of some of these hills.

In one of these picturesque passes, we turned suddenly to contemplate the magnificent scene which we were leaving behind, and, to our great surprise, we saw close to us, and apparently following us step by step, a red Indian.   He was a man of about thirty, tall, and admirably proportioned.   His black and shining hair fell down upon his shoulders, with the exception of two tresses, which were fastened on the top of his head.

His face was smeared with black and red paint. He wore a sort of very short blue blouse. His legs were covered with red *mittas*, a sort of pantaloon which reaches only to the top of the thigh, and his feet were defended by moccasons. At his side hung a knife. In his right hand he held a long rifle, and in his left two birds that he had just killed.

The first sight of this Indian made on us a far from agreeable impression. The spot was ill-suited for resisting an attack. On our right a forest of lofty pines; on our left a deep ravine, at the bottom of which a stream brawled among the rocks, hidden by the thick foliage, so that we approached it, as it were, blindfold! To seize our guns, turn round and face the Indian in the midst of the path was the affair of an instant. . . . . He halted in the same manner, and for half a minute we all were silent.

His countenance presented the characteristics of the Indian race. In his deep black eyes sparkled the savage fire which still lights up those of the half-caste, and is not lost before two or three crossings of white blood. His nose was aquiline, slightly depressed at the end; his cheek-bones very high; and his wide mouth showed two rows of dazzling white teeth, proving that the savage, more cleanly than his neighbor, the American, did not pass his day in chewing tobacco-leaves.

I said, that when we turned round, arms in hand, the Indian stopped short. He stood our rapid scrutiny with perfect calmness, and with steady and unflinching eye. When he saw that we had no hostile intentions, he smiled: probably he perceived that we had been alarmed.

I never before had remarked how completely a mirthful expression changes the savage physiognomy; I have a hundred times since had occasion to notice it. An Indian grave and an Indian smiling are different men. In the motionless aspect of the former there is a savage majesty which inspires involuntary fear. But, if the same man smiles, his countenance takes an expression of simplicity and benevolence, which is really captivating.

When we saw our Indian thus unbend, we addressed him in English. He allowed us to talk as long as we liked, and then made signs that he did not understand us. We offered him brandy, which he readily accepted without thanking us. Still making signs, we asked him for the birds which he carried; he gave them to us for a little piece of money. Having made acquaintance, we bade him adieu, and trotted off.

' At the end of half an hour of rapid riding, on turning round, once more I was astounded by seeing the Indian still at my horse's heels. He ran with the agility of a wild animal, without speaking a single word or seeming to hurry himself. We stopped; he stopped: we went on; he went on. We darted on at full speed; our horses, natives of the wilderness, leaped easily every obstacle: the Indian doubled his pace: I saw him, sometimes on the right, sometimes on the left of my horse, jumping over the brushwood and alighting on the ground without the slightest noise. He was like one of the wolves of the North, which are said to follow horsemen in hope of their falling and thus becoming a more easy prey.

The sight of this strange figure, now lost in the darkness of the forest, and then again appearing in the daylight, and seeming to fly by our side, became at last an annoyance. As we could not imagine what induced him

to follow us at such a rapid rate (he might, indeed, have
long accompanied us before we perceived him for the
first time), it occurred to us that he was leading us into
an ambush.

We were full of these thoughts, when we discovered,
right in front of us in the wood, the end of another rifle;
we soon came alongside of the bearer. We took him at
first for an Indian. He wore a kind of short frock-coat,
tight at the waist, showing an upright and well-made figure. His neck was bare, and his feet covered by moccasons. When we were close to him, he raised his head;
we at once saw that he was an European, and we stopped
short. He came to us, shook us cordially by the hand,
and we entered into conversation.

" Do you live in the desert ? " " Yes; here is my
house." And he showed us, among the trees, a hut even
more miserable than the ordinary log-house. " Alone ? "
" Alone." " And what do you do with yourself here ? "
" I roam about the woods, and I kill right and left the
game which comes in my way; but the shooting is not
good here now." " And you like this sort of life ? "
" Better than any other." " But are you not afraid of
the Indians ? " " Afraid of the Indians ! I had rather
live among them than in the society of white men. No,
no; I am not afraid of the Indians; they are better people than we are, unless we have brutalized them with
strong liquors, poor creatures ! "

We then showed to our new acquaintance the man
who followed us so obstinately, and who at that moment
was standing stock-still a few paces off. " He is a Chippeway," said our friend, " or, as the French would call
him, a ' sauteur.' I would lay a wager that he is returning from Canada, where he has received the annual

presents from the English. His family cannot be far off."

So speaking, the American signed to the Indian to approach, and began to talk to him in his language with great fluency. The pleasure that these two men, so different in race and in habits, took in exchanging their ideas, was a striking sight. The conversation evidently turned upon the relative merit of their arms. After examining carefully the rifle of the savage, the white man said to us, — "This is an excellent musket; the English no doubt gave it to him, that he might use it against us, and he will certainly do so in the first war. This is how the Indians call down upon their own heads their misfortunes,—but they know no better, poor things!" "Are the Indians skilful in the use of these long heavy guns?" "There are no shots like the Indians," replied our new friend, in a tone of the greatest admiration. "Look at the little birds which he sold you, sir; there is but one shot in each, and I am sure that he fired at them only twice. Oh!" he added, "there is no man so happy as an Indian in the districts whence we have not yet frightened away the game; but the larger sorts scent our approach at a distance of more than three hundred miles; and, as they retire, they leave the country before us a waste, incapable of supporting any longer the poor Indians, unless they cultivate the ground."

As we were resuming our journey, our new friend called out to us: "When you pass here again, knock at my door. It is a pleasure to meet white faces in this place."

I have reported this in itself unimportant conversation, in order to give an idea of a description of man that we often met on the borders of the habitable world;

they are Europeans, who, in spite of the habits of their youth, have become enamoured of the liberty of the desert. Attached to the wilds of America by taste and inclination, to Europe by their religion, principles, and ideas, they unite a love for savage life with the pride of civilization, and prefer the Indians to their own countrymen, though without acknowledging them as equals.

We proceeded on our way. We maintained the same rapid pace, and in half an hour reached the house of a pioneer. Before the door of the hut an Indian family had encamped. An old woman, two young girls, and several children, were crouching round a fire, to the heat of which were exposed the still palpitating limbs of a whole kid. A few steps off an Indian was lying quite naked on the grass, basking in the sun, whilst a little child was rolling about in the dust by his side. Here our silent companion stopped ; he left us without bidding us adieu, and sat down gravely among his countrymen.

What could have induced this man to follow our horses for five miles ? We never could guess.

After breakfasting in this spot, we remounted, and pursued our journey through a wood of thinly scattered lofty trees. The underwood had been burnt away, as was evident from the calcined remains on the grass. The ground was covered with fern, extending under the trees as far as the eye could reach.

Some miles farther on, my horse lost a shoe, which caused us great embarrassment. Not far off, happily, we met a planter, who succeeded in putting it on again. If we had not fallen in with him, I doubt if we could have gone on farther, for we had nearly reached the end of the clearings. The settler who enabled us to continue

our journey, advised us to make haste, as the daylight
was beginning to fail, and we were at least five miles
from Flint River, where we intended to sleep.

Soon, indeed, we were enveloped in perfect darkness.
We were forced to push on. The night was fine, but
intensely cold. The silence of the forest was so deep,
the calm so complete, that the forces of nature seemed
paralyzed. No sound was heard but the annoying hum
of the mosquitoes, and the stamp of our horses' feet.
Now and then we saw the distant gleam of a fire, against
which we could trace, through the smoke, the stern and
motionless profile of an Indian.

At the end of an hour we reached a spot where the
roads separated ; two paths opened out in different direc-
tions — which should we take ? The choice was difficult. One led to a stream we did not know how deep ;
the other to a clearing. The moon just rising showed
us a valley full of fallen trees : farther on, we descried
two houses.

It was of so much consequence not to lose our way in
such a place and at such an hour, that we determined to
take advice before proceeding. My companion remained
to take care of the horses, whilst I, with my gun over
my shoulder, descended into the valley.

Soon I perceived that I was entering a new settlement.
Immense trunks of trees, their branches as yet unlopped,
covered the ground. By jumping from one to another,
I soon was near the houses. But the stream separated
me from them. Happily, its course was impeded in this
place by some huge oaks that the pioneer's axe had
no doubt thrown down. I succeeded in crawling along
these trees, and at last reached the opposite side.

I warily approached the two houses which I could see

but indistinctly. I feared they might prove Indian wigwams. They were unfinished. The doors were open, and no voice answered mine. I returned to the edge of the stream whence I could not help admiring for a few minutes the awful grandeur of the scene.

The valley seemed a vast amphitheatre, surrounded on all sides by the dark woods as if by a black curtain. In its centre the moonlight played among the shattered remnants of the forest, creating a thousand fantastic shapes. No sound of any kind, no murmur of life was audible.

At last I remembered my companion, and called loudly to tell him of the result of my search, to advise him to cross the rivulet and to join me. The echo repeated my voice over and over again in the solitary woods, but I got no answer. I shouted again, and listened again. The same death-like silence reigned.

I became uneasy, and I ran by the side of the stream till I reached the place lower down where it was fordable.

When I got there, I heard in the distance the sound of horses' feet, and soon after Beaumont himself appeared. Surprised by my long absence, he had proceeded towards the rivulet. He was already in the shallow when I called him. The sound of my voice, therefore, had not reached him. He told me that he, too, had tried by every means to make himself heard, and, as well as I, had been alarmed at obtaining no. answer. If it had not been for this ford which had served us as a meeting-place, we should perhaps have been looking for each other half the night.

We resumed our journey with the full resolution of not again separating, and in three quarters of an hour

we at last came upon a settlement, consisting of two or
three huts and, what was still more satisfactory, a light.
A violet-colored line of water in the hollow of the valley proved that we had arrived at Flint River. Soon,
indeed, a loud barking echoed in the woods, and we found
ourselves close to a log-house, separated from us only by
a fence. As we were preparing to climb over it, we saw
in the moonlight a great black bear that, standing on his
hind-legs and at the very extremity of his chain, showed
as clearly as he could his intention to give us a fraternal
embrace.

"What an infernal country is this," said I, "where
they keep bears for watch-dogs." "We must call," replied my companion; "if we attempted to get over the
fence, it would be difficult to make the porter listen to
reason."

We holloed at the top of our voices and with such
success, that at last a man appeared at the window. After examining us by the light of the moon : "Enter, gentlemen," he said, "Trink, go to bed ! To the kennel, I say,
they are not robbers."

The bear waddled off, and we got in. We were half
dead with fatigue. We asked our host, if we could have
oats for our horses. "Certainly," he replied, and began
to mow the nearest field with American *sang froid*, and
as if it were noon-day. Meanwhile we unsaddled our
horses, and as there was no stable, fastened them to the
paling which we had just passed through.

Having provided for our travelling companions, we began to think of our own rest. There was but one bed in
the house ; it was allotted to Beaumont. I wrapped myself in my cloak, and lying down on the floor, slept as
soundly as a man does who has ridden forty miles.

On the next day (July 25th) our first care was to in-
quire for a guide.

A wilderness of forty miles separates Flint River from
Saginaw, and the road is a narrow pathway, hardly perceivable.   Our host approved of our plan, and shortly
brought us two Indians whom he assured us that we
could perfectly trust.   One was a boy of twelve or four-
teen; the other a young man of eighteen.   The frame of
the latter, though it had not yet attained the vigor of maturity, gave the idea of agility united with strength.   He
was of middle height; his figure was tall and slender,
his limbs flexible and well-proportioned.   Long tresses
fell from his bare head.   He had also taken care to paint
his face with black and red in symmetrical lines; a ring
was passed through his nose, and a necklace and ear-rings
completed his attire.   His weapons were no less remarkable.   At one side hung the celebrated tomahawk; on
the other, a long sharp knife, with which the savages
scalp their victims.   Round his neck hung a cow-horn,
containing his powder; and in his right hand he held a
rifle.   As is the case with most Indians, his eye was wild,
and his smile benevolent.   At his side, to complete the
picture, trotted a dog, with upright ears and long nose,
more like a fox than any other animal, with a look so
savage as to be in perfect harmony with the countenance
of his master.

After examining our new companion with an attention
which he did not seem to notice, we asked him his price
for the service that he was about to render to us.   The
Indian replied in a few words of his native tongue; and
the American immediately informed us that what he
asked was about equivalent to two dollars.

"As these poor Indians," charitably added our host,

"do not understand the value of money, you will give the dollars to me, and I will willingly give him what they represent."

I was curious to see what this worthy man considered to be equal to two dollars, and I followed him quietly to the place where the bargain was struck. I saw him give to our guide a pair of moccasons and a pocket-handkerchief, that certainly together did not amount to half the sum. The Indian withdrew quite satisfied, and I made no remark, saying to myself, with Lafontaine, — "Ah! if the lions were painters!"

However, the Indians are not the only dupes of the American pioneers. Every day we were ourselves victims to their extreme cupidity. It is true that they do not steal. They are too intelligent to commit any dangerous breach of the law; but I never saw an innkeeper in a large town overcharge so impudently as these tenants of the wilderness, among whom I fancied I should find primitive honesty and patriarchal simplicity.

All was ready: we mounted our horses, and wading across the rivulet (Flint River) which forms the boundary of civilization, we entered the real desert.

Our two guides ran, or rather leaped like wild-cats over the impediments of the road. When we came to a fallen tree, a stream, or a bog, they pointed to the right path, but did not even turn round to see us get out of the difficulty. Accustomed to trust only to himself, the Indian can scarcely understand that others need help. He is willing to serve you in an emergency, but as yet he has not been taught the art of adding value to his services by kindness and solicitude. We might have ventured on some reproofs, but it was impossible to make our companions understand a word. Besides, we felt that we were entirely in their power. Here, in fact, the scale was reversed. Plunged in this impenetrable gloom, reduced to rely on our personal strength, we children of civilization groped blindly on, incapable, not only of threading the labyrinth, but even of finding in it the means of sustenance. In these difficulties lay the triumph of the savage. For him the forest had no secrets, to him it was a home; he walked through it with head erect, guided by an instinct more unerring than the navigator's compass. At the top of the loftiest tree, under the densest foliage, his eye discovered the game, close to which the European would have passed a hundred times in vain.

From time to time our Indians halted. They placed their fingers on their lips, in token of silence, and signed to us to dismount. Guided by them, we reached the spot whence we could see the bird for which we were searching. It was amusing to observe the contemptuous smile with which they led us by the hand like children, and at last brought us near to the object they themselves had discovered long before.

As we proceeded, we gradually lost sight of the traces of man. Soon all proofs even of savage life disappeared, and before us was the scene that we had so long been seeking — a virgin forest.

Growing in the middle of the thin brushwood, through which objects are perceived at a considerable distance, was a single clump of full-grown trees, almost all pines or oaks. Confined to so narrow a space, and deprived of sunshine, each of these trees had run up rapidly, in search of air and light. As straight as the mast of a ship, the most rapid grower had overtopped every surrounding object; only when it had attained a higher region did it venture to spread out its branches, and clothe itself with leaves. Others followed quickly in this elevated sphere ; and the whole group, interlacing their boughs, formed a sort of immense canopy. Underneath this damp, motionless vault, the scene is different.

Majesty and order are overhead — near the ground, all is chaos and confusion : aged trunks, incapable of supporting any longer their branches, are shattered in the middle, and present nothing but a sharp jagged point. Others, long loosened by the wind, have been thrown unbroken on the ground. Torn up from the earth, their roots form a natural barricade, behind which several men might easily find shelter. Huge trees, sustained by the surrounding branches, hang in mid-air, and fall into dust, without reaching the ground.

There is no district with us so scantily peopled as to make it possible for a forest to be so completely abandoned that the trees, after quietly fulfilling the purpose of their existence, attain old age undisturbed, and at last perish from natural decay. Civilized man strikes them while yet in their prime, and clears the ground of their remains. In the solitude of America all-powerful nature is the only instrument of ruin, as well as of reproduction. Here, as well as in the forests over which man rules, death strikes continually ; but there is none to clear away the remains ; they accumulate day by day. They fall, they are heaped one upon another. Time alone does not work fast enough to reduce them to dust, so as to make way for their successors. Side by side lay several generations of the dead. Some, in the last stage of dissolution, have left on the grass a long line of red dust as the only trace of their presence ; others, already half consumed by time, still preserve their outward shape.

Others, again, fallen only yesterday, stretch their long branches over the traveller's path.

I have often at sea enjoyed one of the calm, serene evenings, when the sails, flapping idly from the mast, leave the crew in ignorance even of the quarter whence the breeze will rise. The perfect repose of Nature is as striking in the wilderness as on the ocean. When at noon-day the sun's rays penetrate the forest, there is often heard a long sob, a kind of plaintive cry echoing in the distance. It is the last 'breath of the expiring breeze. Deep silence ensues, and such absolute stillness as fills the mind with a kind of superstitious awe. The traveller stops to contemplate the scene.

Pressed against one another, their boughs interlaced, the trees seem to form one vast indestructible edifice, under whose arches reign eternal darkness. Around are violence and destruction, shattered trees, and torn trunks ; the traces of long elemental war. But the struggle is suspended. It seems to have been suddenly arrested by the order of a supernatural Being. Half-broken branches seem to hold by some invisible link to the trunk that no longer supports them ; trees torn from their roots hang in the air as if they had not had time to reach the ground.

The traveller holds his breath to catch the faintest sound of life. No noise, not even a whisper reaches him. You may be lost in an European forest ; but some noise belonging to life is audible. You hear a church-bell, or a woodman's axe, or the report of a gun, or the barking of a dog, or, at any rate, the indistinct hum of civilized life.

Here not only man is absent, but the voice of no animal is to be heard. The smaller ones have sought the

neighborhood of human dwellings, and the larger have
fled to a still greater distance; the few that remain hide
in the shade. Thus all is motionless, all is silent beneath
the leafy arch. It seems as if the Creator had for a
moment withdrawn his countenance, and all Nature had
become paralyzed.

This was not the only time that we noticed the resemblance of the forest to the ocean. In each case the
idea of immensity besets you. The succession of similar
scenes; their continual monotony overpowers the imagination. Perhaps even the sensation of loneliness and
desolation which oppressed us in the middle of the Atlantic was felt by us still more strongly and acutely in
the deserts of the New World.

At sea the voyager sees the horizon to which he is
steering. He sees the sky. His view is bounded only
by the powers of the human eye. But what is there to
indicate a path across this leafy ocean? In vain you
may climb the lofty trees; others still higher will surround you. In vain you climb a hill; everywhere the
forest follows you, the forest which extends before you to
the Arctic Pole, and to the Pacific Ocean. You may
travel thousands of miles beneath its shade, and, though
always advancing, never appear to stir from the same
spot.

But it is time to return to our journey to Saginaw.
We had been riding for five hours in complete ignorance
of our whereabouts, when our Indians stopped short, and
the elder, whose name was Sagan-Cuisco, traced a line
in the sand. He showed us one end, exclaiming, *Michi*,
Conte-ouinque (the Indian name for Flint River), and
pointing to the other, pronounced the name of *Saginaw*.
Then, marking a point in the middle, he signed to us

that we had achieved half the distance, and that we must
rest a little.

The sun was already high, and we should gladly have
accepted his invitation, if we could have seen water within reach; but as none was near we motioned to the Indian that we wished to halt where we could eat and
drink. He understood us directly, and set off with the
same rapidity as before. An hour later he stopped
again, and showed us a spot where we might find water
about thirty paces off in the forest.

Without waiting for us to answer, or helping us to un-
saddle our horses, he went to it himself; we followed as
fast as we could. A little while before the wind had
thrown down a large tree in this place; in the hollow
that had been filled by the root was a little reservoir of
rain-water. This was the fountain to which our guide
conducted us, without the thought apparently having occurred to him that we should hesitate to partake of such
a draught. We opened our bag. Another misfortune!
The heat had entirely spoilt our provisions, and we found
our dinner reduced to the small piece of bread, which
was all that we had been able to procure at Flint River.

Add to this, a cloud of mosquitoes, attracted by the
vicinity of water, which we were forced to fight with one
hand while we carried our bread to our mouths with the
other, and an idea may be formed of a rustic dinner in a
virgin forest.

While we were eating, our Indians sat cross-legged on
the prostrate trunk that I have mentioned. When they
saw that we had finished, they made signs that they too
were hungry. We showed them our empty bag, they
shook their heads without speaking. The Indian has no
fixed hours for his meals; he gorges food when he can,

and fasts afterwards, till he finds wherewith to satisfy his
appetite: wolves have similar habits. We soon began
to think of starting, but we were dismayed to find that
our horses had disappeared. Goaded, no doubt, by
hunger, they had strayed from the road in which we
had left them, and it was not without trouble that we
succeeded in tracing them ; we blessed the mosquitoes
that had forced us to continue our journey.

The path soon became more and more difficult to
follow. Every moment our horses had to force their
way through thick brushwood, or to leap over the large
fallen trees that barred our progress.

At the end of two hours of an extremely toilsome ride
we at length reached a stream, which though shallow,
was deeply embanked. We waded across it, and from
the opposite side we saw a field of maize and two huts
that looked like log-houses. As we approached we found
that we were in a little Indian settlement, and that the
log-houses were wigwams. The solitude was no less
perfect than in the surrounding forest.

When we reached the first of these abandoned dwellings, Sagan-Cuisco stopped. He examined attentively
everything around him, then laying down his rifle and
approaching us, he again traced a line in the sand and
showed us by the same method as before that we had
accomplished only two thirds of the road; then he rose
and pointing to the sun, signed that it was quickly sinking
into the west, next he looked at the wigwam and shut his
eyes.

This language was easy to understand, he wished us to
sleep in this place. I own that the proposal astonished
as much as it annoyed us. It was long since we had
eaten, and we were but moderately inclined to sleep

without supper. The sombre savage grandeur of scene that we had been contemplating ever since the morning, our utter loneliness, the wild faces of our guides, and the difficulty of communicating with them, all conspired to take away our confidence.

There was a strangeness too in the conduct of the Indians. Our road for the last two hours had been even more untrodden than at the beginning. No one had told us that we should pass through an Indian village, and every one had assured us that we could go in one day from Flint River to Saginaw. We could not therefore imagine why our guides wanted to keep us all night in the desert.

We insisted upon going on. The Indian signed that we should be surprised by darkness in the forest. To force our guides to proceed would have been dangerous. I determined to have recourse to their cupidity. But there is no such philosopher as the Indian. He has few wants, and consequently few desires. Civilization has no hold over him. He neither knows, nor cares for its advantages.

I had, however, remarked that Sagan-Cuisco had paid particular attention to a little wicker-bottle that hung by my side. A bottle that could not be broken. Here was a thing which he had the sense to appreciate. He really admired it. My gun and my bottle were my only European implements that excited his desires. I signed to him that I would give him the bottle if he would take us immediately to Saginaw. He then seemed to undergo a violent struggle. He looked again at the sun; then on the ground. At last he came to a decision, seized his rifle, exclaimed twice, with his hand on his mouth, *Ouh!* *ouh!* and rushed off before us through the bushes.

We followed him at a quick pace, and we soon lost sight of the Indian settlement. Our guides continued to run for two hours faster than before.

Still, night was coming on, and the last rays of the sun had disappeared behind the trees, when Sagan-Cuisco was stopped by a violent bleeding at the nose. Accustomed as the young man, as well as his brother, was to bodily exertion, it was evident that fatigue and want of food had exhausted their strength. We began to fear lest our guides should renounce the undertaking, and insist on sleeping under a tree. We therefore proposed to mount them in turns on our horses.

They accepted our offer without surprise or shame. It was curious to see these half-naked men gravely seated on English saddles, carrying our game-bags and guns slung over their shoulders, while we were toiling on before them.

At last night came. The air under the trees became damp, and icy cold. In the dark the forest assumed a new and terrible aspect. Our eyes could distinguish nothing but confused masses without shape or order; strange and disproportioned forms; the sort of fantastic images which haunt the imagination in fever. The echo of our steps had never seemed so loud, nor the silence of the forest so awful. The only sign of life in this sleeping world was the humming of the mosquito.

As we advanced the gloom became still deeper. Now and then a fire-fly traced a luminous line upon the darkness. Too late we acknowledged the wisdom of the Indian's advice; but it was no longer possible to recede.

We therefore pushed on as rapidly as our strength and the night permitted. At the end of an hour we left the woods, and entered a vast prairie. Our guides uttered three times a savage cry, that vibrated like the discordant notes of the *tam-tam*. It was answered in the distance. Five minutes afterwards we reached a stream; but it was too dark to see the opposite bank.

The Indians halted here. They wrapped their blankets round them, to escape the stings of the mosquitoes; and hiding in the long grass, looked like balls of wool, that one might pass by without remarking and could not possibly suppose to be men.

We ourselves dismounted, and waited patiently for what was to follow. In a few minutes we heard a faint noise, and something approached the bank. It was an Indian canoe, about ten feet long, formed out of a single tree. The man who was curled up in the bottom of this frail bark wore the dress and had the appearance of an Indian. He spoke to our guides, who, by his direction, took the saddles from our horses, and placed them in the canoe.

As I was preparing to get into it, the supposed Indian touched me on the shoulder, and said, with a Norman accent which made me start,—

" Ah, you come from Old France! . . . stop — don't be in a hurry — people sometimes get drowned here."

If my horse had addressed me, I should not, I think, have been more astonished.

I looked at the speaker, whose face shone in the moonlight like a copper ball. " Who are you, then?" I said. " You speak French, but you look like an Indian." He replied, that he was a " Bois-brulé," which means the son of a Canadian and an Indian woman.

I shall often have occasion to mention this singular race of half-castes, which extends over all the frontiers of Canada, and, in fact, over the borders of the United

States. At that time I felt only the pleasure of conversing in my mother-tongue.

Following the advice of my countryman, the savage, I seated myself in the bottom of the canoe, and kept as steady as possible ; my horse, whose bridle I held, plunged into the water, and swam by my side, meanwhile the Canadian sculled the bark, singing in an undertone to an old French tune some verses, of which I caught only the first couplet,—

> " Between Paris and Saint Denis
> There lived a maid," &c.

We reached the opposite bank without any accident ; the canoe immediately returned, to bring over my companion. All my life I shall remember the second time that it neared the shore. The moon, which was full, was just then rising over the prairie behind us, half the disk only appeared above the horizon ; it looked like a mysterious door, through which we could catch a glimpse of the light of another world. Its rays were reflected in the stream, and touched the place where I stood. Along the line of their pale, tremulous light, the Indian canoe was advancing. We could not see any sculls, or hear the sound of rowlocks. The bark glided rapidly and smoothly — long, narrow, and black, resembling an alligator in pursuit of his prey. Crouching at the prow, Sagan-Cuisco, with his head between his knees, showed only his shiny tresses. Farther back, the Canadian was silently sculling, while behind followed Beaumont's horse, with his powerful chest throwing up the waters of the Saginaw in glittering streams.

In the whole scene there was a wild grandeur which made an impression upon us which has never been effaced.

When all had landed, we immediately proceeded to a house that had just become visible in the moonlight about a hundred yards from the river, and which the Canadian assured us would afford us shelter. We contrived, indeed, to establish ourselves tolerably, and we should probably have repaired our strength by a sound sleep if we could have got rid of the myriads of mosquitoes that filled the house; but this was impossible.

The tormentor that in English is called a mosquito, and in Canadian French, a "maringouin," is a little insect much resembling the French "cousin" (gnat). It differs only in size. It is generally bigger, and its trunk is so sharp, and so strong, that only woollen garments can save you from its sting. These insects are the curse of the American wilderness. They render a long stay unendurable. I never felt torments such as those which I suffered from them during the whole of this expedition, and especially at Saginaw. In the day they prevented us from drawing, or writing, or sitting still for an instant; in the night thousands of them buzzed around us, settling on every spot in our bodies that was uncovered. Awakened by the irritation of the bite, we hid our heads under the sheets; their sting went through. Thus persecuted and chased by them we rose and went into the air, till extreme fatigue at last procured for us an uneasy and broken sleep.

We went out very early, and the first objects that struck us were our Indians, rolled up in their blankets near the door, and sleeping by the side of their dogs.

This was our first daylight view of the village of Saginaw, which we had come so far to see. A small, cultivated plain, bounded on the south by a beautiful and gently flowing river; on the east, west, and north, by

the forest ; constitutes at present the territory of the em-
bryo city.

Near us was a house whose character announced the
easy circumstances of its owner. It was the one in
which we had passed the night. A similar dwelling was
visible at the other extremity of the clearing. Between
them, and on the skirts of the woods, two or three log-
houses were half hidden in the foliage.

On the opposite side of the river stretched the prairie,
resembling a boundless ocean on a calm day. A column
of smoke was curling towards the sky. Looking whence
it came, we discovered the pointed forms of two or three
wigwams, which scarcely stood out from the grass of the
prairie. A plough that had upset, its oxen galloping off
by themselves to the field, and a few half-wild horses,
completed the picture.

On every side the eye searches in vain for a Gothic
spire, the moss-covered porch of a clergyman's house, or
a wooden cross by the road-side. These venerable relics of our religion have not been carried into the wilderness. It contains as yet nothing to remind one of the
past or of the future. No consecrated home even for
those who are no more. Death has not had time to
claim his domain, nor to have his close marked out.
Here, man still seems to steal into life. Several generations do not assemble round the cradle to utter hopes
often deceitful, and rejoicings which the future often belies.
The child's name is not inscribed in the register of the
city, religion does not mingle its affecting ceremonies
with the solicitude of the family. A woman's prayers, a
few drops sprinkled on the infant's head by its father's
hand, quietly open to it the gates of heaven.

The village of Saginaw is the farthest point inhabited

by Europeans to the north-west of the vast peninsula of Michigan.   It may be considered as an advanced post; a sort of watch-tower, placed by the whites in the midst of the Indian nations.

European revolutions, the continual noisy clamor of politics, reach this spot only at rare intervals and as the echoes of a sound, the source of which the ear can no longer distinguish nor comprehend.

Sometimes an Indian stops on his journey to relate, in the poetical language of the desert, some of the sad realities of social life ; sometimes a newspaper dropped out of a hunter's knapsack, or only the sort of indistinct rumor which spreads, one knows not how, and which seldom fails to tell that something strange is passing in the world.

Once a year a vessel steams up the Saginaw to join this stray link to the great European chain which now binds together the world.   She carries to the new settlement the products of human industry, and in return takes away the fruits of the soil.

Thirty persons, men, women, old people, and children, at the time of our visit composed this little society, as yet scarcely formed — an opening seed thrown upon the desert, there to germinate.

Chance, interest, or inclination, had collected them in this narrow space.   No common link existed between them, and they differed widely.   Among them were Canadians, Americans, Indians, and half-castes.

Philosophers have thought, that human nature is everywhere the same, varied only according to the laws and institutions of different states of society.   This is one of the opinions to which every page of history gives the lie.   Nations, under all circumstances, have their peculiar physiognomy and their characteristic features, as well as individuals.   Laws, manners, and religion may alter, wealth and power may change ; places, dress, and external appearance may differ ; prejudices may disappear, or be substituted by others.   In the midst of these diversities you still recognize the same race. Though human nature is flexible, it contains elements which are fixed.

The inhabitants of this little oasis belong to two nations which for more than a century have occupied the same country and obeyed the same laws.   Yet they have nothing in common.   They still are as distinctly English and French as if they lived on the banks of the Seine and the Thames.

Within yonder trellised hut you will find a man whose cordial welcome and open countenance show immediately a taste for social pleasures and careless indifference to life.   At first you may take him for an Indian.   Forced to submit to savage life, he has willingly adopted its dress, its customs, and almost its morals : he wears moccasons, an otter-skin cap, and a blanket.   He is an indefatigable hunter ; he sleeps under arms, and lives on wild honey and bison's flesh.   This man is, nevertheless, still French. He is gay, adventurous, proud of his origin, passionately fond of military glory, more vain than selfish, the creature of impulse rather than of judgment, preferring renown to wealth.

In order to fly to the wilderness he has broken every social tie.   He has neither wife nor children.   He may not like this, but he easily submits to it, as he does to everything else.   By nature his tastes are domestic.   He loves his own fireside, and the sight of the steeple of his village.   But he was torn from his peaceful occupations, his imagination fired by novel scenes; another hemisphere became his home : and he was suddenly seized with an insatiable desire for violent emotions, vicissitudes, and perils. The most civilized of Europeans is now a worshipper of savage life. He prefers the savannah to the street, the chase to the plough. He sports with life, and never thinks of the future.

"The white men from France," said the Canadian Indians, "are as good hunters as we are. They despise the conveniences of life, and brave danger and death as we do; God created them to live in the hut of the savage and to dwell in the desert."

A few steps off lives another European who, exposed to the same difficulties, has hardened himself against them. This man is cold, unyielding, and disputatious. He devotes himself to his land, and submits to savage life only so far as is necessary. He is always fighting against it, and every day strips it of some of its attributes. He imports one by one into the desert his laws, his manners and customs, and as much as possible every detail of advanced civilization. The emigrant from the United States cares only for the results of victory ; glory is to him an empty name ; and he considers that man is born only to obtain fortune and comfort. He is brave, but his bravery is the result of calculation ; brave because he has discovered that there are many things more hard to bear than death ; though an adventurer he is surrounded by a family, and yet cares little for intellectual or social enjoyments. Encamped on the other side of the river, amid the beds of the Saginaw, the Indian from time to time casts a stoical glance on the habitations of his brothers from Europe. Do not think that he admires their industry or envies their lot. Though for nearly three hundred years civilization has invaded and surrounded the American savage, he has not yet learnt to know or to appreciate his enemy. In vain, in both races, is one generation followed by another. Like two parallel rivers, they have flowed for three centuries side by side towards the same ocean, only a narrow space divides them, but their waters do not mingle.

It is not natural talent that is wanting in the aborigines of the New World, but their nature seems obstinately to repel our ideas and our arts. From the interior of his smoky hut, wrapped in his blanket, the Indian contemplates with scorn the convenient dwelling of the European. He has a proud satisfaction in his poverty, his heart swells and triumphs in his barbarous independence. He smiles bitterly when he sees˜us wear out our lives in heaping up useless riches. What we term industry, he calls shameful subjection. He compares the workman to the ox toiling on in a furrow. What we call necessaries of life, he terms childish playthings, or womanish baubles. He envies us only our arms. If a man has a leafy hut to shelter his head by night, a good fire to warm him in winter and to banish the mosquitoes in summer, if he has good dogs and plenty of game, what more can he ask of the Great Spirit?

On the opposite bank of the Saginaw, near the European clearings, on the frontier that separates the Old from the New World, rises a hut, more convenient than the wigwam of the savage, more rude than the house of the civilized man: it is the dwelling of a half-caste.

When for the first time we presented ourselves at the door of this half-barbarous cabin, we were surprised at hearing a soft voice from within chanting the penitential psalms to an Indian air. We stopped a moment to listen.

The sounds were slowly modulated and deeply melancholy; it was easy to recognize the plaintive harmony
which characterizes the songs of the desert.

We entered: the owner was absent.   Seated cross-
legged on a mat, in the middle of the room, was a young
woman making moccasons.   With her foot she rocked
an infant, whose copper hue and European features announced a mixed origin.   She was dressed like one of
our peasants, except that her feet were bare and her hair
fell unbound over her shoulders.   When she saw us, she
left off, and looked at us with a mixture of fear and respect.   We asked her if she were French.   "No," she .
replied with a smile.   English?   "No, neither," — drop-
ping her eyes, she added, "I am only a savage."

Child of both races, taught to use two languages,
brought up in different creeds, and nursed in opposite
prejudices, the half-caste forms a compound as inexpli-
cable to himself as to others.   The ideas current in the
world when reflected in his confused brain, seem to him
an inextricable chaos from which he can find no escape.
Proud of his European origin, he despises the desert,
and yet loves its savage freedom; he admires civilization, but cannot completely submit to its restraints.   His
tastes contradict his ideas, his convictions are opposed to
his habits.   Unable to guide his steps by the uncertain
light of his reason, his mind struggles painfully in the
toils of universal doubt: he adopts opposite customs, he
prays at two altars; he believes in the Redeemer of the
World and in the amulets of the juggler; and he arrives
at the term of his days without having been able to solve
the mystery of his existence.

Thus, in this unknown corner of the earth, Providence has sowed the seeds of divers nations.   Already

many distinct races are ' to be found here side by side.

A few exiles from the great human family have met in these vast forests. They have the same wants. They have to resist wild animals, hunger, and rough weather. Scarcely thirty of them are collected in one spot in this intractable wilderness, and they look upon each other with nothing but hatred and suspicion. Diversity of color, poverty or comfort, ignorance or cultivation, have already set up amongst them ineffaceable distinctions. National prejudices, and those of education and birth, divide and isolate them.

Thus a narrow frame contains a complete picture of the contemptible side of our nature. Still one feature is wanting.

The strong lines of demarcation, traced by birth and prejudice, are not confined to the present life. They reach beyond the grave. Six different religions, or sects, share the faith of this infant society.

Catholicism, with its formidable immutability, its absolute dogmas, its terrible anathemas, and its vast rewards; the reformed faith, with its movement and continual changes; and even the old paganism, all find here their disciples. They adore in different ways the One Eternal Being who made man in His own image. They fight for the heaven to which each sect claims to be exclusively entitled. Even amidst the privations of exile, and actual suffering, man exhausts his imagination in conceiving indescribable horrors for the future. The Lutheran damns the Calvinist, the Calvinist the Unitarian, and the Catholic includes them all in one common reprobation.

More tolerant in his rude faith, the Indian is content

with excluding his European brother from the happy hunting-fields reserved for himself. Constant to the traditions bequeathed to him by his ancestors, he easily consoles himself for the evils of life, and dies dreaming of the ever-verdant forest untouched by the axe of the pioneer, where he will chase the deer and the beaver through the unnumbered days of eternity.

After breakfast we went to see the richest land-owner in the village, Mr. Williams. We found him in his shop engaged in selling to the Indians a number of little articles of small value, such as knives, glass necklaces, ear-rings, &c. It was sad to see how these poor creatures were treated by their civilized brother from Europe.

All however, whom we saw there were ready to do justice to the savages. They were kind, inoffensive; a thousand times less given to stealing than the whites. It was only a pity that they were beginning to understand the value of things. But why a pity? "Because trade with them became every day less profitable." Is not the superiority of civilized man apparent in this remark? The Indian in his ignorant simplicity would have said, that he found it every day more difficult to cheat his neighbor; but the white man finds in the refinement of language, a shade which expresses the fact, and yet saves his conscience.

On our return from Mr. Williams's we went a short way up the Saginaw to shoot wild ducks. A canoe left the reeds, and its Indian occupants came up to us to examine my double-barrelled gun. This weapon, which is common enough, always attracted especial attention from the savages. A gun that can kill two men in a second, can be fired in the wet and damp, was to them a marvel, a masterpiece beyond all price. These men showed, as usual, great admiration. They asked whence my gun came. Our young guide replied, that it was made on the other side of the great water, where the Fathers of the Canadians lived: and, as may be supposed, this answer did not make it less precious in their eyes. They remarked, however, that, as the aim was not in the centre of the barrel, it could not be sure : an observation which, I own, I could not answer.

When evening came, we returned to our canoe, and trusting to the experience that we had acquired in the morning, we rowed, unaccompanied, up an arm of the Saginaw, of which we had had only a glimpse.

The sky was without a cloud, the atmosphere pure and still. The river watered an immense forest ; it flowed so gently that we could scarcely tell the direction of the current.

We always thought that to have an accurate idea of the American forests, we ought to follow the course of some of their rivers. These rivers are the great highways with which Providence has pierced the desert and rendered it accessible to man. In the roads cut through the woods the view is circumscribed, and the path itself is the work of human hands. Rivers do not show the traces of human labor, and you see freely the grandeur of the wild and luxurious vegetation of their banks.

The wilderness was before us just as, six thousand years ago, it showed itself to the fathers of mankind.

It was a delicious, blooming, perfumed, gorgeous dwelling, a living palace made for man, though as yet, the owner had not taken possession. The canoe glided

noiselessly and without effort.   All was quiet and serene.
We ourselves soon felt softened by the scene.   Our
words became fewer and fewer ; our voices sank to a
whisper ; at last, we lapsed into silence ; and, raising
our oars, we each fell into a peaceful and inexpressibly
delicious reverie.

How is it that language, which finds an equivalent for
every sorrow, is incapable of expressing the simplest and
sweetest emotions ?

How is it possible adequately to describe those rare
moments when the luxury of sensation leads to mental
calm, and universal harmony seems to pervade creation ;
when the mind, only half awake, fluctuates between the
present and the future, the actual and the possible ; when,
amidst the exquisite repose of nature, inhaling the soft
still air, a man listens to the even beating of his own
heart, every pulse marking the lapse of time flowing drop
by drop into eternity !

Many men may have added one year to another of a
long life without once having felt anything resembling
what I have just described.   They will not understand
me.   But there are others, I am sure, who will fill up
my sketch from their hearts and memories, and in whom
these lines will awaken the remembrance of some fleeting
hours which neither time nor the real cares of life have
been able to obliterate.

The report of a gun in the woods roused us from our
dream.   At first it sounded like an explosion on both
sides of the river ; the roar then grew fainter, till it was
lost in the depth of the surrounding forest.   It sounded
like the prolonged and fearful war-cry of advancing civilization.

One evening in Sicily we lost ourselves in the extensive marsh, the site of the ancient Himera. The impression produced on us by the desert, all that was left of that famous city, was deep and strong. It was a striking testimony to the instability of human creations, and to the imperfection of human nature.

Here also was solitude; but the imagination, instead of recurring to the past, sprang forward, and lost itself in a boundless future. We asked ourselves, by what singular fate it happened that we, to whom it had been granted to look on the ruins of extinct empires, and tread the deserts made by human hands, — we children of an ancient people, should be called on to witness this scene of the primitive world, and to contemplate the as yet unoccupied cradle of a great nation.

These are not the more or less probable speculations of philosophy. The facts are as certain as if they had already taken place. In a few years these impenetrable forests will have fallen; the sons of civilization and industry will break the silence of the Saginaw; its echoes will cease; the banks will be imprisoned by quays; its current, which now flows on unnoticed and tranquil through a nameless waste, will be stemmed by the prows of vessels. More than 100 miles sever this solitude from the great European settlements; and we were, perhaps, the last travellers allowed to see its primitive grandeur. So strong is the impetus that urges the white man to the entire conquest of the New World.

It is this idea of destruction, with the accompanying thought of near and inevitable change, that gives to the solitudes of America their peculiar character, and their touching loveliness. You look at them with mournful pleasure. You feel that you must not delay admiring them. The impression of wild and natural greatness so

soon to expire, mingles with the lofty thoughts to which
the progress of civilization gives rise — you are proud
of being a man; and yet you reflect, almost with re-
morse, on the dominion which Providence allots to you
over nature.   You are distracted by conflicting ideas and
feelings.   But every impression received is sublime, and
leaves a deep trace.

We wished to quit Saginaw on the next day, the 27th
July, but one of our horses was galled by the saddle, and
we resolved to remain a day longer.   To pass the time,
we shot over the prairies which border the Saginaw below the clearings.

These prairies are not marshy as might have been
expected.   They are more or less extensive plains on
which no tree grows, though the soil is excellent; the
grass is dry, and springs to a height of three or four feet.
We found but little game, and we came back early.   The
heat was stifling, as if a storm were in the air, and the
mosquitoes more annoying than usual.   As we walked
we were enveloped in a cloud of these insects, and had
to fight our way.   Woe betide the loiterer! he is abandoned to a merciless enemy.   I remember being forced
to load my gun running, it was so painful to stand still
for an instant.

As we were returning across the prairie we remarked
that our Canadian guide followed a narrow path, and
looked very carefully where he placed his feet.   " Why
are you so cautious," I said, " are you afraid of the
damp?"   " No," he replied, " but when I walk in the
prairie I have acquired the habit of always looking at
my feet lest I should tread on a rattlesnake."   " Diable,"
I exclaimed, with a start, "are there any rattlesnakes
here?"   " Oh, yes, indeed!" answered my American

Norman with perfect indifference, "the place is full of them."

I found fault with him for not telling us sooner; he declared that as we were well shod, and the rattlesnake never bites above the heel, he did not think that we ran any great danger. I asked him if the bite of the rattlesnake were mortal; he replied, "Always in less than twenty-four hours, unless recourse be had to the Indians. They know of a remedy which, given in time, saves the patient."

However that might be, during the rest of the way we imitated our guide, and looked, as he did, at our feet.

The night which followed this burning day was one of the most disagreeable that I ever passed. The mosquitoes had become so troublesome, that though overpowered with fatigue, I could not close my eyes.

Towards midnight the storm which had long been threatening broke. As there was no longer any hope of sleeping, I rose and went to the door of our hut to breathe the cool night air.

The rain had not begun. The air seemed still. But the forest was already in motion — from time to time a deep sigh or a long cry escaped from it. Now and then a flash of lightning illumined the sky. The gentle flow of the Saginaw, the little clearing on each side of its banks, the roofs of five or six huts, and the belt of trees that surrounded us, appeared then for a moment like a revelation of the future. All vanished again in perfect darkness, and the awful voice of the desert was once more heard.

I was looking with emotion at this grand spectacle, when I heard a sigh close to me, and the lightning showed to me an Indian leaning, as I was, against the wall of our dwelling. No doubt the storm had disturbed him, for he cast a fixed and perturbed glance on all around.

Was he afraid of the lightning? or, could he see in the shock of the elements something beyond a passing convulsion of nature? Those fleeting pictures of civilization springing up, as it were, of themselves in the wilderness, were they to him prophetic? Those sobs of the forest which seemed to struggle in an unequal combat, did they reach his ears as a secret warning from Heaven; a solemn revelation of the fate finally reserved for the savage races? It was impossible to say. But his trembling lips appeared to murmur a prayer, and his features were stamped with superstitious terror.

At five A. M. we resolved to start. Every Indian from the neighborhood of Saginaw had disappeared. They were gone to receive the annual presents from the English; the Europeans were engaged in the harvest. We were, therefore, obliged to make up our minds to recross the forest without a guide.

The undertaking was not so arduous as it might appear. In general, there is but one path through these vast wildernesses; if you do not lose sight of it you must reach your journey's end.

So, at five A. M. we recrossed the Saginaw. We received the farewell and last advice of our host, and turning our horses' heads, found ourselves alone in the forest.

I own that it was not without a solemn sensation that we began again to penetrate its damp recesses. The forest stretched behind us to the Pole and to the Pacific. But one inhabited spot was between us and the boundless desert, and we had just quitted it. These thoughts, how-

ever, made us only press on our horses, and in three
hours we reached a deserted wigwam on the lonely
banks of the river Cass. A grassy bank overhanging
the water, shaded by large trees, served for a table ; and
we breakfasted, looking on the reaches of the river, which
wound among the trees as clear as crystal.

On leaving the wigwam, we found several paths. We
had been told which we were to take. But such direc-
tions are not always full or precise. We had been told
of two paths : there were three. It was true that of
these three roads two, farther on, joined together in one ;
but of this we were not aware, and our perplexity was
great.

After due examination and discussion, we could think
of nothing better than to throw the bridle on our horses'
necks to leave them to solve the difficulty. In this way
we forded the river as well as we could, and were carried
rapidly in a south-westerly direction. More than once
the roads became nearly invisible in the brushwood. In
other places the path appeared so untravelled, that we
could hardly believe that it led to more than an abandoned wigwam ; our compass indeed showed that we
were proceeding in the right direction, yet we were not
completely reassured till we reached the spot where we
had dined three days before.

We knew it again by a gigantic pine, whose trunk, shattered by the wind, we had before admired. Still we rode
on with undiminished speed, for the sun was getting low.
Soon we reached the clearing which usually betokens a
settlement. As night was coming on, we came in sight
of the river Flint ; half an hour later we were at the
door of our house. This time the bear received us as
old friends, and rose upon his hind legs to greet our
happy return.

During the whole day we had not met a single human face; the animals, too, had disappeared. No doubt they had retired from the heat. All that we saw, and that at rare intervals, was now and then, on the bare top of a withered tree, a solitary hawk standing motionless on one leg, and sleeping quietly in the sun, as if cut out of the wood on which he was resting.

In this absolute solitude, our thoughts suddenly recurred to the revolution of 1830, the first anniversary of which fell on this day. I cannot describe the violence with which the recollection of the 29th of July seized my mind. The cries and the smoke of the battle, the booming of the cannon, the rattle of musketry; the still more awful peal of the tocsin; that whole day enveloped in its flaming atmosphere, seemed suddenly to rise out of the past, and become a living picture before my eyes. It was as instantaneous as it was vivid, fleeting as a dream; for when I lifted my head, and looked round me, the vision had disappeared. But the silence of the forest had never struck me as so frigid, the shadows as so black, or the solitude as so absolute.

FRANCE BEFORE THE REVOLUTION.

THE following pages contain the article contributed by
M. de Tocqueville to the *Westminster Review*, of April,
1836, and translated by Mr. J. S. Mill. It is inserted in
this place as a preface to the two chapters on the French
Revolution, which unhappily are all that we at present
possess.

On comparing this Essay with the celebrated work on
the *Ancien Régime*, published by M. de Tocqueville
twenty years afterwards, it will be found to contain
fewer historical details and more general views. The
writer had not then passed whole years among the provincial archives of France. He drew his inferences
rather from consciousness than from observation, rather
from his wonderful power of reflection, from the sagacity
with which he conjectured what, under certain circumstances, would be the thoughts and feelings and actions
of men, than from a laborious investigation of the evi-
dences as to what they actually felt, and thought. That
investigation he afterwards made, and we have its results
in his *Ancien Régime*. They confirm most remarkably
the theories of this Essay. But they are far from super-
seding it. I am inclined to think that to an English
reader, who cares little for the details of the *ancien régime*, and much for its results, this Essay will be, if pos-

sible, more instructive than the book into which many years afterwards it was expanded. I cannot conclude without expressing my gratitude to Mr. Mill for the permission which he kindly gave me to make use of his admirable translation. — Tr.

FRANCE BEFORE THE REVOLUTION.

THE ideas and feelings of every age are connected with those of the age that preceded it, by invisible but almost omnipotent ties. One generation may anathematize the preceding generations, but it is far easier to combat than to avoid resembling them. It is impossible, therefore, to describe a nation at any given epoch, without stating what it was half a century before. This is especially necessary when the question relates to a people who, for the last fifty years, have been in an almost continual state of revolution. Foreigners who hear this people spoken of, and who have not followed with an attentive eye the successive transformations which it has experienced, only know that it has undergone great changes, but are ignorant what portions of its ancient state have been abandoned, and what have been preserved, in the midst of such prolonged vicissitudes.

It is proposed in this article to give some explanation of the state of France previously to the great Revolution of 1789, for want of which her present condition would be difficult to comprehend.

Towards the close of the ancient monarchy, the Church of France presented a spectacle analogous in some respects to that which the Established Church of England offers at the present day.

Louis XIV., who had destroyed all powerful individual existences, and annihilated or humbled all corporate bodies had left to the clergy alone the outward marks of independence. The clergy had preserved their annual assemblies, in which they taxed themselves ; they possessed a considerable portion of the landed property of the kingdom ; and they thrust themselves, in a thousand different ways, into the public administration. Without abandoning their adherence to the principal dogmas of the Roman Catholic Church, the French clergy had nevertheless assumed a firm and almost a hostile attitude towards the papal throne.

In detaching the French priesthood from their spiritual chief, leaving them at the same time riches and power, Louis had merely followed the despotic tendency which is perceptible in every act of his reign. He knew that he should ever be the master of the clergy, whose chiefs he himself chose ; and he believed it to be his interest that the clergy should be strong, in order that they might aid him in ruling over the minds of the people, and that they might resist with him the encroachments of the popes.

The Church of France, under Louis XIV., was both a political and a religious institution. In the interval between the death of this prince and the French Revolution, the religious faith of the people having been gradually weakened, the priest and the people gradually became strangers to one another. This change was produced by causes which it would take too much time to enumerate. At the end of the eighteenth century the French clergy still possessed their vast wealth — still mixed themselves up in all the affairs of state ; but the spirit of the population was becoming everywhere estranged from them, and the Church had now become much more a political than a religious institution.

It will perhaps be not without some difficulty that we shall convey to the English reader of the present day a clear conception of the old *noblesse* of France. The English language has no word which expresses exactly the old French idea of a *noblesse*. The word "nobility" expresses more, the word "gentry" less. Neither is the word "aristocracy" one which can be applied to the case without explanation. By aristocracy, taking the word in its ordinary sense, is commonly understood the aggregate of the higher classes. The French *noblesse* was an aristocratic body, but we should be wrong in saying that it alone formed the aristocracy of the country, for by its side were to be found classes as enlightened, as wealthy, and almost as influential as itself. The French *noblesse*, therefore, was to aristocracy as it is understood in England, what the *species* is to the *genus*; it formed a *caste*, and not the entire aristocracy. In this respect it resembled the *noblesse* of all the nations on the continent. Not that a man could not be made noble in France by the purchase of certain offices, or by the prince's will; but the fact of being ennobled, though it removed him from the ranks of the *tiers-état*, did not, properly speaking, introduce him into those of the *noblesse*. The noble of recent date halted, as it were, on the confines of the two orders; somewhat above the one, but below the other. He perceived afar the promised land which his posterity alone could enter. Birth, therefore, was in reality the only source whence the *noblesse* sprung. Men were born noble — they did not become so.

About 20,000 families* spread over the surface of the kingdom composed this great corporation. These families recognized among themselves a species of theoretic equality, founded on their common privilege of birth. " I am," said Henry IV., " but the first nobleman in my kingdom."† This expression is an indication of the spirit which still reigned among the French *noblesse* towards the close of the eighteenth century.‡ There existed, nevertheless, great differences of condition among the nobles. Some still possessed large landed estates, others had scarcely the means of subsistence in their paternal manor-house. Some passed the greater part of their time at court, others proudly cherished, at the extremity of their province, a hereditary obscurity. To some, custom opened the road to the highest dignities of the state, whilst others, after having attained the utmost limit of their hopes, a moderate rank in the army, returned peaceably to their homes, to quit them no more.

---

* The labors of Messrs. Moheau and De la Michodière, and those of the celebrated Lavoisier, have shown that in 1791 the number of nobles only reached 83,000 individuals, of whom only 18,323 were capable of bearing arms. The *noblesse* at that time would have formed only about the three-hundredths part of the population of the kingdom. Notwithstanding the authority which the name of Lavoisier imparts to these calculations, we have some difficulty in believing in their perfect accuracy. It seems to us that the number of the nobles must have been greater. See *De la Richesse Territoriale du Royaume de France, par Lavoisier*, p. 10.

† " *Je ne suis que le premier gentilhomme de mon royaume.*" A *gentilhomme* is a man whose family has been noble for at least two generations preceding himself.

‡ Of this the reader may convince himself by perusing the *cahiers* of the order of the *noblesse* (their instructions to their representatives) in 1789 : he will there perceive that the equality of the nobles among themselves is continually laid down as a principle.

To depict faithfully, therefore, the order of the *noblesse*, it would have been necessary to resort to numerous classifications. The *noblesse d'épée* must have been distinguished from the *noblesse de robe* — the noble of the court from the noble of the provinces — the ancient from the modern *noblesse*. In this smaller society were almost as many shades and distinctions, as in the general society of which it was but a section. A certain community of spirit nevertheless existed among all the members of this great body. They agreed in obeying certain fixed rules, in governing themselves by certain invariable usages, and in holding some ideas which were common to them all.

The French *noblesse*, having originated, like all the other feudal aristocracies, in conquest, had, like them, and even in a still greater degree, enjoyed enormous privileges. It had monopolized almost all the intelligence and wealth of society. It had possessed all the land, and been master of the inhabitants.

But at the close of the eighteenth century, the French *noblesse* presented but a shadow of its former self. It had lost its influence over both the prince and the people. The king still chose from its ranks the principal officers of Government, but in this he rather followed instinctively an ancient custom, than recognized an acquired right. It was long since any nobles had existed who had power to excite the fears of the monarch, and extort from him a share in the Government. Upon the people the influence of the *noblesse* was still less. Between a king and a body of nobles there is a natural affinity, which draws them, even unconsciously, towards each other: but a union of the aristocracy and the people is not in the ordinary course of events;

only by sustained efforts can it be brought about and maintained.

In truth, there are but two modes by which an aristocracy can maintain its influence over the people; by governing them, or by uniting with them for the purpose of checking the Government. The nobles must either remain the people's masters, or must become their leaders.

The French *noblesse* was far from placing itself at the head of the other classes in resistance to the abuses of the royal power; on the contrary, it was the kings who formerly united themselves, first with the people to struggle against the tyranny of the nobles, and afterwards with the nobles to maintain the people in obedience.

On the other hand, the *noblesse* had long ceased to take an active part in the details of Government. The general government of the State was usually in the hands of nobles; they commanded the armies, and filled the chief offices in the ministry and about the courts; but they took no share in the detailed business of administration — in that part of the public business which comes into immediate contact with the people. Shut up in his château, unknown to the prince, a stranger to the surrounding population, the noble of France remained immovable in the midst of the daily movement of society. Around him were the king's officers, who administered justice, levied taxes, maintained order, and did whatever was done for the well-being or the guidance of the people. The irksomeness of their obscure leisure induced those nobles who still retained large estates to repair to Paris, and live at the court, the only place which could supply any aliment to their ambition. The lesser nobles, confined to the provinces by narrow circumstances, led an

idle, useless, and restless existence. Those, therefore, of
the nobles, who in default of political power might by
their wealth have acquired some influence over the
people, voluntarily withdrew themselves from them;
whilst those who were compelled to live among them,
only displayed before their eyes the uselessness and inconvenience of an institution of which they were the only
visible representatives.

In thus abandoning to others the details of the public
administration, and aspiring only to the more important
offices of the State, the French *noblesse* had shown that
they were more attached to the semblance of power than
to power itself. The effect which the central government produces on the interests of individuals is remote
and comparatively obscure. The foreign policy of the
State, and its general system of laws, exercise chiefly an
indirect, and often not very obvious, influence on the welfare of each citizen. The local administration, on the
other hand, meets them daily and hourly; it incessantly
touches them in their most sensitive points; it operates
upon every one of those smaller interests of which the
great interest we take in life is made up; it is the principal object both of the hopes and fears of the people at
large; it connects itself with them by a thousand invisible ties, which bind them, and draw them on, without
their being aware. It is in governing the village that an
aristocracy lays the foundation of the power which afterwards serves it to control the State.

Fortunately for the aristocracies which still exist, the
power which seeks to destroy them knows almost as little
as themselves the secret of their influence. For our
part, were we plotting the destruction of some great
aristocratic power firmly established in any country, our

struggle would not be to drive its representatives from around the throne; we should be in no haste to attack the aristocracy in its most dazzling privileges, nor should we begin by contesting even its great legislative functions; we would endeavor to remove it to a distance from the dwelling of the poor — to deprive it of influence over the daily interests of the citizens. We would rather permit it to participate in making the general laws of the State, than to regulate the police of a single city. We should, with less regret, abandon to its control the direction of the greater affairs of society, than that of the smaller. Leaving to it all the more conspicuous marks of its grandeur, we would deprive it of the people's attachment, the true source of political power.

The French nobles had preserved a certain number of exclusive rights, which distinguished them from, and raised them above, the rest of the citizens; but it was easy to discover that among the privileges of their fathers, the French *noblesse* had only retained those which make aristocracies hated, and not those which cause them to be respected or beloved.

The nobles enjoyed the exclusive right of furnishing officers to the army. This would, doubtless, have been an important privilege, if the nobles had preserved a certain degree of individual importance, or a powerful *esprit de corps*. But as they had no longer either the one or the other, they were in the army but what they were everywhere else, passive instruments in the hands of the monarch. To him alone they looked for advancement and favor, and whether on the field of battle or at the court, to please him was their sole ambition. The privilege, therefore, which we have just mentioned, whilst it was advantageous to the pecuniary interests of noble

families, was of no service to the *noblesse* as an order in
the state.   In an essentially warlike nation, where military glory has ever been considered as the most important of all possessions, the privilege in question excited
against those who enjoyed it violent hatred and implacable jealousy : instead of placing the soldiery at their
disposal, it made the soldier the natural enemy of the
noble.

The nobles were exempt from some of the taxes, and
they levied from the inhabitants of their domains, under
divers names, a great number of annual contributions.
These rights did not increase to any great extent the
wealth of the nobles, but they erected the order of nobility into an object of general hatred and envy.

The most dangerous of all privileges, to those who
enjoy them, are pecuniary privileges.   Every one can
appreciate them at a glance, and sees clearly how much
he is injured by them.   The sums which they produce
furnish an exact standard by which the unprivileged are
able to measure the hatred which the privilege ought to
excite.   There are but a limited number of men who
crave after honors, or who aspire to govern the State, but
there are few who do not desire to be as rich as they
can.   Many persons care but little to know who rules
over them, but there are none who are indifferent to what
affects their private fortunes.   The privileges, therefore,
which confer pecuniary profit, are at once less valuable
and more dangerous to the possessor than those which
confer power.   The French nobles, by preserving the
former in preference to the latter, had maintained that
feature of inequality of condition which is offensive, and
renounced that which is serviceable.   They oppressed
and impoverished the people, but did not rule over them.

They stood in the midst of the people as strangers favored by the prince, rather than as their leaders and chiefs. Having nothing to bestow, they did not act upon the people's affections through their hopes ; while, being limited in their exactions by certain rules, which in all cases were previously fixed, they excited hatred, but did not produce fear.

Independently of these lucrative privileges, the French *noblesse* had retained a vast number of purely honorary distinctions, such as titles, order of precedence in public, and the privilege of adopting a certain costume, and wearing certain arms. Some of these privileges they had formerly enjoyed as the natural adjuncts of their power — the others had risen since the weakening of that power, and as a compensation for its loss ; both were alike incapable of being of the slightest service, and might be productive of danger.

When once the reality of power has been abandoned, to wish to retain its semblance is to play a dangerous game. The outward aspect of vigor may sometimes sustain an enfeebled body, but more frequently serves to complete its downfall. Those who possess the appearance of power, without its substance, seem, to the general eye, of sufficient consequence to be hated, while they are no longer capable of protecting themselves against the hatred they excite. Those, therefore, whose power is in its infancy, and those with whom it is in its decline, should rather shun all honorary privileges than seek them. It is only a power firmly established, and which has attained to maturity, that can safely permit itself the use of them. ·

All that we have said of laws and customs may be extended to opinions.

The modern nobles had abandoned most of the ideas of their ancestors, but there were still several of a very hurtful character to which they were obstinately attached. At the head of these must be placed the prejudice which interdicted to persons of noble birth the pursuits of commercial industry.

This prejudice had been generated during the Middle Ages, when the possession of the land and the government of its inhabitants were one and the same thing. In those ages the idea of landed property was identified with that of power and greatness : the idea of mere movable property, on the contrary, called up the idea of inferiority and weakness. Although the possession of land afterwards ceased to confer power in the State, and the other kinds of wealth had prodigiously increased, and acquired an entirely new importance, the feelings of the noble class had remained unchanged ; the prejudice had survived the causes which gave birth to it.

The consequence of this was that the families of the *noblesse*, while they were liable in common with others to the chances of ruin, were precluded from the ordinary means of increasing their fortunes. The *noblesse*, therefore, taken as a body, was gradually becoming impoverished : and thus, after having abandoned the direct road to power, they remained equally strangers to the by-roads which might possibly conduct to it.

Not only were the nobles precluded from increasing or repairing their own fortunes by commerce and industry, but custom forbade them even to appropriate by marriage wealth so acquired. A nobleman would have deemed himself degraded by an alliance with the daughter of a rich *roturier*. Nevertheless such unions were not uncommon among them ; for their fortunes decreased more rapidly than their desires. These plebeian alliances while they enriched certain members of the *noblesse*, put the finishing stroke to the ruin of that influence over opinion, which was the only power the body, as a body, retained.

We must consider what are men's motives, before we applaud them for having elevated themselves above common prejudices. To judge of their conduct, we must place ourselves at their own point of view, and not at the point of view of abstract truth. To run counter to a common opinion because we believe it to be false, is noble and virtuous ; but to despise a prejudice merely because it is inconvenient to ourselves, is nearly as dangerous to morality as to abandon a true principle for the same reason. The nobles were wrong in the first place, when they believed themselves degraded by marrying the daughters of *roturiers*. They were still more wrong in the second place, by marrying them under that persuasion.

In the eighteenth century the feudal laws relative to entails were still in vigor, but these laws had little effect in keeping together the fortunes of the nobles.

We suspect that the influence which such laws can exercise is frequently exaggerated. To produce important consequences, a concurrence of circumstances is required, which those laws do not produce, and which depends on quite other causes.

When the nobles are not tormented by the desire of enriching themselves, and when the other classes of the nation are tolerably content with the lot which Providence has assigned to them, the law of entail being then in complete accordance with the tendency of opinions and habits, the result of the whole is a universal slumber and immobility. Commoners having scarcely a greater chance of acquiring wealth than the nobles, and the nobles having no chance of losing theirs, all the advantage remains with the latter, and each generation of nobles maintains without difficulty the rank which the preceding generation occupied.

But in a nation where all except the nobles are seeking to enrich themselves, the territorial possessions of the *noblesse* become a sort of prize which all the other classes endeavor to catch at. The ignorance of the nobles, their passions, their foibles, all are put in requisition to draw into the general current of circulation the mass of landed property which they possess: and in a short time the *noblesse* themselves seldom fail to assist in the work.

The commons having only the privilege of wealth to oppose to the privileges of all kinds which their rivals enjoy, do not fail to display their opulence with every kind of ostentation. This excites the emulation of the nobles, who desire to imitate their splendor without having the same means to supply it. Embarrassment soon manifests itself in the fortunes of the nobles; their incomes become inadequate to their wants; and they themselves, ultimately feeling inconvenienced by the very laws which are made to keep them rich and powerful, seek by every means in their power to elude those laws. We will not positively assert, that even then, entails do not somewhat retard the ruin of the nobles; but we believe that they cannot prevent it. There is something more powerful than the constant operation of the laws in one direction; it is, the constant operation of human passions in the contrary direction.

At the breaking out of the French Revolution, the laws of France still assigned to the eldest son of a noble almost all the family estates. He was, in his turn, compelled to transmit them to his descendants unimpaired.

Nevertheless, many domains of feudal origin had already passed from the hands of the *noblesse,* and many others had been divided.*

Not only did the *noblesse* comprise in its ranks very rich and very poor men — a circumstance which by no means conflicts with the notion of an order of *noblesse* — but it included very many persons who were neither rich nor poor, but possessed moderate fortunes. This state of things already savored more of democracy than of aristocracy; and if the composition of the French *noblesse* had been closely examined, it would have been found to be in reality a sort of democratic body, clothed in relation to all other classes with the privileges of an aristocracy.

But the danger which menaced the nobles arose much more from what was passing around them, than from what occurred within their own circle.

At the same time that the wealth of the French *noblesse* was dwindling, and their political and social influence fading away, another class of the nation was rapidly acquiring moneyed wealth, and even coming into contact with the government. The *noblesse* was thus losing ground in two ways. It was becoming both positively and relatively weaker. The new and encroaching class, which seemed to be elevating itself on the ruins of the other, had received the name of *tiers-état.*

As it is difficult to make Englishmen comprehend the nature of the French *noblesse,* so it is by no means easy to explain to them what was understood by *tiers-état.*

* It is stated in the *cahiers* of the *noblesse,* in 1789, that "the country is covered with *châteaux* and mansions formerly inhabited by the *noblesse* of France, but now abandoned." — *Résumé des Cahiers,* tom. ii. p. 206.

At the first glance it might be thought that in France the *tiers-état* was composed of the middle class, and stood between the aristocracy and the people. But this was not the case. The *tiers-état* included, it is true, the middle classes, but it also comprised elements which were naturally foreign to these classes. The richest merchant, the most opulent banker, the most skilful manufacturer, the man of letters, the man of science, might form part of the *tiers-état*, as well as the small farmer, the shopkeeper, and the peasant who tilled the ground. Every man, in short, who was neither a priest nor a noble belonged to the *tiers-état*. It included rich and poor, the ignorant and the instructed. The *tiers-état* had thus within itself an aristocracy of its own. It contained within itself all the elements of a people; or rather it formed of itself a complete people, which coexisted with the privileged order, but which was perfectly capable of existing by itself, apart from them. It had opinions, prejudices, and a national spirit of its own. This is clearly discoverable in the *cahiers* drawn up in 1789, by the order of the *tiers-état*, to serve as instructions to its deputies. The *tiers-état* were almost as much beset with the fear of being mixed up with the *noblesse*, as the latter could have been of being confounded with them. They complained of the custom of ennobling by purchase, which permitted some of their body to penetrate into the ranks of the nobles. At the elections which preceded the assembling of the States-general, Lavoisier, the celebrated chemist, having wished to vote among the *tiers-état*, was rejected from the electoral college, on the ground that, having purchased an office which conferred nobility, he had forfeited the right of voting with *roturiers*.

Thus the *tiers-état* and the *noblesse* were intermixed on

the same soil; but they formed, as it were, two distinct nations, which, though living under the same laws, remained strangers to each other. But of these two nations the one was incessantly recruiting its strength, the other was losing something every day, and never regaining anything.

The creation of this new people in the midst of the French nation threatened the very existence of the *noblesse.* The state of isolation in which the nobles lived was a still greater source of danger to them.

This complete division between the *tiers-état* and the nobles not only accelerated the fall of the *noblesse,* but threatened to leave in France no aristocracy whatever.

It is not by chance that aristocracies arise and maintain themselves. Like all other phenomena, they are subject to fixed laws, which it is not, perhaps, impossible to discover.

There exists among mankind, in whatsoever form of society they live, and independently of the laws which they have made for their own government, a certain amount of real or conventional advantages, which, from their nature, can only be possessed by a small number. At the head of these may be placed birth, wealth, and knowledge. It would be impossible to conceive any social state in which all the citizens, without exception, should be noble, highly intellectual, or rich. These three advantages differ considerably from one another, but they agree in this, that they are always the lot of a few, and give, consequently, to those who possess them, tastes and ideas of a more or less peculiar or exclusive kind. They therefore form so many aristocratic elements, which, whether separated or united in the same hands, are to be found amongst every people and at every period of history.

When the governing power is shared by all those who possess any of these exclusive advantages, the result is a stable and powerful aristocracy.

During the eighteenth century the French *noblesse* possessed within itself a portion only of the natural elements of an aristocracy. Some of those elements remained with the classes beyond their pale.

In isolating themselves from the aristocracy of wealth, and from that of intellect, the nobles believed they were remaining faithful to the example of their fathers. They did not remark, that in imitating the conduct they were missing the aim of their ancestors. In the Middle Age, it is true, birth was the principal source of all social advantages; but in the Middle Age the nobles were also the rich, and had called into alliance with them the priests, who were the instructed. Society yielded, and could not but yield, to these two classes of men a complete obedience.

But in the eighteenth century many of the wealthy class were not noble, and many of the nobles were no longer rich. The same might be said in respect to intelligence. The *tiers-état* formed one member of what may be called the natural aristocracy, separated from the main body; a member which could not fail to weaken it, even by withholding its support, and was sure to destroy it by declaring war against it.

The exclusive spirit of the nobles tended not only to detach from the general cause of the aristocracy the chiefs of the *tiers-état*, but also all those who hoped one day to become such.

The greater number of aristocracies have perished, not because they established political and social inequality, but because they insisted upon maintaining it in favor of certain individuals, and to the detriment of certain others. What mankind detest is not so much inequality itself, as a particular kind of inequality. Neither must it be thought that an aristocracy commonly perishes by the excess of its privileges. On the contrary, it may happen that the greatness of those privileges sustains it. If every one may hope one day to enter into the exalted body, the extent of the privileges of that body is often the very thing which renders it dear to those who have not yet become members of it. In this manner the very vices of the institution sometimes constitute its strength. Let it not be said that each man's chances are small. This is of little consequence, where the object to bè attained is brilliant. What excites human desires is much less the certainty of moderate, than the possibility of splendid, success. Increase the greatness of the object to be attained, and you may without fear diminish the probabilities of obtaining it.

In a country where it is not impossible that a poor man may come to the highest offices of the State, it is much easier to continue excluding the poor from any share of control over the government, than in those countries where all hope of rising to a higher rank is denied them. The idea of the imaginary grandeur to which he may one day be called, places itself continually between the poor man and the contemplation of his real miseries. It is a game of chance, where the enormous possible gain lays hold of the mind in spite of the almost certainty of loss. He is charmed with aristocracy as with the lottery.

The division which existed in France between the different aristocratic elements, established in the aristocracy itself a sort of intestine war, by which democracy

alone was destined to profit. Rejected by the *noblesse*, ·
the principal members of the *tiers-état* were obliged, in
combating those adversaries, to arm themselves with
principles, convenient for their immediate purpose, but
ultimately dangerous to themselves, even by reason of
their efficacy. The *tiers-état* was one portion of the
aristocracy which had revolted against the rest; and
was obliged to profess the general principle of equality,
as a means of overthrowing the particular barrier which
was opposed to themselves.

Even within the pale of the *noblesse*, inequality was
daily attacked; if not in its principle, at least in some
one or other of its numerous applications. The military
nobles accused the *noblesse de robe* of arrogance, and the
latter complained of the preponderance accorded to the
former. The court noble affected to rally the rural
nobles upon their petty seignorial rights, and the latter
were annoyed at the favor bestowed upon the courtiers.
The ancient noble contemned the recently ennobled, who
in turn envied the honors of the other. All these re-
criminations and jealousies between the different sections
of the privileged class were extremely injurious to the
general cause of privileges.

The people, disinterested spectators of the quarrels of
their chiefs, adopted only as much of their language and
doctrines as suited them. The idea thus spread itself by
degrees through the nation, that equality alone was con-
formable to the natural order of things, and was the
foundation on which all well-regulated society should be
built. These theories found their way into the minds of
the nobles themselves, who, though still in the full enjoyment of their privileges, began to look upon the possession of them as a lucky accident, rather than as a right
entitled to respect.

Custom, in general, follows much more closely than law, the changes of opinion.   The aristocratic principle still triumphed in political institutions ; but manners had already become democratic, and a thousand different ties had established themselves between men whom their social position would naturally have separated.

A circumstance which favored singularly this mixture of classes in society, was the position gradually acquired by the literary class.

In a nation where wealth is the sole, or even the principal foundation of aristocracy, money, which in all society is the means of pleasure, confers power also.   Endowed with these two advantages, it succeeds in attracting towards itself the whole imagination of man; and ends by becoming, we may almost say, the only distinction which is sought.

In such a country literature is little cultivated, and literary merit therefore scarcely attracts the attention of the public.   But in the nations where the aristocracy of birth predominates, the same universal impulse towards the acquisition of wealth does not exist.   The human mind, not being driven in one direction by a single passion, abandons itself to the natural variety of its inclinations.   If such nations are highly civilized, a large number of citizens are to be met with who prize mental enjoyments, and honor those who are capable of bestowing them.   Many ambitious men, who despise wealth, and whose plebeian origin shuts them out from participation in public affairs, take refuge in the study of letters, and seek literary glory, the only kind that is open to them.   They thus occupy, beyond the limits of politics, a brilliant position, which is seldom disputed with them.

In those countries where money is the source of power, the importance of a man is in proportion to the wealth he possesses ; and wealth being liable to be acquired or lost at any given moment, the members of the aristocracy are perpetually beset by the fear of falling from their rank, or of seeing other citizens rise to a participation in their privileges. The constant changeableness which thus prevails in the political world, throws their minds into a sort of permanent agitation. Even their enjoyment of their fortune is not untroubled ; they seize with haste the advantages which riches can bring. They are incessantly contemplating their position with an unquiet eye, to ˙discover if they have not lost ground. On all other persons they cast looks of jealousy and fear, to find out whether anything is changed around them ; and all that is elevating itself ends by giving them umbrage.

Aristocracies founded solely on birth display much less inquietude at the sight of anything illustrious without their circle ; because they are possessed of an advantage which from its nature can neither be divided nor lost. A person may *become* rich, but it is necessary to be born noble.

The French *noblesse* had at all times held out their hands to literary men, and liked to associate with them ; but this was especially the case in the eighteenth century, a period of leisure, when men of rank found themselves almost as much relieved from the cares of government as the *roturiers* themselves, and when the spread of intelligence had communicated to all the refined taste of literary pleasures. Under Louis XIV. the nobles were accustomed to honor and protect writers, but did not in reality mingle with them. The two were distinct classes, which often approached each other, but without being in any one instance confounded. Towards the close of the eighteenth century this was no longer the case. It was not that writers had been admitted to a share in the privileges of the aristocracy, nor that they had acquired an acknowledged position in the political world. The *noblesse* had not called them into its ranks; but many of the nobles had placed themselves in theirs. Literature had thus become a species of neutral ground, on which equality took refuge. The man of letters and the *grand seigneur* met there, without having sought and without fearing each other; and there, beyond the limits of the real world, reigned a species of imaginary democracy, where every individual was reduced to his natural advantages.

This state of things, so favorable to the rapid development of science and letters, was far from satisfying the men who cultivated these pursuits. They occupied, it is true, a brilliant position, but one which was ill defined, and perpetually contested. They shared in the pleasures of the great, and remained strangers to their rights. The nobles were sufficiently near to them to exhibit to them in detail all the advantages reserved for superiority of birth, but at the same time kept themselves sufficiently distant to prevent them from participating in, or even tasting those advantages. Equality was thus placed before their eyes as a phantom, which fled before them in proportion as they approached to seize it. Accordingly the class of literary men thus favored by the *noblesse* formed the most discontented portion of the *tiers-état*, and might be heard railing at privileges even in the palaces of the privileged.

This democratic tendency made itself manifest not

only among the men of letters who frequented the society of the nobles, but also among those nobles who had become men of letters. The greater number of the latter warmly professed the political doctrines generally received among literary men : and, far from introducing the aristocratic spirit into literature, they transported what might be called the literary spirit into a portion of the *noblesse.*

Whilst the upper classes were gradually lowering themselves, the middle classes were gradually raising themselves, and an insensible movement was bringing them daily nearer to each other. Changes were going on in the distribution of property which were of a nature to facilitate, in a most singular manner, the growth and ultimate rule of democracy.

Almost all foreigners imagine that, in France, the division of landed property first commenced from the epoch when the laws relating to descent experienced a change, and when the greater part of the domains belonging to the nobles were confiscated. This is an error. At the moment when the revolution broke out, the lands, in a great number of provinces, were already considerably divided. The revolution did but extend to the whole territory what had previously been peculiar to some of its parts.

There are many causes which may tend to make landed property accumulate in few hands. The first of these is physical force. A conqueror seizes the lands of the conquered, and divides them among a small number of his partisans. In this way the ancient proprietors are deprived of their rights; but there are other cases in which they themselves voluntarily cede them.

Let us imagine a people amongst whom industrial and

commercial enterprises are numerous and productive, and intelligence sufficiently developed to enable every person to perceive the advantages of fortune which may be acquired by trade and industry. Let us suppose that by a combination of causes — laws, manners, and ancient ideas — landed property is still amongst this people the principal source of consideration and power. The shortest and most rapid way of becoming enriched, would be to sell any land which may happen to be possessed, and employ the purchase-money in trade. The best means, on the other hand, of enjoying a fortune when acquired, would be to withdraw it from trade and invest it in land. Land in that case becomes an object of luxury — of ambition, and not of pecuniary speculation. The ends sought to be obtained by its acquisition are not harvests, but honors and power. This being the case, small landed properties will be offered for sale, but purchasers can be found only to throw them into larger ; for the object, as well as the position, of the seller differs considerably from that of the buyer. The first, compared with the second, is a poor man going in quest of a competence ; the other is a rich man, who has a large superfluity, and desires to apply it to his pleasures.

If to these general causes we add the particular operation of legal arrangements, which, while they give great facilities to the alienation of movable property, render the conveyance of land so difficult and onerous, that the rich, who alone have the desire to possess landed property, have also exclusively the means of acquiring it, we shall comprehend without difficulty that among such a people small landed properties must have a perpetual tendency to disappear, by being merged into a small number of large estates.

In proportion as industrial processes are perfected and multiplied, and as the diffusion of intelligence renders the poor man more aware of what these new instruments can do for him, the movement which we have just described, naturally becomes more rapid. The prosperity of trade and industry will, more forcibly than ever, induce the small proprietor to sell; and this same cause will be constantly creating large masses of wealth, which will permit those who possess them to acquire immense domains. It would thus seem that the aggregation of the land of a country in large masses may be found at the two extremes of civilization; first, when men are in a state of semi-barbarism, and do not prize, indeed do not know, any other kind of wealth; and lastly, when they have become highly civilized, and have discovered a thousand other means of enriching themselves.

The picture which we have drawn may serve for a representation of England. No part of what we have said has ever been applicable to France.

It is extremely doubtful whether, at the conquest of France by the barbarians, the land was divided among the conquerors in a general and systematic manner, as was the case in England after the invasion of the Normans. The Franks were much less civilized than the Normans, and much less skilful in the art of systematizing their violence. The Frankish conquest moreover goes back to a much remoter epoch, and its effects became earlier weakened. There is reason to believe that in France many domains have never been subject to the feudal law; and those which were subject to it appear to have been of more moderate extent than in several others of the European states. The land consequently had never been very much agglomerated, or at least had for a long time ceased to be so.

We have seen that long before the French revolution, landed property had come to be no longer the principal source of consideration and of power. During the same period industry and commerce had not made a very rapid progress; and the people, already sufficiently enlightened to conceive and desire a better condition than their own, had not yet acquired intelligence to disclose to them the most ready means of attaining it. The land, whilst it ceased to be an object of luxury to the rich, became an object, or, to say truth, the only object of industry to the poor. The former disposed of it, to facilitate and increase his pleasures; the other purchased it, to improve his circumstances. In this manner landed property was silently passing out of the hands of the nobles, and becoming divided among the people.

While the ancient proprietors of the soil were thus losing their estates, a multitude of commoners came gradually to acquire considerable property. But they only did so by great efforts, and by the aid of most imperfect processes. Thus the large territorial fortunes daily diminished, without much contemporaneous amassing of large capitals; and in the place of a few vast domains were created many small ones, the slow and painful fruit of labor and economy.

These changes in the distribution of landed property facilitated in a singular manner the great political revolution which was on the eve of taking place.

Whoever thinks to succeed in permanently establishing perfect equality in the political world, without introducing at the same time an approach to equality in society itself, appears to us to fall into a dangerous error.

You cannot with impunity place men in a position in which they have alternately the feelings of strength and those of weakness — you cannot make them approach to complete equality on one point, and leave them to suffer extreme inequality on others, without their shortly aspiring to be strong, or becoming weak, on all points. But the most dangerous species of social inequality is that which results from the accumulation of landed property in large masses.

The possession of land gives to men a certain number of peculiar ideas and habits, which it is very important to take into account, and which the possession of movable wealth either does not produce, or produces in a minor degree.

Great territorial properties localize, if we may so speak, the influence of wealth; and forcing it to exert itself always in the same place and over the same persons, give it by that means a more intense and a more permanent character. Inequality of movable property creates rich individuals; inequality of landed property makes opulent families. It connects the wealthy with one another; it even unites different generations; and creates at length in the state a little community apart from the nation, which invariably comes to obtain a certain degree of power over the larger community in the midst of which it is placed. This is precisely the thing which is most hurtful to a democratic government.

There is nothing, on the contrary, more favorable to the reign of democracy than the division of the land into small independent properties. The possessor of a small moneyed fortune almost always depends more or less on the passions of others. He is compelled to bend either to the rules of an association or to the desires of an individual; he is exposed to every vicissitude in the commercial or industrial condition of his country; his existence is incessantly troubled by alternations of prosperity and distress; and it is rare that the fluctuation which rules his destiny does not introduce disorder into his ideas and instability into his tastes. The small landed proprietor, on the contrary, receives no impulse but from himself. His sphere is confined, but he moves within it in perfect liberty. His fortune increases slowly, but it is not subject to sudden risks. His mind is tranquil as his destiny; his tastes regular and peaceful as his labors; and not being absolutely in want of anybody's assistance, he maintains the spirit of independence even in the midst of poverty.

One cannot doubt that this mental tranquillity of a large number of the citizens — this calmness and simplicity in their desires — this habit and relish of independence — favors in a singular manner the establishment and the maintenance of democratic institutions. For our part, should we see democratic institutions established among a people where great inequality of fortune prevailed, we should consider such institutions as a passing accident. We should think that both the owners of property and the laboring classes were in peril: the former exposed to the risk of losing their property by violence, the last of losing their independence. It is, therefore, strongly the interest of those nations who desire to arrive at a democratic government, that great inequality of fortune should not exist amongst them; but above all, that such inequality should not prevail in landed property.

In France, at the close of the eighteenth century, the principle of the inequality of rights and conditions still

ruled despotically in political society. The French not
only had an aristocracy, but a *noblesse:* that is to say, of
all the systems of government of which inequality is the
basis, they had preserved the most exclusive, and, if we
may use the expression, the most intractable. A man
must be noble before he could serve the state. Without
nobility a man could scarcely approach the prince, who
was forbidden all contact with *roturiers* by the puerili-
ties of etiquette.

The details of the French institutions were in accordance with this principle. Entails, the right of pri-
mogeniture, the seignorial rights, the corporations — all
the remains of the ancient feudal society still existed.

France had a state religion, the ministers of which
were not only privileged, as they still are in some other
aristocratic countries, but were alone tolerated by law.
The Church, being, as in the Middle Ages, proprietor of
a large portion of the country, naturally took a considerable share in the government.

In France, nevertheless, everything had for a long
time been in progress towards democracy. He who,
without resting in first appearances, had pictured to himself the state of moral impotence into which the clergy
had fallen — the impoverishment and degradation of the
noblesse — the wealth and intelligence of the *tiers-état* —
the remarkable division of landed property which already existed — the great number of middling, and the
small number of large fortunes ; who had recollected the
theories professed at this epoch, the principles tacitly but
almost universally admitted — he, we repeat, who had
embraced in one view all these different objects, could
not have failed to conclude that the France of that day,
with her *noblesse,* her state religion, her aristocratic laws

and customs, was already, taken altogether, the most really democratic nation of Europe: and that the French at the close of the eighteenth century, by their social state, their civil constitution, their ideas and their manners, had already outstripped greatly even those among the nations of the present day who tend most conspicuously towards democracy.

It is not only in the progress she was making towards equality of conditions, that France in the eighteenth century approximated to the France of our day. Many other features of the national physiognomy, which are usually looked upon as new, had already made their appearance.

It may perhaps be laid down as a general truth, that there is nothing more favorable to the establishment and durability of a system of municipal and provincial institutions independent of the general government than a territorial aristocracy.

There are at every point of the territory occupied by such an aristocracy, one or more individuals who, being already placed above the rest by their birth and their riches, naturally assume, or upon whom is naturally conferred, the management of the affairs of their neighborhood. In a society, on the contrary, where there exists great equality of conditions, the citizens, being so nearly equal among themselves, are naturally led to place the details of administration in the hands of the only power which stands forth conspicuously in an elevated situation above them all ; namely, the central government of the state. And even when they may not be disposed thus to delegate the management of all their affairs to the central government, they are often compelled, by their individual weakness, and the difficulties which oppose their acting in concert, to suffer that government to usurp it.

It is true that when once a nation has admitted the principle of the sovereignty of the people — when intelligence has diffused itself — when the art of government has been brought to considerable perfection, and the evils of an administration too much centralized have been felt — then, indeed, the inhabitants of the country, and of the country towns, are often seen endeavoring to create a collective power among themselves for the direction of their local affairs. Sometimes even the supreme power itself, bending under the weight of its own prerogatives, endeavors to localize the business of government, and seeks, by combinations more or less skilful, to found artificially in all the different points of the country a kind of elective aristocracy. A democratic people tends towards centralization, as it were by instinct. It arrives at provincial institutions only by reflection.

But provincial self-government thus founded is always exposed to great hazards. In an aristocratic country, local authorities often subsist in spite of the hostility of the central power, and always without depending upon the interference of the latter to preserve them; but in a democratic country, the local government is often a creation of the central power, which suffers itself to be deprived of some of its privileges, or strips itself of them of its own accord.

This natural tendency of a democratic people to centralize the business of government becomes chiefly manifest, and has the most rapid growth, in an epoch of struggle and transition, when the aristocratic and the democratic principles are disputing with each other for ascendency.

The people, at the moment when they begin to feel their power, finding that the nobles direct all local affairs, become discontented with the provincial government, less as provincial than as aristocratic. The provincial power once torn from the hands of the aristocracy, there remains the question, in whose hands it shall be placed.

In France it was not only the central government, but the king in particular, who was exclusively vested with this power. This arises from causes which it may be well to explain.

We have already expressed our opinion that the democratic portion of society have a natural tendency to centralize the management of all their joint concerns : but we are far from contending that their inclination leads them to centralize it in the person of the king alone ; that depends upon circumstances. When unfettered in their choice, the people will always prefer to confide the powers of administration to an assembly or a magistrate of their own choosing, rather than to a prince placed beyond their control. But this liberty is often wanting to them.

The democratic portion of society, at the time when it begins to feel its strength, and wishes to exert it, is as yet composed only of a multitude of individuals, equally weak and equally incapable of struggling single-handed against the great individual existences of the nobles. It has an instinctive desire to make itself felt in the government, without having the command of any of the instruments by which the government can be influenced. These numerous individuals, being also widely scattered and little accustomed to concert, feel instinctively the necessity for finding, somewhere out of themselves, and yet distinct from the aristocracy, an authority already constituted, round which they can rally, and, by combining as a whole, obtain that influence which is denied to them individually.

The popular power having as yet no constitutional organization, the only power already constituted, independently of the aristocracy, of which the people can avail themselves, is the prince. Between the prince and the nobles there is, no doubt, a natural affinity of inclination, but not a perfect identity; if their tastes and habits are alike, their interests are often contrary. The nations, therefore, which are in progress towards democracy commence ordinarily by increasing the royal power. The prince inspires less jealousy and less fear than the nobles; and, besides, in periods of revolution, it is something gained to change the depositaries of power, even if it be only taken from one enemy to be vested in another.

The great triumph of the English aristocracy has been their long success in making the democratic classes believe that the common enemy was the prince; thus constituting themselves the virtual representatives of the people, instead of remaining conspicuously their principal adversaries.

In general, it is only after having, by the assistance of the king, completely destroyed the power of the aristocracy, that a democratic people begins to think of rendering the king himself accountable for the power which it has allowed him to assume, and attempts either to render him dependent upon itself, or to remove the authority with which it has invested him into other and more dependent hands.

But, even when the democratic classes, after having succeeded in placing the powers of government in the hands of their own representatives, become desirous to divide those powers among several distinct authorities, this is often not easily effected : whether from the difficulty always found in withdrawing power from those who are once in possession of it, or from the uncertainty of knowing where best to place it.

The democratic classes can always find among themselves a sufficient number of able and enlightened men to compose a political assembly or a central government; but it may happen that they do not find a sufficient number to be organized into provincial bodies. It may happen that the people of the provinces are not willing to allow themselves to be governed by the aristocracy, and are not yet in condition to form a government for themselves. In the mean time, the powers of local administration can only be exercised by the central authority.

A considerable time, moreover, elapses before a people, just escaped from the hands of an aristocracy, feel the advantage, and experience the desire, of *un*centralizing the management of their common concerns.

In the nations subject to an aristocracy, every individual belonging to the inferior classes has contracted, almost from his birth, the habit of looking in his immediate neighborhood for the man who is the principal object of his jealousies, hopes, or fears. He is accustomed to consider the central government as the natural umpire between himself and his local oppressor ; and he contracts the habit of attributing to the first a great superiority of intelligence and wisdom. These two impressions often subsist when the causes which have given birth to them have perished.

Long after the aristocracy has been destroyed, the

citizens still look with a kind of instinctive fear upon all who are elevated above them in their own neighborhood; they are with difficulty induced to believe that skill in affairs, impartiality in rendering justice, or respect for the laws, can be found in an authority at their own doors. They are jealous of neighbors who have become their equals, because they have been jealous of neighbors who were their superiors; they distrust even men of their own choice; and, though they no longer consider the central government as their shelter against the tyranny of the nobles, they still look upon it as a safeguard against their own mistakes. Thus, then, nations whose social condition is becoming democratic, almost always begin by concentrating all power in the prince; and when, afterwards they acquire the necessary energy and force, they destroy the instrument, but continue to centralize the power in the hands of an authority which has now become dependent upon themselves.

When they become stronger, better organized, and more enlightened, they make a new effort, and, taking away from their general representatives some portion of the business of administration, they confide it to a secondary class of elective functionaries. Such appears to be the natural, the instinctive, and, we may add, the inevitable progress which those societies follow who, by their social condition, their ideas, and their manners, are travelling towards democracy.

In France, the extension of the royal power to embrace every part of the public administration regularly kept pace with the rise and progressive development of the democratic classes. In proportion as conditions became more equalized, the king penetrated more deeply and more habitually into the management of the local affairs;

the towns and the provinces lost their privileges, or by degrees neglected to make use of them.

The people and the *tiers-état* assisted these changes with all their force, and even gave up, voluntarily, all their rights, where it so happened that they possessed any, in order to draw into a common ruin those of the nobles. The independent local authorities, and the power of the nobles, were therefore both weakened in the same manner and at the same time.

The kings of France had been singularly assisted in this tendency by the support which, during so many ages, had been afforded to them by the lawyers. In a country like France, where there existed privileged orders, a *noblesse* and a clergy, who had within themselves a large portion of the intelligence and almost all the riches of the country, the natural chiefs of the democracy were the lawyers. Until the French lawyers themselves aspired to govern in the name of the people, they labored assiduously to ruin the *noblesse* for the aggrandizement of the throne. They lent themselves to the despotic purposes of the kings with singular readiness and with infinite art.

This is not peculiar to France; and we may be permitted to believe that, in serving the regal power, the French lawyers obeyed the instincts of their own position, as much as they consulted the interests of the class of which they found themselves accidentally at the head.

There exist, says Cuvier, natural analogies between all the parts of an organized body, by which, from the examination of a detached portion of any one of them, we may in imagination correctly reconstruct the whole. By a similar process of investigation to that which detected these analogies, many of the general laws which govern the universe might be discovered.

If we study what has passed in the world since men began to preserve the remembrance of events, we soon discover that, in civilized countries, by the side of a despot who governs, there is almost always a lawyer who regularizes, and strives to render consistent with one another, the arbitrary and incoherent decrees of the monarch.

The general and indefinite love of power which animates kings is, by the lawyers, tempered with a love of method, and with the skill which they naturally possess in the management of business. Kings can constrain, for the time being, the obedience of men; lawyers can bend them almost voluntarily to a durable obedience. Kings furnish the power; lawyers invest that power with the form and semblance of a right. Kings seize upon absolute power by force; lawyers-give it the sanction of legality. When the two are united, the result is a despotism which scarcely allows a breathing-place to human nature.

He who conceives the idea of the prince, without that of the lawyer, sees only one of the aspects of tyranny; to conceive it as a whole, it is necessary to contemplate them both at once.

Independently of the general causes of which we have spoken, there existed in France many of an accidental and secondary nature, which hastened the concentration of all power in the hands of the king. Paris had, from an early period, acquired a singular preponderance in the kingdom. There existed in France several considerable towns; but there was only one great city, which was Paris. From the Middle Ages Paris had already begun to be the centre of the intelligence, the riches, and the power of the kingdom. The centralization of political power in Paris continually augmented the importance of that city; and its increasing importance facilitated in turn the concentration of power. The king drew all the public business to Paris, and Paris drew all the public business to the king.

France had formerly been made up of provinces, acquired by treaties or conquered by arms, and which long remained in the position of foreigners towards one another. In proportion as the central power was enabled to subject these different portions of territory to a uniform system of administration, the differences which previously existed among them vanished; and, in proportion as these differences subsided, the central power found greater facilities in extending its sphere of action over all parts of the country. Thus the unity of the people facilitated the unity of the government, and the unity of government aided in blending the people into one nation.

At the end of the eighteenth century, France was still divided into thirty-two provinces, in which thirteen *parlements*, or supreme courts of justice, interpreted the laws according to various conflicting systems. The political constitution of these provinces varied considerably. Some had preserved a sort of national representation, others had never possessed any. In some, the feudal laws were still observed, in others the Roman. All these differences, however, were superficial, or, properly speaking, only external. The whole of France had already, in a manner, but one mind; the same ideas were prevalent from one end of the kingdom to the other; the same customs were in vigor — the same opinions were professed; the human mind was cast in the same mould — had the same general tendencies. The French, in short, with their provinces, their *parlements*, the diversity of their civil laws, the fantastic variety of their customs, composed, nevertheless, the nation of Europe the most firmly bound together in all its parts, and the most capable, in case of need, of moving as one man.

In the centre of this great nation, composed of elements so homogeneous, was a royal power, which, after having possessed itself of the direction of the greater affairs of the public, aspired also to the regulation of the smaller.

All strong governments strive to centralize the administration; but they succeed more or less in the attempt, according to their own nature.

When the predominant power resides in an assembly, the centralization is more apparent than real. The assembly can interfere only by the enactment of laws, and laws cannot foresee everything; or, even if they did, they cannot be carried into execution but by means of agents, and with the aid of a continual *surveillance* of which a legislative assembly is incapable. The legislative branch of the government, consequently, is centralized, but not the administrative.

In England, where parliament is considered entitled to take cognizance of all the affairs of society, whether great or small, administrative centralization is little known; and the great representative body leaves to the will of individuals a great independence in detail. This does not originate in any natural moderation on the part of this great body; it does not pay deference to local liberty from any peculiar respect to it, but because its own constitution does not afford it any efficacious means of interfering with the exercise of that liberty.

When, on the other hand, the predominant power resides in the executive (the man who commands having the means of causing the minutest details of his will to be executed), the central power may gradually extend itself to everything ; or, at least, there is nothing in its own constitution which limits it. If this preponderant executive power is placed in the midst of a people among whom everything has already a natural tendency toward the centre — where no citizen is in a condition to resist individually — where numbers cannot legally combine their resistance — and where all, having nearly the same habits and manners, bend without difficulty to a common rule — it is not easy to see what limits can be set to administrative tyranny, nor why (not content with directing the great interests of the state) the agents of government may not at last assume to regulate the affairs of families.

The above picture represents correctly the state of France before 1789. The royal power had assumed, directly or indirectly, the management of everything, and had no longer, to speak correctly, any limits but in its own will. In most of the towns and provinces it had destroyed even the semblance of a local government, and to the others it had left nothing more than the semblance. The French, while they formed of all the nations of Europe that in which the greatest national unity existed, were also that in which administrative business had been brought into the most systematic form, and where what has since been called centralization existed in its highest degree.

We have shown that, in France, the constitution tended to become more despotic every day. Nevertheless, by a singular contrast, habits and ideas became constantly more liberal. Liberty disappeared from institutions, and maintained itself more than ever in manners : it seemed to be more cherished by individuals in proportion as the secu-

rities for it were less; and one might have thought, that
the independence, which had been snatched from the
great bodies of the state had been conferred upon its individual members.

After having overturned its principal adversaries, the
royal power had stopped as it were of itself; it had
been softened by victory, and appeared to have con-
tended for the possession of power rather than for its
exercise.

It is a great, though a common, error to believe that
the spirit of liberty in France had its birth with the revolution of 1789. It had always been one of the distinctive
characters of the nation; but this spirit had only shown
itself at intervals, and, as it were, by fits. It had been
an instinct rather than a principle; irregular, and at once
violent and feeble.

Never was a nobility more proud, and more independent in its opinions and in its actions, than the French
noblesse of the feudal times. Never did the spirit of
democratic liberty show itself with more energy than
in the French *communes* of the Middle Ages, and in the
states-general which assembled at different periods up to
the commencement of the seventeenth century (1614).
Even when the royal power had substituted itself for all
other powers, the national spirit submitted to it, but without servility.

It is necessary to distinguish the fact of obedience from
the various causes of that fact. There are nations who
bend to the arbitrary will of the prince, because they believe that he has an absolute *right* to command over them.
Others, again, see in him the representative of the idea
of country; or the image of God upon earth. There
are others, who adore a royal power which succeeds to a

tyrannical oligarchy of nobles, and experience, in giving obedience to it, a mixed feeling of gratitude and pleasant repose. In all these kinds of obedience, there is, no doubt, a mixture of prejudice; they denote insufficiency of intelligence, but not degradation of character.

The French of the seventeenth century submitted to *royalty* rather than to *the king*, and obeyed royalty not because they merely judged it to be powerful, but because they believed it to be a beneficent and a legitimate power. They had, if we may so speak, a *free* principle of obedience. They also mixed with their submission a kind of independence, of firmness, of delicacy, of caprice, of irritability, which demonstrated clearly that, in adopting a master, they had retained the spirit of liberty.

The king, who in certain cases could, without restraint, dispose of the fortunes of the state, would have been quite impotent in certain other cases, even to control, in the smallest trifles, the actions of his subjects, or to suppress the most insignificant of opinions; and, in case of resistance to such encroachment, the subject would have been better defended by the state of usages and manners, than the citizens of free countries are often protected by their laws.

But these are sentiments and ideas which nations that have always been free, or even that have become so, do not comprehend. The former have never known them, the latter have long since forgotten them. They both see, in obedience to an arbitrary power, nothing but degradation; and, amongst the people who have lost their liberty after having once enjoyed it, obedience has really that character. But there often enters into the submission of a people who have never been free, a principle of morality which must not be overlooked.

At the close of the eighteenth century this spirit of independence, which had always characterized the French,
had not only singularly developed itself, but had entirely
changed its character. During this century, a sort of
transformation had taken place in the notion which the
French had of liberty.

Liberty may be conceived by those who enjoy it, under
two different forms : as the exercise of a universal right,
or as the enjoyment of a privilege. In the Middle Ages,
those who possessed any liberty of action, viz. : the feudal
aristocracy, figured to themselves their liberty under the
latter type. They desired it, not because it was what all
were entitled to, but because each considered himself as
possessing, in his own person, a peculiar right to it. And
thus has liberty almost always been understood in aristocratic societies, where conditions are very unequal, and
where the human mind, having once contracted the thirst
for privileges, ends by ranking among privileges all the
good things of this world.

This notion of liberty as a personal right of the individual who so conceives it, or at most of the class to
which he belongs, may subsist in a nation where general
liberty does not exist. It even sometimes happens that,
in a certain small number of persons, the love of liberty
is all the stronger in proportion to the deficiency of the
securities necessary for the liberties of all. The exception is the more precious in proportion as it is more rare.

This aristocratic notion of liberty produces, among
those who have imbibed it, an exalted idea of their own
individual value, and a passionate love of independence;
it gives extraordinary energy and ardor to their pursuit
of their own interests and passions. Entertained by individuals, it has often led them to the most extraordinary

actions; — adopted by an entire people, it has created the most energetic nations that have ever existed.

The Romans believed that they alone of the human race were fitted to enjoy independence; and it was much less from nature than from Rome that they thought they derived their right to be free.

According to the modern, the democratic, and, we venture to say, the only just notion of liberty, every man, being presumed to have received from nature the intelligence necessary for his own general guidance, is inherently entitled to be uncontrolled by his fellows in all that only concerns himself, and to regulate at his own will his own destiny.

From the moment when this notion of liberty has penetrated deeply into the minds of a people, and has solidly established itself there, absolute and arbitrary power is thenceforth but a usurpation or an accident; for, if no one is under any moral obligation to submit to another, it follows that the sovereign will can rightfully emanate only from the union of the wills of the whole. From that time passive obedience loses its character of morality, and there is no longer a medium between the bold and manly virtues of the citizen and the base compliances of the slave.

In proportion as ranks become equalized, this notion of liberty tends naturally to prevail.

France, nevertheless, had long emerged from the ignorance of the Middle Ages, and had modified her ideas and manners in a democratic direction, before the feudal and aristocratic notion of liberty ceased to be universally received. Every one, in protecting his individual independence against the claims of despotism, had still much less in view the assertion of a common right, than the

defence of a particular privilege; and the question between him and his oppressor was much less one of principle than one of fact. In the fifteenth century some adventurous spirits had a glimpse of the democratic idea of
liberty, but it was almost immediately lost sight of. It
was during the eighteenth only that the transformation
began to operate.

The idea that every individual, and by extension
every people, is entitled to the direction of its own interests — this idea, still vague, incompletely defined, and
not yet expressed in any correct language, introduced
itself by slow degrees into all minds. It became fixed,
as an opinion, among the enlightened classes — it penetrated, as a species of instinct, even among the body of
the people.

From this resulted a new and more powerful impulse
towards liberty. The taste which the French always
had for independence became at length an opinion resting on reason and conviction, which, spreading from one
person to another, ended in attracting towards it the
royal power itself, which, still absolute in theory, began
to acknowledge tacitly by its conduct that public feeling
and opinion were the first of powers: " It is I who nom-
inate my ministers," said Louis XV.; " but it is the
nation which dismisses them." Louis XVI. in prison,
retracing his last and most secret thoughts, made use of
the term, *"My fellow-citizens,"* in speaking of his subjects.*

Speaking as the organ of one of the first tribunals of
the kingdom, Malesherbes said to the king, in 1770,
twenty years before the revolution : —

* See the testament of Louis XVI. written the day previous to his
death.

" You hold your crown, Sire, from God alone ; but you will not refuse yourself the satisfaction of believing that, for your power, you are likewise indebted to the voluntary submission of your subjects.   There exist in France some inviolable rights, which belong to the nation.   Your ministers will not have the boldness to deny this ; but, if it were necessary to prove it, we need only invoke the testimony of your Majesty.   No, Sire, in spite of all their efforts, they have not yet been able to persuade your Majesty that there is no difference between the French nation and a nation of slaves."

And further on he adds : —

" Since all the intermediate bodies are impotent or annihilated, interrogate the nation itself ; — there only remains the nation to be consulted by you." *

The spirit of liberty manifested itself, indeed, by writings rather than by actions — by individual efforts rather than by collective enterprises — by an *opposition*, often puerile and unreasonable, rather than by a grave and systematic resistance.

This force of opinion, acknowledgèd even by those who often trampled it under foot, was subject to great alternations of strength and weakness ; all-powerful to-day, almost imperceptible on the morrow ; always irregular, capricious, undefined ; a body without an organ ; a shadow of the sovereignty of the people rather than the thing itself.

It will be always thus with a people who have the taste and the desire for liberty without having yet known how to establish popular institutions.

It is not that we believe men may not enjoy a species of independence, even in countries where no such insti-

* See "Remonstrances de la Cour des Aides, 1770."

tutions exist. Customs and opinions may sometimes, to a certain extent, suffice; but, in these circumstances, men are never secure of the durability of their freedom because they are never assured that they shall at all instants be ready to assert it. There have been times when the nations most in love with their independence have suffered themselves to consider it only as a secondary object. The great utility of popular institutions is, to sustain liberty during those intervals wherein the human mind is otherwise occupied — to give it a kind of vegetative life, which may keep it in existence during those periods of inattention. The forms of a free government allow men to become temporarily weary of their liberty without losing it. When a people are determined to be slaves, it is impossible to hinder their becoming so; but, by free institutions, they may be sustained for some time in independence, even without their own assistance.

A nation which comprised fewer poor, fewer rich, fewer powerful individuals, and fewer absolutely impotent, than any other nation in the world; — a people with whom the theory of equality had taken root in their opinions, the taste for equality in their dispositions; — a country already more homogeneous and united in its parts than any other; subject to a government more centralized, more skilful, and more powerful than any other; and yet in which the spirit of liberty, always vivacious, had recently assumed a new character, more enlarged, more systematic, more democratic, and more restless than in any other country; — such was France — such were the principal features which marked her physiognomy at the end of the eighteenth century.

If we now close the page of history, and, after having

allowed half a century to elapse, come to consider what the intervening time has produced—we observe immense changes; but, in the midst of new and unheard-of things, we easily recognize the same characteristic features which struck us half a century earlier. The effects, therefore, said to be produced by the French Revolution are usually exaggerated.

Without doubt, there never was a revolution more powerful, more rapid, more destructive, and more creative than the French Revolution. It would, however, be deceiving ourselves strangely to believe that there arose out of it a French people entirely new, and that an edifice had been erected whose foundation had not existed before. The French Revolution has created a multitude of accessary and secondary things; but, of all the things of principal importance, it has only developed the germs previously existing. It has regulated, arranged, and legalized the effects of a great cause, but has not been itself that cause.

In France conditions were already more equalized than elsewhere; the Revolution carried still farther that equality, and introduced it into the laws. The French had, at an earlier period and more completely than any other country, abandoned the minute subdivisions of territory, the innumerable independent authorities, of the feudal system; the Revolution completed the union of the whole country into one body. Already the central power had, more than in any other country, extended its interference to the management of local affairs; the Revolution rendered that power the more skilful, stronger, and more enterprising. The French had conceived, before all others, and more clearly than all others, the democratic idea of liberty; the Revolution gave to the nation itself, if not all the reality, at least all the appearance of sovereign power. If these things are new, they are so only in form, and in their degree of development, not in their principle and in their essence.

All that the Revolution has done would have been done, sooner or later, without it. It was but a violent and rapid process, by the aid of which the changes already effected in society were extended to the government; laws were made to conform themselves to manners; and the direction already taken by opinions was communicated to the outward world.

FRANCE BEFORE THE CONSULATE.

Two Chapters of a Work which was to have been a continuation of
"FRANCE BEFORE THE REVOLUTION OF 1789" (L'ANCIEN
RÉGIME ET LA RÉVOLUTION).

CHAPTER I.

HOW THE REPUBLIC WAS READY TO ACCEPT A MASTER.

ONE of the most extraordinary subjects of contemplation among the shifting scenes of human life is the interior of the Republic before which all Europe trembled.

The government, which had at its disposal the most formidable army, and perhaps the greatest generals that had appeared in the world since the downfall of Rome, tottered at every instant, steadying itself with difficulty, always on the point of falling under the weight of its vices and its follies, devoured by innumerable diseases, and in spite of its youth, consumed by the nameless evil which in general attacks only old governments — a sort of general feebleness, of senile consumption, of which there can be no other definition than an inability to live. Attempts were no longer made to overturn it; but it seemed to have lost the power of standing upright.

After the 18th Fructidor, more power was conferred

on the directory than had ever belonged to the dynasty which the Revolution had overthrown; in fact, it had become despotic, and it followed a revolution which had destroyed every barrier formerly opposed by law, habit, and manners, to the abuse, and sometimes to the use of power. The press was mute. France had returned the representatives designated by the government; local administrators who were not submissive had been superseded; the legislature, humbled and powerless, desired only to obey.

Still the directory was incapable of governing. It occupied the seat of government, but could not wield the power. It never could give regularity to the administration, order to the finances, or peace to the country. The whole of its reign was an anarchy tempered by violence. Not for a single day was its duration expected by one of its supporters. Political parties never took it for an established government — they kept alive their hopes, and, above all, their antipathies.

The Government itself was only a party — always restless and violent, it was the least numerous and most contemptible party of all. It was a coterie of regicides, composed almost entirely of second-rate revolutionists, who, by following in the wake of great criminals, or by committing none but obscure crimes, had escaped both under the Reign of Terror and the reaction which followed the 9th Thermidor. These men looked upon the republic as their refuge, but in reality the majority cared for nothing but the power and pleasure which they enjoyed under it. Both sceptical and sensual, all that they had preserved of their former selves was their vigor. It is remarkable that almost all the men whose moral sense had been destroyed in the course of this long revolution, still retained, in the midst of the vices that they acquired, some remnant of the ungoverned and wild courage which had enabled them to take a part in making that revolution. Often, amid their cares and their dangers, they had contemplated and desired a return to the Reign of Terror. They thought of it after Fructidor, they tried to reëstablish it after Prairial, but in vain. This fact suggests important reflections.

At the beginning of a violent revolution, the laws, passed in ordinary times, are milder than public opinion suddenly rendered harsh by the influence of new passions. But, at a later period, law becomes more stringent than public opinion, which, in its turn, paralyzes the action of the law. At first terror reigns, as it were, without the legislator's interference, afterwards he often spends his strength in endeavors to create it. The most cruel of the laws of 1793 are less barbarous than many of those passed in 1797, 1798, and 1799. The laws which banished without trial the representatives of the people and the newspaper writers to Guiana, that which authorized the directory to imprison or transport at will any priests whom it should consider dangerous; the graduated income-tax, which, under the name of the forced loan, deprived the rich of the whole of their revenues; and lastly, the famous law of hostages; have a finished and skilful atrocity that did not belong even to the laws of the convention, and yet they did not reawaken terror. The men who proposed them were as bold, as unscrupulous, and perhaps more intelligent than their predecessors, in the devices of tyranny; and it is still more striking that these measures were voted almost without discussion, and promulgated without resistance. While most of the laws that prepared and established the Reign of

Terror were warmly contested, and excited the opposition of a great part of the country, the laws of the directory were silently accepted. But they never could be completely enforced, and (this observation deserves especial attention) the same cause aided their birth and deadened their effect. The Revolution had lasted so long that France, enervated and dispirited, had neither surprise nor reprobation left to manifest when the most violent and cruel laws were propounded; but this very moral debility made the daily application of such laws difficult. Public opinion no longer lent its aid; it opposed to the virulence of the government a resistance, languid indeed, but on account of its languor almost impossible to put down. The directory wasted its strength in the endeavor.

It is true that this government, though fruitful in the invention of revolutionary measures, was strangely awkward and incapable in all questions of organization. It never learned to supply the absence of popular enthusiasm by an ably constituted administrative machinery. Its tyranny was always in want of instruments, and its victims escaped because its agents would not seize them. The directory never understood the great maxim which we soon shall see applied, that to command and to maintain obedience, tyrannical laws, capriciously followed, are less efficacious than mild ones, enforced regularly and almost mechanically every day and against every person, by a skilful administration.

This deadness of the passions, this languor in public opinion, did not show itself merely in the application of revolutionary laws, but in the selection of punishments. For the scaffold was substituted transportation, a penalty often severer than death, but which the people do not see executed, so that while vengeance is satisfied, the unpleasant sight of suffering is avoided.

Towards the end of the directory, the Jacobins reopened their club. They resumed their badges, their phrases, and their habits, for political parties seldom change, and it is a phenomenon worth remarking that they are more inflexible, both in theory and practice, than the individuals who compose them. The Jacobins then acted precisely as they had acted under the Reign of Terror, without being able to bring it back. The fear which they inspired had the effect only of making the nation more eager to give up its freedom.

The directory, after having governed without opposition and almost without control, having interfered with everything, having tried everything, with the absolute power bestowed on it by the events of Fructidor, seemed gradually to expire of itself, and without an effort. (June, 1799; in the language of that time, 30th Prairial, an VII.) The same legislative body that it had decimated, in part recomposed, and always treated as its slave, regained the mastery and resumed the government. But soon the victor knew not what to do with his conquest. Hitherto the administrative machinery had worked irregularly, now it seemed to stand still. It was evident that assemblies, which are of admirable use sometimes in strengthening, and at other times in moderating the government, are more incapable than the worst governments of directing public affairs.

No sooner had the sovereign power returned to the *corps législatif*, than universal debility pervaded the administration throughout the country. Anarchy spread from private individuals to officials. No one resisted — no one obeyed. It was like a disbanding army. The taxes, instead of being ill paid, were not paid at all. In every direction, conscripts preferred highway robbery to rejoining the army. At one time it seemed as if not only order, but civilization itself, were to be overturned. Neither persons, nor property, nor even the high roads were safe. In the correspondence of the public function-aries with the government, still preserved in the national archives, is a description of these calamities; for, as a minister of that time said, " The accounts given to the nation should be reassuring; but in the retreat, not ex-posed to the public eye, where the government deliber-ates, everything ought to be told."

I have before me one of these secret reports, that of the Minister of Police, dated the 30th Fructidor, an VII. (the 16th of September, 1799), on the condition of the country. I gather from it, that, at that time, of the eighty-six departments into which France (properly so called, for I except the recent acquisitions by conquest) was divided, forty-five were abandoned to disorder and civil war. Troops of brigands forced open the prisons, assassinated the police, and set the convicts at liberty; the receivers of taxes were robbed, killed, or maimed; municipal officers murdered, land-owners imprisoned for ransom or taken as hostages, lands laid waste and dili-gences stopped. Bands of two hundred, of three hun-dred, and of eight hundred men overspread the country. Gangs of conscripts resisted everywhere, arms in hand, the authorities whose duty it was to enroll them. The laws were disobeyed in all quarters; by some to follow the impulse of their passions — by others to follow the practices of their religion; some profited by the state of affairs to strip travellers — others to ring the long-silent church-bells, or to carry the banners of the Catholic faith through the deserted church-yards.

The means used to suppress disturbances were at once violent and insufficient. We read in these reports, that often when a refractory conscript tried to escape from the soldiers, they killed him as an example. The private dwellings of citizens were continually exposed to public domiciliary visits. Moving columns of troops, almost as disorderly as the bands which they pursued, scoured the country, and extorted ransoms for want of pay or rations.

Paris was cowed. She slept, but uneasily and disturbed by painful dreams. A thousand different prophecies of some terrible outbreak are circulated through the city. Some say that a great movement will be made against the directory, in favor of democracy — others think that it will be on the royalist side; a huge fire is to give the signal. Men have been heard to say, "It is foolish to pay one's rent, for a blow will be struck that will settle every debt; blood will shortly be shed." Such is the language of the reports.

It is curious to observe the despair into which the sight of this universal confusion throws the reporters; the causes that they assign, and the remedies which they propose. The citizens are in absolute apathy, say some; public spirit is utterly destroyed, say others. Here we find it asserted, that the brigands find asylums everywhere; in another place it is said, that the manœuvres of different parties and the impunity of crime are viewed by patriots with deplorable indifference. A few ask for measures against the supporters of fanaticism; many wish for still more stringent laws against emigrants, priests, and nuns. The greater number are full of astonishment, and consider all that is going on as incomprehensible. The secret disease which surprised the agents of the directory, the unknown and hidden evil that was sapping

the life of authority, was the state of public opinion and
public morals — France refused to obey her government.

It is easy to mistake the signs which betoken great
convulsions in revolutions of long duration, for these signs
vary with the different periods. They even change their
nature as the revolution advances. In the beginning
public opinion is excited, lively, intolerant, presumptuous,
and capricious; in the decline it is patient and sad. After
having tolerated nothing, there seem to be no bounds to
its powers of endurance. But submission is accompanied
by implacable resentment; irritation increases, contempt
becomes every day more inveterate, and hatred more
bitter, in the midst of obedience. The nation has no
longer, as in the commencement of the revolution, force
and energy sufficient to push its government towards the
precipice, but it rejoices to see it fall over.

Such was the state of France in 1799. She despised
and detested, yet obeyed, her government.

This secret moral resistance sufficed to paralyze a
government which had no internal force or vitality.
Often, in our own day, we have seen the executive
survive the legislative functions. While the paramount
powers in the state were expiring or already overthrown, the subordinate powers still continued to conduct affairs with regularity and firmness. They were
times of revolution, but not of anarchy.

The reason is, that now in France the actual executive government forms, to a considerable extent but independently of the sovereign, a special administrative
body, with habits, rules, and instruments of its own, so
that it is able for a certain period to present the phenomenon of a headless trunk still proceeding on its
way. This was the work of Napoleon. We shall see

how, by the construction of this powerful machine, he made revolution at the same time more easy and less destructive.

Nothing similar existed at the time of which we are speaking. The old authorities were overthrown without any other being in reality as yet substituted. The administration was as incoherent and disorderly as the nation; as much without rules, without a hierarchy, and without traditions. The Reign of Terror had been able to work with this ill-made and ill-adjusted machinery. To return to it had become impossible, and in the failure of public spirit the whole political machine fell at once into pieces.

We then presented a sad spectacle; in every direction France bore the traces of the sort of moral decay produced in the long run by the wear and tear of revolutions. All revolutions, even the most necessary, have indeed for a time this effect, but it was stronger, I think, in our case than in any other, and I do not find in history a single event that contributed more to the well-being of succeeding generations, or more entirely demoralized the generation that brought it to pass. Many reasons for this may be assigned, and especially the immense mass of property confiscated by the winning party. The French Revolution multiplied, to an extent never before witnessed in any civil war, the number of doubtful properties guaranteed by law but not by conscience. The sellers of confiscated estates were not quite sure of their right to alienate them, nor the buyers of their right to acquire them. With both parties it generally happened that idleness or ignorance prevented their forming a correct opinion on this important point, and interest prevented most of them from looking too closely into the matter. Bad feelings were often excited among millions of men. During the great revolution which preceded the Reformation, in the sixteenth century — the only revolution that can be compared with the French Revolution — the property of the Church was confiscated, but it was not brought to the hammer. A few great nobles seized it. With us, on the other hand, not only the estates of the Church, but those of almost all great land-owners — not the property of a single corporation, but the patrimonies of 100,000 families, were disposed of. It is to be remarked, too, that men did not grow rich merely by the purchase at a low price of confiscated estates, but by the pretended satisfaction of a large amount of incumbrances; the profit was perfectly legal and perfectly dishonest.

Risking the comparison further, I find that the revolution in the sixteenth century threw doubt upon only one set of human opinions, and disturbed established habits on only some points. The moral sense, which in most men is founded less upon reason than upon custom and prejudice, was then only shaken, whereas the French Revolution attacked at the same time political and religious faith, desired to reform simultaneously the individual and the state, tried to change ancient customs, received opinions, and fixed habits on every subject, and all at once; all which produced a universal perturbation in morals, and conscience tottered on every point.

But in long-continuing revolutions, men are morally ruined less by the faults and the crimes that they commit in the heat of passion or of their political convictions, than by the contempt that in the end they acquire for the very convictions and passions which moved them; when wearied, disenchanted, and undeceived, they turn against themselves and consider their hopes as having been childish — their enthusiasm, and above all, their devotion, absurd. None can conceive how often the main-spring of even the strongest minds is broken by such a catastrophe. Man is so crushed by it that not only can he no longer attain to great virtues, but he seems to have become almost incapable of great crimes. Those who saw France reduced to this state imagined that in future it would be impossible for her to make any great moral effort, but they deceived themselves; for if our virtues never satisfy the moral philosopher, our vices never leave him without hope; the truth is, that we never tread either path so decidedly as to be unable to leave it.

The French nation, after having been passionately attached to liberty in 1789, loved her no longer in 1799, though no other object had engaged their affections. Having at one time bestowed on her a thousand imaginary charms, they now could not see even the merits that she really possessed; they could feel only her inconveniences and her dangers. For the last ten years, indeed, they had found in her little else. According to the strong expression of a contemporary, the republic had been nothing but a restless slavery. At what other period in history had the habits of men been so violently interfered with, and when did tyranny enter so deeply into the details of private life? What feelings and what actions had been left free? What habits or what customs had been respected? The private citizen had been forced to change his days of work and rest, his calendar, his table of weights and measures, even his terms of speech. While obliged to bear his part in ceremonies which appeared to him ridiculous and profane, he was not allowed to worship except in secret. He broke the law whenever he obeyed his conscience or indulged his taste. I know not if a similar state of things could have been endured for so long by any other nation, but there is no limit to our patience, nor again to our resistance, on different occasions.

Often during the course of the Revolution the French thought that they were on the point of finding a happy termination of this great crisis; sometimes they trusted in the constitution, sometimes in the assembly, and sometimes in the executive itself. Once or twice they trusted in their own exertions, which is always the last resource. All these hopes had been deceived, all these attempts had been made in vain. The march of the Revolution was not arrested. Great changes, indeed, were no longer effected, but a continual agitation was kept up. The wheel, it is true, carried nothing with it, but it seemed likely to go round and round forever.

It is difficult to imagine, even in these days, the extreme fatigue, apathy, indifference, or rather contempt, for politics, into which such a long, terrible, and barren struggle had thrown men's minds. Many nations have presented a spectacle of the same nature, but as every nation brings its own peculiar character into a situation resembling that in which others have been placed, on this occasion the French appeared to abandon themselves to fate, with a feverish passionate intoxication. Despairing of escape from their misfortunes, they determined not to think about them. The amusements in Paris, says a contemporary, are now not interrupted for a single instant, either by the terrible events that take place, or by the fear of future calamities. The theatres and public places were never so crowded. At Tivoli you hear it said, that things will soon be worse than ever; patriotism is sneered at,* and through it all we dance. One of the police reports says, that on the pedestal of the statue of Liberty has been placed this inscription: " Our Government resembles the Funeral Service; there is no Gloria, no Credo; a long Offertory, and no Benediction at the end." Fashion was never so despotic nor so capricious. It was a strange phenomenon that despair revived the frivolity of former times. New features, however, were introduced. Our manners became eccentric, disorderly, in fact revolutionary; trifles, as well as serious things, no longer knew rule or limit.

Institutions are like religions — observances generally survive faith. It was curious to see the government of a nation, which no more cared for liberty than it believed in the continuance of the Republic, in whom all revolutionary zeal seemed to have expired, still obstinately persevering in all the ceremonies introduced by the Revolution. In May it attended solemnly the Fête of the Sovereignty of the People; in the spring it was present at the Fête of Youth; in summer at that in honor of Agriculture; in autumn at the Fête of Old Age. On the 21st of January, all the public functionaries were assembled round the altar dedicated to the country, to swear fidelity to the constitution and hatred to tyrants.

François de Neufchâteau, who was Home Minister in 1799, when France was devoured at home by anarchy and threatened abroad by foreign enemies, was chiefly occupied in arranging these civic *fêtes;* most of his

---

* " On appelle la Patrie la Patraque," are the French words. *Patraque* is slang for an old worn-out machine. — TR.

circulars are on this subject. He depends greatly on
pageants, he says, for reviving patriotism and all private
virtues. As no one would regard these ridiculous *fêtes*
in earnest, a law was passed (the 17th Thermidor, 6th
year) to force the shopkeepers, on pain of fine or imprisonment, to close their establishments on *fête*-days and on
the decades ; and to forbid, under the same penalty, any
work to be done on these days on the high roads or
within the public view. As the appellation of *citizen*
had become vulgar and had fallen out of use, the
government posted up in large letters in all the public
places these words: " Here men are proud of the title
of citizen." The revolutionary, which was the governing
party, kept up likewise in its official language all the
commonplaces of the Revolution. The last thing abandoned by a party is its phraseology, because among
political parties, as elsewhere, the vulgar make the language, and the vulgar abandon more easily the ideas
that have been instilled into it than the words that it
has learnt. When one reads the harangues of the time,
it seems as if nothing could be said simply. Soldiers
are called warriors ; wives — faithful companions ; children — pledges of love. Duty is never mentioned, virtue
takes its place ; no one ever promises less than to die
for his country and for liberty. The contemptible part
is, that most of the orators who delivered these speeches
were themselves almost as wearied, as disgusted, and as
cold as their hearers ; but it is a sad necessity to violent
passions in their decline, that long after they have lost
all influence over the heart, the expressions that once
were natural to them survive. Any one who had derived
all his information from the newspapers might have imagined that he lived in the midst of a nation passionately

fond of liberty and interested in public affairs. Their
language had never been more inflated, nor their demands
more clamorous, than when they were on the eve of a
fifteen years' silence. To ascertain the real power of
the press, attention should be paid, not to what it says,
but to the way in which the public listens. Its very
vehemence is sometimes a forerunner of its entire extinction; its clamors are often the proof of its perils. It
screams only because its audience is growing deaf, and
this very deafness makes it safe to silence it.

Although the people were from this time excluded
from the conduct of affairs, it must not be thought that
they were indifferent to their personal danger. Exactly
the contrary was the case. The French had never perhaps so dreaded the consequences to themselves of
political events, as when they were no longer able to
direct them. In politics, fear is a passion that grows
at the expense of all others; everything terrifies when
nothing is any longer ardently desired. The French,
too, have a sort of joyous desperation, which deceives
their rulers; they laugh at their own misery, but they
feel it no less. At this time, though full of their own
petty affairs and dissipated by pleasure, they were worn
by political anxieties. Suspense that was almost unbear-
able, terror that seems to us incredible, took possession
of every mind.

Although the dangers of that time were, on the whole,
infinitely less than those of the beginning of the Revolution, they inspired terror that was more intense and
more general, because the nation had less energy, feebler
passions, and more experience. All the evils that had
overpowered the people for ten years were combined in
their fancy to form a picture of the future; and after

having permitted to take place, without alarm and even without foreboding, the most terrible catastrophes, they trembled at their own shadows. On reading the edicts of the time, it is evident that the most opposite things were feared; some dreaded the abolition of property, and others the return of feudal rights. Often the same man, after fearing one of these evils, immediately appre- hended the other; in the morning a Restoration, in the evening a return of the Reign of Terror. Many were afraid of showing their fear; and it was not till after the crisis of the 18th Brumaire that it was possible to measure, by the extent of their satisfaction and the excess of their joy, the depth of pusillanimity into which the Revolution had plunged these enervated souls.

Although experience ought to prepare us for any amount of caprice in men, some surprise may be per- mitted to us at seeing so great a change in the disposition of a nation; so much selfishness succeeding to such devotion; so much indifference, to such vehemence; so much cowardice, to so much heroism; such utter con- tempt for what they had desired so ardently and paid for so dearly. Such a complete and sudden revolution can- not be explained by ordinary moral laws. The charac- ter of our nation is so peculiar, that the study of human nature in general does not embrace it; those even who have most studied it are continually taken by surprise; for our nation is gifted beyond any other with capacity to appreciate great things, and even to do them; it is equal to any single effort, however extraordinary, but unable to remain strung up to a high pitch for any length of time; because we act upon impulse, not on principle, and our instincts are better than our moral qualities; we are the most civilized people in the world, and yet, in certain respects, we have retained more of the savage than any other nation ; for the great characteristic of the savage is, to be influenced by the sudden impressions of the present, without recollection of the past or thought of the future.

CHAPTER II.

HOW THE NATION, THOUGH IT CEASED TO BE REPUBLICAN, REMAINED REVOLUTIONARY.

THE Royalists, seeing the disgust conceived against liberty by the nation, fancied that it was anxious to return to the old* system. Almost all parties whose day has gone by are apt to imagine that because their successors are hated they must be loved, not perceiving how much easier it is for men to be constant in their antipathies than in their affections. France, though she no longer loved the Republic, was still strongly attached to the Revolution. Such important consequences follow from this fact, that it deserves to be considered at some length.

As time passed on, and the *ancien régime* faded in the distance, the people grew more and more resolved not to return to it. The phenomenon was remarkable. The Revolution seemed to become dear to the nation in proportion to the suffering which it inflicted. From the writings of the time it is evident, that this it was which most astonished the enemies of the Revolution. When they contrasted the evils that it produced with the attachment that it retained, France seemed to them to have become raving mad.

These opposite effects, however, were due to one cause.

* " Ancien Régime."

Men suffered more and more from the Revolution the longer the bad government which had risen out of it lasted, while this very duration made the habits that it had planted take root, and increased the number and variety of the interests which it sustained. As the nation advanced, barrier after barrier rose up behind and impeded a return. Most Frenchmen had taken an active share in affairs since the beginning of the Revolution, and had attested their adherence to it by public acts; they felt almost themselves responsible for the calamities that had ensued. This responsibility seemed to strengthen with the increase and duration of the evils. Thus the Reign of Terror gave to many, even of its victims, an unconquerable aversion to the reëstablishment of old rights, the owners of which would have so many injuries to resent.

Something like this has been witnessed in every revolution. Even the most oppressive render a return to a former state intolerable to the nation, if they only last long enough. Our revolution, besides, did not oppress the whole country in an equal degree; some suffered little by it, and among those even who bore the burden many had found considerable advantages mixed with the evils that it had caused. I believe that the comfort of the lower classes was much less disturbed than is commonly supposed. At least they had great alleviations of their misfortunes. Great numbers of workmen having willingly, or by compulsion, joined the army, those who remained in France obtained much higher pay. Wages rose in spite of public and private calamities, for the working class diminished still more quickly than the demand for their services.* One of the principal foes of

---

* Similar causes produced a similar phenomenon at the close of the Empire. The condition of the working classes improved in the midst of our disasters.

the Revolution, Mallet-Dupan, writes in 1796: "The working men earn more now than in 1790." Sir Francis d'Ivernois, who for ten years imposed on himself the task of proving once a year to England that France, exhausted by misery, had only six months to live, acknowledges in his last pamphlet, written in 1799, that wages had risen everywhere since the Revolution, and that the price of wheat had fallen.

As for the peasantry, I need not repeat that they were able to purchase much land at a low price. It is impossible to set down precisely in figures the gain that they made, but it is well known that it was considerable. All the world knows that the Revolution abolished many heavy and vexatious taxes, such as tithes, feudal dues, forced labor, the salt-tax, some of which were never reimposed, and others only partially, and at a much later period. At this day we can scarcely imagine how hateful many of those taxes were to the people, either on account of their oppressiveness, or from the ideas with which they were connected.

In the year 1831 I was in Canada, and when conversing with the peasants of French extraction, I found that in their language the word *taille* (poll-tax) was synonymous with misery and evil. They call any great misfortune "a regular *taille*." The tax itself I believe to have never existed in Canada; at any rate it had been abolished for more than half a century. Its meaning was even lost, the name alone remained in the language as a lasting proof of the horror that it had inspired.

Another fact, which has not sufficiently been noticed, is the less direct and regular, but not less real benefit conferred by the Revolution on many poor debtors. Their debts were not actually abolished in law, but soon afterwards they were reduced in fact by the issue of paper-money.

It is now known that in many provinces in France the number of small proprietors was considerable, even before 1789. There is reason for thinking (although the fact cannot be absolutely proved) that most of these small land-owners were involved in debt, for at that time they bore the chief burden of taxation. Now even, when the weight of contributing to the revenue is laid on all equally, that class still falls most into debt. The possessors of small incumbered estates nearly filled the towns, for France has always been a country abounding more in vanity and in wants than in wealth. We must note, that before the Revolution, as in our own day, the farmers formed a numerous class, because our farms are in general small. The rapid depreciation of paper-money operated universally, as if all securities had been thrown into the fire, and rents reduced to nothing. The disorder of the times, and, still more, the weakness of the administration, prevented even the debt to the state from being regularly or fully paid. The financial records of the Republic show that neither the old taxes which were retained, nor the new ones that were imposed, were ever completely collected. The state was maintained by means of *assignats* by payment in kind, and by the spoils of Europe. M. Thibeaudeau said with reason in his memoirs, "that the discredit of *assignats*, while it ruined the great proprietors and annuitants, made the fortunes of the peasants and farmers."

"The country," wrote, in 1795, M. Mallet-Dupan, whom I have already quoted, "grows rich by the poverty of the towns; fabulous profits are made in it. A sack of flour pays the farmer's rent. The peasantry

have become calculating and speculating; they fight
with each other for the lands of emigrants, and pay no
taxes."

A foreigner, evidently a man of talent, who was travelling in France at this period, wrote in his journal, "In
France, at the present day, the rich aristocracy is the
aristocracy of farmers and peasants."

It is true that the peasant had to set against these
advantages some oppressions incident to the times, the
billeting of soldiers and requisitions in kind; but these
partial and momentary evils did not prevent his enjoying
the benefits of the Revolution. On the contrary, he became more and more attached to them, and he bore these
annoyances as he bore storms and floods, for which a
good estate is never abandoned, though they make the
owner long for a fair season that will enable him to turn
it to good account.

When one considers the means by which the origina-
tors of our first revolution succeeded in gaining the hearts
of the agricultural classes, and with what substantial
gifts they obtained the enthusiastic suffrage of the small
farmers and lower classes (that is, of the masses) for
their work, in spite of the misery and desolation of the
period, one wonders at the simplicity of some democrats
in our own day who thought that it would be easy to
persuade a highly civilized people to submit patiently
to the inconvenience inseparable from a great political
change, by the bribe of freedom instead of that of plunder
and profit.

The middle class (*la Bourgeoisie*), especially that of
the towns, who began the revolution, was, of the victorious party, the class that had chiefly to bear the burden.
Its personal sufferings were greater, and its substantial

losses relatively almost as great as those of the nobles.
Its trade was partially, its manufactures were totally,
destroyed. The small government employments, and
many other privileges belonging to it, were abolished,
but the events which ruined it made it the governing
class. The power of the state passed to it immediately,
the fortune of the state soon followed. The greater part
of the innovations which were suddenly produced by the
violent and disorderly tyranny of the Revolution had
been expected, extolled, and longed-for all through the
eighteenth century. They satisfied the judgment and
charmed the imagination even of those with whose interests they interfered. The only fault found with these
innovations was that they had cost too dear. Even the
price that had been paid rendered some of them still*
more precious. Much as France, therefore, feared and
suffered, there was always one thing which seemed worse
than present pain and anxiety; it was a return to the
past.

Some ingenious modern writers have undertaken the
defence of the *Ancien Régime*. My first remark is that
it is a small proof of the excellence of a government when
men wait to praise it till they have ceased to believe in
the possibility of its restoration. But I judge of it, not
from my own ideas, but from the feelings that it inspired
in those who endured and overthrew it. All through the
course of that cruel and tyrannical revolution I see hatred
towards the *Ancien Régime* surpass in the heart of every
Frenchman every other hatred, and so deeply rooted as
to survive the object of its abhorrence, and from a passing
impulse become a permanent instinct. I observe that
during the most dangerous vicissitudes of the last sixty
years, fear of the return of the *Ancien Régime* has always

extinguished in our restless, excitable minds, every other fear. This is enough for me. The experiment, in my opinion, has been made.

The impossibility of forcing the French back into the former state of things was seen, indeed, almost immediately after they had escaped from it. Mirabeau proclaimed it from the first, and by many of the greatest enemies to the new institutions it soon was discovered. The following extract is from a little pamphlet published during the emigration, by M. de Montlosier (in 1796), and perhaps the most remarkable production of his vigorous and eccentric mind.

" Monarchy," he said, "has sunk with the weight of our rights and privileges which clung to it for salvation. We must sacrifice our rights and privileges before it rises to the surface. We are assured that every one curses the Revolution; I am quite willing to believe it. I am only trying to find out if there is not some difference between cursing the Revolution and wishing to restore the ancient state of things. France wishes only to remain as she is, and to be at peace. No one will consent to lose the fruit of his talents or of circumstances. Generals will not again be privates, judges do not choose again to be constables, the mayors and residents of the department are not willing to be once more laborers or artisans, those who have obtained our fortunes are not likely to give them up. The thing is done, the Revolution cursed by the whole of France has spread over the whole of France. We must take this confusion as it is, find our places in it, and convince ourselves that it will not value us at our former price." *

* In a report on the debts of the emigrants, made in 1798 by the head of the " Bureau de liquidation," Bergerat, we read that the debts

Most of the emigrants had different ideas. The mistakes of these royalists living abroad would appear to be inconceivable, if we did not know that they were brought up in the prejudices and illusions of an unpolitical aristocracy, and that they had long lived in exile. The punishment of exile is especially cruel in this respect, that, while it inflicts suffering, it teaches nothing.

It crystallizes, as it were, the minds of its victims, fixes in them the notions acquired in childhood, or those that were in vogue when they were exiled. For them the facts that occur, the new customs that are established in their country, do not exist. They stand still like the hands of a watch at the hour when it stopped. This is said to be an infirmity peculiar to the minds of certain exiles. I believe that it is a malady incident to exile, from which few escape.

The emigrants, then, lived in the imaginary enjoyment of their privileges, long after these privileges had been lost to them forever. They were always thinking of what they would do when they should be reinstated in the possession of their estates and of their vassals, without remembering that Europe trembled before those vassals. Their chief uneasiness was not lest the republic might last, but lest monarchy should not be restored precisely such as it had been before its fall. They hated the constitutionalists more than the terrorists ; they talked only of the just severity that they would exercise when they should return to power, and in the mean time they

of the emigrants from the Department of the Seine alone equalled in amount all the debts left by the emigrants in the other departments, because all the great land-owners in France lived in Paris. Nothing can show better than this fact that the nobles had ceased to be a political aristocracy, and become merely a select society; they had exchanged real power for court favor.

persecuted each other; in short, they omitted nothing
that might maintain the detestation in which they were
held; or that might give an idea to France of an *ancien
régime* more odious than that which had been destroyed.
Divided between fears of the royalists and of the Jacobins,
the mass of the nation sought for an escape. The Revolution was loved, but the Republic was feared lest it
should bring back the royalists or the Jacobins. We
may even say that each of these passions nourished the
other; it was because the French set great value upon
certain benefits conferred upon them by the Revolution,
that they felt all the more keenly the inconvenience that
would result from a government which should interfere
with their enjoyment of them. Of all the privileges that
they had won or obtained during the last ten years, the
only one that they were willing to surrender, was liberty!
They were ready to give up the liberty which the Revolution had only promised, to enjoy at length in peace the
other advantages that it had given to them.

All parties, indeed, reduced, cold, and weary, longed to
rest for a time in a despotism of any kind, provided that
it were exercised by a stranger, and weighed upon their
rivals as heavily as on themselves. This stroke finishes
the picture. When great political parties begin to cool
in their attachments, without softening their antipathies,
and at last reach the point of wishing less to succeed than
to prevent the success of their adversaries, one must prepare for slavery — the master is near. It was easy to
see that this master could rise only from the army.

It is interesting to follow throughout the different
phases of this long revolution, the gradual advance of
the army towards sovereign power. In the beginning,
the army was dispersed by an unarmed populace, or,

rather, fell to pieces in the rapid changes of public opinion. For a long time it stood aloof from all internal affairs. The population of Paris usurped the power of making and unmaking the rulers of France. Still the revolution goes on. The enthusiasm which it had inspired fades; the able men who had directed its course in the assembly retire or die. The government relaxes; public opinion, stern in the early days of the Revolution, becomes weak, anarchy spreads in every direction. Meanwhile the army acquires consistency, experience, and fame; great generals are formed. It retains a common object and common passions, while the nation has them no more. In short, the military and the civilians grow into two entirely distinct societies, within the same period and in the heart of the same nation. The chain that binds the one is drawn closer, while that which unites the other relaxes its hold.

On the 13th Vendémiaire, 1795, the army, for the first time since 1789, took part in internal affairs. It caused the victory of the Convention, and the discomfiture of the middle class in Paris.

In 1797, on the 18th Fructidor, it assisted the directory in the conquest, not only of Paris, but of the legislative body, or rather of the whole country, by which that body had been chosen. On the 30th Prairial, 1799, it refused to support the very directors whom it held responsible for its own reverses, and they fell before the assembly.

After the 13th Vendémiaire, no government was possible without the army. Soon after, there could be no government except through the army. Having reached this point, it chose to assume the government itself. One step induced the other. Long before they were really masters, the soldiery adopted the tone and habits of command. A German-Swiss, a great partisan of the Revolution and friend to the Republic, who travelled in France in 1798, remarks with regret, that to judge from the military parade at the public festivals, the tyranny of the soldiers, and the insolence with which they repulsed the public, one would think that never in the royal fêtes had so little respect been shown to the people.

The friends of the Republic, who perceived the growing influence of the army, consoled themselves by considering that the military had always exhibited ultra-republican passions, by which it seemed still to be violently agitated, while they had disappeared in the rest of the nation. What they took for love of the Republic was chiefly love for the Revolution. In fact, the army was the only class in France of which every member, without exception, had gained by the revolution, and had a personal interest in supporting it. Every officer owed his rank to it, and every soldier his hopes of becoming an officer. The army was, in truth, the Revolution roused and in arms. When it still wildly exclaimed, — " Long live the Republic ! " it was only as a challenge to the *ancien régime*, whose adherents cried, — " Long live the King ! " In reality it cared nothing for the liberties of the nation. Hatred to foreigners, and a love of his native land, are in general the only elements of the soldier's patriotism, even in free countries ; still more must this have been the case in a nation in the then state of France. The army, like almost every other army in the world, could make nothing of the slow and complicated movements of a representative government ; it detested and despised the assembly, because it was incapable of understanding any power that was not strong and simple, and all that it wanted was national independence and victories.

The recent revolution having thus prepared the way, it must not be supposed that a clear idea was formed of what was coming. There are moments when the world resembles one of our theatres before the curtain rises. We know that we shall see a new play. We already hear the preparations on the stage; the actors are close to us, but we cannot see them, and we know not what the piece is to be. In like manner, especially toward the end of the year 1799, the approach of a revolution was heard in every direction, though none knew whence it was to come. It appeared to be impossible for the existing state of things to continue, and seemed equally impossible to escape from it. In every correspondence of the time is this sentence: "things cannot remain as they are" — no more is added. Even imagination was exhausted. Men were tired of hoping and predicting. France abandoned herself to her fate; filled with dread, but overcome by languor, she looked wearily from side to side to see if no one could come to her aid. It was evident that this deliverer must rise from the army. Who could it be? Some named Pichegru, some Moreau, others thought that it would be Bernadotte.*

"Retired into the country in the heart of the Bour-

---

* Towards the last, the approach of the catastrophe became so evident that even the amusements were interrupted in Paris. At the end of Fructidor, about two months before the 18th Brumaire, we find, in a literary journal of fashion, among various attempts at poetry, this advertisement, in which the frivolity, the anxieties, and the monstrous taste of the time are well painted: "We shall publish no new fashions till this crisis is over. At present fear and anxiety appear to have usurped the empire over our polished countrymen."

bonnais," writes M. Fiévée in his memoirs, "one fact only recalled me to politics; every peasant whom I met in the fields, the vineyards, or the forest, stopped me to ask if there were any news of General Bonaparte, and why he did not return to France; I was never asked any question concerning the directory."

LETTERS.

Amiens, 1824.

Your letter, dear friend, made me laugh heartily, especially the coolness, so worthy of us, with which you write on the margin : " Idle away the rest of our time ; " that single touch paints us. . . . . The plan that I had formed was most preposterous, but therefore only the more delightful.* Though we were to have been only a week away, our tour would have cost as much as if it had lasted a fortnight. But the results would have been magnificent, we were to go straight to London. We were to take the public conveyance as far as Calais. There get on board the packet, which in twenty-four hours would take us to London, sailing up the Thames, through the double line of vessels, and all the wealth that covers its waters. In London we spend two days. Williams assures me, that with the complete information which he would give us, two days would be enough, on the third we reënter France. Here is a superb plan ! what a pity that it is so little practicable. In the first

---

* At the ages of nineteen and twenty, Alexis de Tocqueville and Louis de Kergorlay took it into their heads to visit England. Against this plan there were several obstacles; among others, 1st, that they knew not how to obtain passports; 2d, they had no money; 3d, they did not know how to gain their parents' consent, or how to do without it. These early letters, of which only two fragments have been found, are curious proofs of the restless disposition, and of the remarkable activity of mind, of A. de Tocqueville.

place it must have been done, as we have done some
other things, incognito, and told about afterwards as a
sudden fancy that seized us on the sea-coast. I have
already told my father that I should go with you to
Calais and Lille. All that is easy; the great, the chief
obstacle is, that one must have a passport to go abroad.
I cannot get one here. If you could procure one in
Paris it would be capital. If it were made out for you
and your servant it would be still better. At the worst
I might provide myself with Williams's English passport,
as his height and appearance tally with mine. Once in
England we want no passport. It is only on leaving and
returning to France. Very likely we might be arrested,
and in this lies the extravagance of the plan. But one
must risk something. I own that I should like above
all things to take a voyage of forty miles in your company, and to see for once those rascally English, who, we
are told, are so strong and so flourishing. I send to you
the plan arranged by Williams, and an estimate of the
cost of a fortnight's tour. I make it about 12*l.* apiece.

Rome, January 20, 1827.

Nothing ever produced a greater effect upon me than
the sight of the Campagna of Rome, on which a curse
seems to have fallen; imagine, under a splendid sky,
hills of a reddish hue, absolutely barren, and enclosed in
a circle of the most lovely mountains. No trees, no vegetation, no dwellings; the scene animated only by a few
shepherds and cow-herds, whose countenances wear a
sinister expression to be seen only here. The stones
covering the fields, the ruined tombs, above all the unac-
countable sterility, fill you with religious awe. When
you perceive on the horizon a column of smoke, and an

Italian voice cries " Roma," you are plunged into a chaos of ideas and sensations. If instead of gradually approaching Rome through this desert, you came upon the ancient city suddenly, and saw the Coliseum and the Pantheon, and the heaps of ruins around : you might go mad. But modern Rome destroys the charm; and the Romans dressed like Frenchmen, spoil everything. On entering the town the heart sinks and does not recover. Less than anything else can one forgive the Romans for modernizing their ruins; it is like an old man putting on rouge.

Versailles, July 23, 1827.

. . . . You ask me how I like my new position. I cannot answer in a single word : I cannot say that I absolutely like it or dislike it, — it has both its good and its bad side ; and the only way of treating the question is to separate the two. We will begin by considering the bad : first, I thought that I knew a great deal about law, and I grossly deceived myself. My knowledge of law was about equal to that which a young man who has just left college has of science. I have the raw material in my head, and that is all. When I have to apply the principles I am quite bewildered; my incompetence throws me into despair. I am certainly more ignorant than any of my colleagues ; and though my vanity, which is as great as that of others, tells me that when I shall have worked as long as they have done, I shall be quite equal to them, I still feel hurt. I have on most occasions an ambition to be first, which will be the torment of my whole life. I have another defect, which annoys me at present; I find a difficulty in acquiring the habit of speaking in public; I pause for words, and I attach too much importance to my ideas. At my side I see men who reason ill and speak well; and I despair. I think myself their superior, and I come out their inferior.

I have told you part of the bad. Now for the good side. I no longer suffer from *ennui*. No one that has not tried it can imagine what it is to turn one's attention seriously to a subject; in the end one cannot help being interested in one's work. So with law, — its theory disgusted me, but its practice does not. When trying to solve a point, or find a clew, I feel my mind work with all its powers. In the second place, my companions are a greater resource to me than at first I expected. Their friendliness and good-fellowship are very agreeable. I think that I have already established my character among them. . . . .

To sum up, my dear friend, I begin to think that I shall enter into the spirit of my profession. That is the important point. There are still moments when I regret bitterly that I did not choose another path; but generally speaking, I become more and more engrossed by my business, and see so little of my acquaintances or my friends, that I sometimes fear that I shall grow in time into a sort of law-machine, like most of the members of my profession, devoted to their own special line, as incapable of judging a great movement, or of guiding a great undertaking, as they are capable of drawing an inference, or discovering an analogy. I had rather burn my books! Who, however, can foresee the effects of daily influence, and who can be sure of escaping them?

Versailles, March 27, 1828.

I thank you heartily for your letter, my dear friend. I never felt more deeply than while I read it, the value of our friendship. Let us hold it with all our might, dear Louis: nothing else is firm in this world. As long as we can thus lean on each other, we shall not falter; and if one of us should fall, the other will lift him up. When we were children, you may have noticed in me a singular effect of the false experience which is given by books. I distrusted all generous sentiments. I yielded to them reluctantly, believing their very beauty to be a proof of their instability. This was my conception of friendship. I thought it a fancy of early youth. But the farther I advance in life, the more I am convinced that friendship, even such as I conceived it, can exist and preserve its charms, not in every heart, but in some hearts. One cannot make friends late in life; but when once friendship has taken root, I do not see why age should wither it, or in any way affect it; especially if, appreciating its true value, we watch over it, and do not deprive it of its necessary food — confidence in all things, little as well as great. In this respect, dear Louis, we must always be on our guard; and I own that I trust more to myself than to you. There are chambers in your mind into which I have never penetrated. Your discretion, which cannot but increase, often gives me pain; especially as I do not see that I have a right to complain of a quality founded on good feeling, and on principles that cannot be controverted. One of these days I must talk to you on this among other subjects.

Paris, May 10, 1828.

I am free for an instant, my dear friend, and I write to you, which I ought long ago to have done. You have been much neglected by me lately. Neither indifference, as you well know, nor idleness has been the cause, but an instinct that I often feel though I cannot define it, which inclines me to shut myself up in my own thoughts, even though they be sad. Pride, perhaps, may be at the bottom of it. I am ashamed to speak of an irremediable evil, and one too that I have brought upon myself. Between what I have attained, and what I aimed at, I see an immense distance. It does not discourage me, but it deprives me of the support of ardent hope. Then how is one to know one's self? This thought occurs to me twenty times a day. The world swarms with happy fools who sincerely admire themselves (I am sure that I do not belong to this category), and also with fools, who, aware of their own condition, feel its disadvantages without its pleasures. Sometimes I fancy that I belong to the latter class, and the idea is by no means agreeable.

I hear that you are coming in January. What are your plans, my dear Louis? Will you travel, or stay at home? Among the circumstances that I envy in your position, are the long intervals of absolute liberty succeeding to severe duties. How much you must enjoy your freedom! We have not such hard work; but we never have such complete rest. . . . . My old taste for a life of excitement and wandering is not extinguished. It seems to me, that I should set off on a long adventurous journey with more pleasure than ever, and that after roaming for some time I should wish again to be settled. Experience has taught me to expect this ebb and flow. Longing for action, longing for rest, I have oscillated between them, for the last six or seven years.

Versailles, Sept. 6, 1828.

. . . . I have heard of the safe arrival of Stoffels. He has, no doubt, told you that our time was well spent, without any extraordinary gayeties indeed, but in an intimacy which to me, and I think also to him, was better than all other pleasures. Friendship, dear Louis, is all that is worth having here on earth. The taste which I have had of other emotions, has gradually convinced me of this. I cannot conceive the existence of men able to live without a friend. It seems to me incredible; if there be such men, they cannot be worth much. . . . . Stoffels and I talked much of you. He is attached to you with the warm friendship of which you know that he is capable, and our conversation constantly turned upon you.

Versailles, . . . 1828.

I could not write yesterday, as M. de Lamoricière * was not able to come to breakfast, and after we had met it was too late for the post. I must tell you that I was delighted with him; he seemed to me to have all the marks of a really distinguished man. Accustomed as I am to live with people who are satisfied by mere words, I was surprised by his anxiety for clearness and precision. The calm way in which he stopped me, to ask me to explain one idea before I passed on to another, sometimes disconcerted me; his manner of talking on the subjects which he understands gave me a higher opinion of him than I almost ever formed of a man on first acquaintance. I told him that I hoped that we should meet again, and it was not a compliment.

We talked much of you. I own, dear Louis, that, in spite of all my efforts, I have no clear view of your position: many premises are wanting to me in order to form an opinion: —

* Now General Lamoricière. He entered the École Polytechnique with Louis de Kergorlay, who introduced him to Tocqueville. This interview first brought together men who were again to meet in public life.

1st. — I do not know whether the foot artillery has any advantage over the horse artillery . . . . one thing only I see clearly: if you choose the foot and the Montpellier regiment, you will have two chances of employment; even if the expedition to the Morea should be feebly carried on, as is possible, without being probable, you might hope to be sent there to replace those who die or those who return, for it is said, that there are perpetual changes in the artillery regiments.

2dly. — The Turks seem to be victorious just now. If their success continues, I think that Europe will have peace. However, it might happen that the Turks, puffed up by their victories over the Russians, might direct an army on Attica and the Peloponnesus; and then the war in the Morea would become serious. . . . I do not see that, in this case, it would be for the interest of any European nation to make war: we should, no doubt, be left to help ourselves out of the difficult enterprise which we have undertaken; in this event, not only the Montpellier regiment would be sent but probably many others.

3dly. — There is a third chance, which did not occur to me at first; it is not probable, but it is possible, that if the Morea were evacuated, we might attack Algiers, for that ridiculous business must be settled. . . .

However, my dear friend, I own to you, that I do not share your fears for the future; no, you will have opportunities of fighting, if your life is spared; be sure of that. Europe cannot long remain at peace. Do you not see that, in France especially, the exhaustion produced by war and revolution is rapidly vanishing; that a new generation brings with it new passions and hopes. With our strength, our pretensions will increase. Heaven grant that this activity may not turn inwards. It certainly will spread its influence in some way. . . .

* Yonkers, June 20, 1831,
(twenty miles from New York).

I begin a letter to you, dear friend, but I know not when I shall finish it. I did not write to you before, because I had nothing particular to say; I hate to speak of France from such a distance. I should talk of things which would be forgotten when you got my letter; the circumstances on which I should dwell would have changed ten times in the interval. Then I wished to know a little more of this country than I did when I first arrived. I find that I have not gained much by waiting. Every foreign nation has a peculiar physiognomy, seen at the first glance and easily described. When afterwards you try to penetrate deeper, you are met by real and unexpected difficulties; you advance with a slowness that drives you to despair, and the farther you go the more you doubt. I feel that at this moment my head is a chaos of contradictory notions. I tire myself in seeking for some clear and decisive results; I find none. In this frame of mind writing to you is agreeable and useful. Perhaps my ideas may be reduced to some order by the effort to express them. Even if they should turn out to be no better than vague theories and unsupported conclusions, I still should send them to you without scruple. One of the privileges of our friendship is that we know each other so perfectly, and are so convinced of each other's sincerity, that we may express our dawning opinions without the fear of committing ourselves, for each knows that in writing,

* A small village on the Hudson, near New York.

his friend gives him an exact picture of the state of his mind at the time.

In your last letter you ask me if this country has any *convictions.* I do not know the precise sense that you attach to that word. What strikes me is that the majority have certain opinions in common. Up to the present time, this is what I most envy in America. Thus I have not heard a single person in any rank express a doubt as to a republic being the best possible form of government, or on the right of a nation to choose its own government. The greater number take republican principles in the most democratic sense. In a few you see peeping out an aristocratic tendency, which I shall presently try to explain. But that a republic is a good form of government, and that it is a form of government to which society naturally tends, are facts admitted by clergymen, by magistrates, by tradesmen, and by artisans. This opinion is so general and so seldom questioned, even in a country where there is entire freedom of speech, that it may almost be called a *conviction.*

Another idea is prevalent, apparently in an equal degree; a belief in the wisdom and good sense of mankind; the perfectibility of the human race is contradicted by few, if by any. No one denies that the majority may sometimes be mistaken; but they think that in the end it must be right; that it is not only the sole judge of its own interests, but even the safest, the nearest to infallibility. The result is the belief that education should be bestowed freely on the people; that they cannot be sufficiently enlightened. You remember how often in France we (among others) have puzzled our brains with the question, whether it were to be desired or feared that knowledge should penetrate every class of society. Though so difficult to solve in France, the doubt seems here never to have occurred. I have already propounded the question a hundred times to the most thoughtful men in this country. I saw by their summary method of dealing with it that they had never considered it; and that it should even be asked, struck them as shocking and absurd. The diffusion of intelligence, they said, is our only protection against the outbreaks of the mob.

These are what I should call the convictions of this people. They believe firmly in the excellence of their government; they believe in the wisdom of the masses, provided they be educated; and do not seem to be aware that there is a certain cultivation which can never be shared by the masses, but may yet be essential for the rulers of a state.

As for what we generally consider as making up the convictions of a nation, such as the moral standard, old traditions, recollections, of these I see as yet no traces. I even doubt whether religious opinions have as much influence as appears at first sight. The religious condition of this country is, perhaps, the most interesting subject of inquiry. I will try to tell you what I know about it when I resume my letter, which I am now forced to lay aside, perhaps for some days.

Calwell, forty-five miles from New York.

My mind has been so much excited since I began my letter to you this morning, that I feel obliged to take it up again, though I know not exactly what I shall say. I was speaking of religion. Sunday is rigorously observed. I have seen the streets barred in front of the churches during divine service. The law forbids labor; and opinion, which is much more powerful, obliges every one to appear in church, and to eschew amusement.

Hitherto my observations incline me to think that the Catholics increase in numbers. They are considerably recruited from Europe, and there are many conversions. New England and the valley of the Mississippi begin to fill with them. It is evident that all the naturally religious minds among the Protestants, the men of strong and serious opinions, disgusted by the vagueness of Protestantism, yet ardently desirous to have a faith, give up in despair the search after truth, and submit to the yoke of authority. They throw off, with pleasure, the heavy burden of reason, and they become Catholics. Again, Catholicism captivates the senses and the imagination, and suits the masses better than the reformed religion; thus the greater number of converts are from the working classes. We will pass now to the opposite end of the chain. On the confines of Protestantism is a sect that is Christian only in name. I mean the Unitarians. They all deny the Trinity, and acknowledge but one God; but among them are some who believe Christ to have been an angel, others a prophet, and others a philosopher like Socrates. The last are pure Deists. They quote the Bible because they do not wish to shock too much public opinion, which supports Christianity. They have a service on Sundays. I went to it. Verses are read from Dryden, and other English poets, on the existence of God, and the immortality of the soul. There is a sermon on some moral subject, and the service is over. This sect makes proselytes in about the same proportion as Catholicism; but its recruits come from the higher ranks of society.

Both sects grow rich on the spoils of Protestantism. It appears that the Protestants of cold, logical minds, the argumentative classes, men of intellectual and studious habits, seize the opportunity of joining an entirely philosophical sect, which allows them to make an almost public profession of pure theism. This sect, however, has no resemblance to the St. Simonians in France. It rests on different principles, and there is nothing exaggerated or absurd in its worship or in its doctrine. They endeavor as much as possible to resemble the Christian sects. No sort of ridicule is attached to them. No party-spirit urges them on or restrains them. Their demeanor is unaffectedly serious, and their ceremonies are simple. So you see that Protestantism, which is a mixture of reason and authority, is attacked on each side by these two uncompromising principles. The attentive observer will see that this is taking place, more or less, everywhere; but in America it is obvious at the first glance. It is obvious, because in this country no established laws or opinions interfere with the intelligence or the passions of men on this subject. They follow their natural inclinations. It seems to me to be certain that at no distant time the two extremes will have no barrier between them. What then will be the result? Here I lose myself in uncertainties from which I can see no way out.

But to return to the present state of the public mind in America; you must not take what I have said in too positive a sense. I have spoken of tendencies not of facts that have already taken place. Christianity rests here on a firmer foundation than in any other country in the world which I know, and I have no doubt but that the religious element influences the political one. It induces morality and regularity; it restrains the eccentricities of the spirit of innovation; above all, it is almost fatal to the mental condition, so common with us in which men leap over every obstacle *per fas et nefas* to gain their point. Any party, however anxious to obtain its object, would in the pursuit feel obliged to confine itself to means apparently legitimate, and not in open opposition to the maxims of religion, which are always more or less moral even when erroneous. . . .

I enter on another subject. I heard it said in Europe that there was an aristocratic tendency in America. It is a mistake; I am more sure of this than of most things. Democracy is rapidly advancing in some states, and fully developed in others. It is rooted in the habits, in the laws, and in the opinions of the majority. Its opposers hide their heads, and if they wish to rise are forced to borrow its colors. In New York, the beggars alone are without electoral rights. The effects of a democratic government are obvious — they are perpetual changes of men and of institutions, extreme external equality, manners without distinction, and ideas always commonplace.

We ourselves, my dear friend, are drifting towards complete democracy. I do not say that it is a good thing; what I see in this country convinces me that it will not suit France, but we are being driven on it by an irresistible force. No effort to stop its march will produce more than a halt. To refuse to admit these facts is weakness, and I cannot help believing that the Bourbons, instead of trying to fortify the aristocratic element, which is dying out with us, ought to have devoted all their energies to making it the interest of the democratic party to maintain order and stability.

In my opinion our parochial and municipal administration ought, from the first, to have attracted all their attention. Instead of living from day to day with the parochial institutions established by Napoleon, the Bourbons ought immediately to have modified them, to have gradually initiated and interested the people in the management of its own affairs; to have created local interests, and above all to have founded, if possible, the habit of submitting willingly to law, which, in my opinion, is the only counterpoise to democracy. These measures would, perhaps, have rendered the present movement less dangerous both to the state and to its rulers.

Democracy, in short, seems to me to be a fact which the government may hope in future to regulate, but not to reverse. I assure you that it was not without difficulty that I resigned myself to this idea. My view of this country does not prove to me that, even under the most favorable circumstances, and they existed here, the government of the people is a desirable event. All are pretty well agreed that in the early days of the republic, the statesmen and members of congress were much more distinguished men than they now are. They nearly all belonged to the class of country gentlemen, a race which diminishes every day. The country no longer selects so well. It chooses in general those who flatter its passions and descend to its level. This effect of democracy, joined to the extreme instability, the entire absence of coherence or permanence that one sees here, convinces me every day more and more, that the best government is not that in which all have share, but that which is directed by the class of the highest moral principle and intellectual cultivation.

However, it is impossible to deny that this country presents, on the whole, an admirable aspect. I frankly own, that it convinces me of the superiority of a free government over every other. I feel more certain than ever, that all nations are not fitted for the same amount of liberty, but also I am more inclined than ever to regret that such should be the case. It is impossible to give an idea of the universal satisfaction of this nation with the existing government. The lower classes are undeniably higher in the moral scale than with us; every man has a consciousness of his independent position and of his personal dignity which, without perhaps adding suavity to his manners, leads him to respect himself and others. The two things that I chiefly admire here are these: — First, the extraordinary respect entertained for law: standing alone, and unsupported by an armed force, it commands irresistibly. I believe, in fact, that the principal reason is, that they make it themselves and are able to repeal it. We see thieves who have violated all public laws obey those that they have made for themselves. I think that there is a similar feeling among nations. The second thing for which I envy these people is, the ease with which they do without being governed. Every man considers himself interested in maintaining the safety of the public and the exercise of the laws. Instead of depending on the police he depends on himself. The general result is that, without ever showing itself, a police is everywhere. You will scarcely credit the order kept by this people from the feeling that they themselves are the only safeguard against themselves.

You see that I give you as exact an account as I can of all my impressions. On the whole, they are more favorable to America than they were when I first arrived. There are many blots in the picture, but the general effect seizes the imagination. I fancy that it must act with irresistible power over minds that are at the same time reasoning and superficial, a combination which is not rare. The principles of the government are so simple, and the results are so sure, that if one is not on one's guard, one is carried away by the charm. One is forced to reflect, to struggle against one's impressions to discover that these simple and reasonable institutions would not suit a great nation, which must have a strong internal government, and a fixed foreign policy; that the government of this country is in its nature perishable; that a nation adopting it should long have been used to liberty and have reached a point of intellectual cultivation acquired seldom and by slow degrees. And after repeating all this to one's self, one still thinks that a free government is a grand institution, and that it is to be regretted that the moral and physical constitution of man should impede his enjoying it at all times and in all places.

Paris, Nov. 13, 1833.

. . . I have absolutely nothing new to tell you of myself. My life is as regular as that of a monk. From early morning till dinner-time my existence is purely intellectual; I pass the evening at Mrs. Belam's,* where I enjoy long conversations with Marie, of which I never tire. The next day I do the same over again, and so on with wonderful uniformity; for since my return from England, my books and Marie form all my existence.

Like you, I become more and more alive to the happiness which consists in the fulfilment of duty. I believe that there is no other so deep and so real. There is only one great object in this world which de-

---

* Aunt of the Miss Mottley whom he married two years afterward.

serves our efforts, that is the good of mankind. Some persons try to be of use to men while they despise them, and others because they love them. In the services rendered by the first there is always something incomplete, rough, and contemptuous that inspires neither confidence nor gratitude. I should like to belong to the second class, but often I cannot. I love mankind in general, but I constantly meet with individuals whose baseness revolts me. I struggle daily against a universal contempt for my fellow-creatures. I sometimes succeed, at my own expense, by a minute uncompromising investigation into the motives of my own conduct. Sometimes I find personal calculations which others do not see, and which had escaped my own observation. Sometimes I find that I have done wrong from a good motive, and still oftener, judging of myself as if I were an indifferent spectator or an opponent. I can account for the severity of a sentence pronounced on me in spite of its injustice. All this is enough to make me doubt my own powers, and in judging other men to impute more blame to their heads than to their hearts. I think that it is almost impossible to serve them if one judges of them as one is tempted to do at the first glance; and I had rather drop a little in my own esteem than place them too low. . . .

Paris, June 25, 1834.

I received your letter only two days ago. While it was running after me in Brittany, I was on my way back to Paris.

You put me out of patience by lamenting over the little sympathy which you find for your intellectual projects. What does it signify? Do you not know yourself? Are you not acquainted with the natural bent of your tastes and habits? And as for success, who ever can be sure of it till he has succeeded? On this point the whole universe can afford no certain information. You know, beyond a doubt, that you have reached the age when your powers should be developed in action; that political events prevent your employing your powers in the public service; that your character will not allow you to content yourself with the petty cares of private life, and yet that it is absolutely necessary for you to turn the activity of your mind to some object lest you should sink even below the level of those who manage their own affairs with success.

I have just been spending six weeks in the country, a thing that I had not done since I was nine years old. I know now what a country life is. I felt somewhat as I do when I meet some man of a very religious character; a great wish to think and feel as he does, with the conviction that to me it is impossible. I know not what will happen to me; but I feel certain that I am more likely to start for China, to enlist as a soldier, or to risk my life in any hazardous, imprudent enterprise, than to condemn myself to the existence of a potato, like the good people whom I have just been with. . . . .

Dublin, July 6, 1835.

On my arrival at this place, I found two letters from you. I was beginning to wonder at your silence, to be uneasy, but not to grumble; for we have never been touchy in our friendship. As you did not write, I fancied that you had perhaps already started on your long journey. You see that there is a communion in our souls, although distance separates us, and that one of us cannot be full of a subject without its influence extending to the other. I was going to write to you about it from Liverpool. I waited only in the hope of finding letters from you here.

The idea of this long tour fills me with sorrow and anxiety; but, after all, I am not sure that I should not do the same in your place. This is all I have to say. It would take too long to explain the whole meaning of these words; but you will have no difficulty in understanding them. I should never advise you to undertake a journey of such length and of so much risk; I am not sufficiently convinced of its utility; my opinion is rather negative than affirmative. But if you make up your mind to it, my thoughts will follow you without repining. May God be with you, dear and true friend, and allow us to meet again in happier times! As I advance in life I see it more and more from the point of view which I used to fancy belonged to the enthusiasm of early youth; as a thing of very mediocre worth, valuable only as far as one can employ it in doing one's duty, in serving men, and in taking one's fit place among them. Amidst the greatest trials these thoughts raise my courage. I know that you share them, for they have been the ideas that have governed our lives. They have grown with our friendship. They were the fruit of the most delightful intercourse that ever subsisted between two men. Whatever happens to you, you may be sure that my heart sympathizes entirely with yours. However differently we may *reason* on some subjects, we shall always *feel* in the same way; a noble sentiment uttered by you, or a generous, disinterested action resolved on by you, will always give me a thrill of pleasure; and if I have the happiness to experience similar emotions, I shall believe that in giving myself up to their influence, I am acting in a way that you would approve. What a cold, sad, and trivial life this would be, if by the side of this every-day world, full of selfishness and cowardice, the human mind could not build for itself another, where devotion, courage — virtue, in a word, may breathe at ease! But such a world can be formed only out of such elements as exist in minds like yours. . . . .

How I long for an opportunity, if Heaven would only grant it, of directing the fire that burns within me without an object, to the achievement of great and noble ends, no matter through what dangers I might have to pass!

Baden, August 5, 1836.

I am writing to you from the little town of Baden. The following circumstance brought me to it. Marie is suffering much from neuralgic pains. While we were at Berne many of our acquaintances assured us that the Baden waters were useful in such cases; we heard the same from the first physicians. I have, therefore, determined on passing the month of August here; we shall afterwards extend our tour a little. You must, therefore, write to me again, directing to Baden, Canton d'Argovie (Suisse).

Your letter of the 20th July reached me at Berne. It interested me deeply; you need not have told me to keep it. This letter proves to me more than ever the truth of what I have already said to you, that you must beware of spoiling your style when you polish it too highly. Your carefully-finished writings have, indeed, all the appearance of being torn from the book of an author of the seventeenth century, but not from that of a first-rate author; your familiar style, on the other hand, with all its faults, has often first-rate merits, and these merits incline me to give it the preference, in spite of its defects. But we must consider the subject again.

What you say on material enjoyments has always seemed to me to be true, and all the more just now when I am reading Plato. The philosophers of his school do not, I think, make the marked division which you complain of, in the pleasures of sense. Immorality and luxury are in their eyes, if not synonymous, at least analogous, and of the two they are more indulgent to the former than to the latter. . . . . ⁻

Your ideas are expressed with great originality; in substance they are rather recent than new. The Platonists and the fathers of our church have said, I think, something like them before; but I do not remember having ever seen expressed so strongly and so clearly the strong resemblance that exists between the various sensual pleasures. They were satisfied with condemning all. Now I will state my own opinion. Whatever we do we cannot prevent men from having a body as well as a soul, as if an angel occupied the form of an animal. . . . A system of philosophy or of religion that chooses entirely to ignore the one or the other may produce some extraordinary cases, but will never exercise any general influence over mankind : this I believe and deplore, for you know that though the animal is not more subdued in me than in most people, I adore the angel, and would give anything to make it predominate. I am, therefore, continually at work to discover a middle course which men may follow without becoming disciples either of Heliogabalus or of St. Jerome ; for I am convinced that the great majority will never be persuaded to imitate either, and less the saint than the emperor. I am, then, not so much shocked as you are by the *deco-*

rous materialism of which you complain so bitterly ; not that it does not excite my contempt as much as it does yours; but I consider it practically, and I ask myself whether, if not exactly this, something like it, be not, in fact, all that one can expect, not of any particular man, but of the species in general? Reflect on these ideas, and give me an answer. Now I will turn to another subject, for I have not much to do here, and I have grea pleasure in writing to you.

The Machiavelli of the " History of Florence " is to me the same Machiavelli who wrote the " Prince." I cannot understand the perusal of the first work leaving any doubt as to the object and meaning of the second. Machiavelli, in his history, often praises great and noble actions : but with him this is obviously an affair of the imagination.   The foundation of his ideas is, that all actions are morally indifferent in themselves, and must be judged according to the skill they display and the success they secure.   For him the world is a great arena, from which God is absent, in which conscience has nothing to do, and where every one must manage as well as he can.   Machiavelli is the grandfather of M——. I need say no more.

As for the events that he relates, I own that his picture of those times startles me, and leads me to think that our own may be unjustly censured.   The Italian republics in the Middle Ages, had, indeed, a sort of coarse energy, but how little real virtue ! What brutal violence joined to refinement of vice ! What selfishness ! What disregard of right ! What scepticism in the higher, and what superstition in the lower classes ! What utter corruption without cultivation, in society !

I am aware, however, that what was true of the

Italians in the sixteenth century, was not the case with the other European nations. Still I imagine that the times immediately before the Reformation were everywhere periods of great corruption. Ignorance and bigotry in the lower classes, doubt and unbelief in the higher; in short, the evils of barbarism and of civilization combined. This proves to me more than ever, that when once the religious belief of a nation is shaken, no time should be lost in educating its reasoning faculties. For if an intellectual but sceptical nation presents a sad spectacle, there can be none so frightful as that of a people at the same time ignorant, brutal, and incredulous.

But I begin to tire of writing. Good-by. Answer quickly. Your letters always give great pleasure to me: here more than elsewhere. Marie sends her kind regards. We often talk of you. I wish that you could hear us.

Nacqueville,* October 10, 1836.

I write from Nacqueville, where I am spending a few days. Your letter from Châlons reached me here. I suppose that my answer should be directed to Berlin, lest my letter should miss you at the intermediate address that you have given me. Your present journey is deeply interesting to me, not alone on your account, though I believe that it will be useful to you, but also on my own. You will see things which greatly excite my curiosity. After England, the country that I have always most wished to travel in, is Prussia. All that I have heard makes me think that there is none more deserving careful observation. Many things that I have

---

* The country-seat of his brother, Hippolyte de Tocqueville, near Cherbourg.

been told about it are very striking, among others this : — the Prussian government, acting either from principle or instinct, tries, they say, to make its subjects forget that they have not real freedom, by granting them liberally all the lesser liberties that are compatible with absolute monarchy ; so that voluntarily it prepares the people to stand alone, and without any violent change to govern themselves. To me it is interesting to study the indirect influence exercised by the free states of the west of Europe over the great despotic monarchies in the East and the North. It somewhat resembles the state of affairs in the sixteenth century, when the reformed countries modified Catholicism in those which still remained Catholic.

I point this out to you, not as being in itself, perhaps, the subject most interesting generally, but as being that which most interests me. In detail, I would ask you to obtain as precise information as you can on the Prussian provincial and municipal systems, as well as on the extent of its centralization. I attach great importance to this. It is not with arguments taken from republican or half republican nations that we can hope to attack with advantage French centralization. The examples that can produce a real impression on the ordinary crowd of illiberals must be taken from nations with an absolute government. I should like you, then, to get me all the documents that you can, and also to enter yourself into the spirit, and understand the system of administration, or you will not be able to explain it, nor I to comprehend it.

As to general advice about your travels, recollect that it is most important to mix with as many people as possible ; and by making each talk on what he knows best,

to draw out of him all that you can in the shortest possible time. It is good, too, to make men talk of one
another. This sort of information is precious; and as
you do not intend to communicate it, you may innocently
obtain it. Your name and letters of introduction will
secure your reception among the aristocracy. All your
endeavors should therefore be directed to becoming acquainted with the middle and literary classes. I should
also, as an experienced traveller, advise you to listen to
every one and take part with no one. You are a foreigner; you need not have an opinion on Prussian affairs.
Only say enough to make your interlocutor develop
fully his ideas. Above all, be on your guard against a
tendency natural to you, which even in France you carry
to an extreme, that of associating only with those whom
you esteem. Write a great deal; you cannot write too
much. In writing you become aware of the vagueness
of your ideas, and you see whence they sprang. Do not
hesitate, therefore, to send me as much MS. as you like.
It will be useful to you and interesting to me. For such
a purpose to regard expense would be absurd. I
need not add that you may put into the packet as many
sealed letters as you please. As you so well said, the
singular and in a moral point of view really elevated side
of our friendship, is to have combined so much independence of thought and action with so much intimacy. Now,
I think that I have said all. I will add, however, as
a general remark, that you should vigorously shake off
during your tour the disposition to carelessness to which
almost all travellers are subject, and you especially, because you are given to dreaming. Be as active therefore as possible. Never lose an opportunity of seeing
things, or above all of making acquaintances. . . .

Our visit to Switzerland has done Marie good in many respects. Still it tired her, and has left her with a sort of general physical irritation which we find a difficulty in subduing. If, however, our tour was not entirely satis-factory as far as health is concerned, it at least drew our minds closer together, if possible, than before. I cannot tell you the inexpressible charm which I found in living so continually with Marie, nor the treasures that I was perpetually discovering in her heart. You know that in travelling, still more than at other times, my temper is uneven, irritable, and impatient. I scolded her frequently and almost always unjustly, and on each occasion I dis-covered in her inexhaustible springs of tenderness and indulgence; and then I cannot describe to you the hap-piness yielded in the long run by the habitual society of a woman in whose soul all that is good in your own is reflected *naturally*, and even improved. When I say or do a thing which seems to me to be perfectly right, I read immediately in Marie's countenance an expression of proud satisfaction which elevates me. And so when my conscience reproaches me her face instantly clouds over. Although I have great power over her mind, I see with pleasure that she awes me; and as long as I love her as I now do, I am sure that I shall never allow myself to be drawn into anything wrong. You asked me, my dear friend, to speak of myself and of Marie; I have opened to you my whole heart. There is one idea connected with this subject which often troubles me. You will soon be married, and I cannot help trembling lest the kind and friendly relations that would be so favorable to our inti-macy should not be established between our wives; for experience will teach you how difficult it is to separate one's self in any way from one's partner. In this respect

Beaumont's recent marriage is sure to be very agreeable to me. I see that a real friendship is likely to spring up between Marie and Madame de Beaumont, and from that minute our intimacy will be secure for the rest of our lives. Take notice that I speak of intimacy not of friendship, which can be affected by no external circumstances. Good-by, my paper is out.

Baugy,* October 10, 1836.

A few days ago I received your letter of the 27th October, dated from Geislingen, in which you complain of finding nothing from me. When you reached Berlin you must have found that I was not in fault. More than a month ago I wrote to you at the latter address, fearing lest my letter should run after you, and at last lose you, as has often happened to me in travelling. I hope, therefore, that you now are no longer angry, and that you are prepared to write to me at length while you remain in Prussia.

Your letter from Geislingen interested me much. There was a passage on the intellectual somnolence of our time, that I think excellent and full of spirit. Why do you not always write with the same liveliness and originality? I agree with you entirely as to the fact, but it is difficult to ascribe it entirely to the reason which you give. Do you not think that, independently of King Louis Philippe, our unnatural horror of intellectual exertion arises from the exhaustion produced by a protracted revolution, every outbreak in which was preceded by great mental excitement, by theories, ideas, and principles more or less true or plausible, and yet in the end producing results so little satisfactory, as to inspire disgust for all intellectual activity, and to cause the frightful consequences that you de-

* The country-seat of his brother, Edward Vicomte de Tocqueville.

scribe? Louis Philippe gives no impulse to the production
of new ideas: true; but he does not stifle them.   Try to
bring out the cause that you assign, try to place it in a
strong light and high relief, and you will have made great
progress in the political inquiries of our day; but I doubt
your being able to do so.

On the subject of Louis Philippe, no doubt you heard
long ago of the Strasburg attempt.   That our greatest
dangers would come from the army we had long foreseen; and I myself think that not only our present but
our future dangers will arise in the same quarter; and
that not only the existing government, but all future governments, will long continue to be threatened by them.
This subject has long occupied my thoughts, and it seems
to me that the same reasons that incline a democratic
people to wish for peace and quiet, ought to induce a
democratic army to desire war and tumult.   The same
wish to get on, and the same possibility of doing so, drives
the citizens in one direction and the soldiers in the other.
The cause is the same, the effects only are different; and
the cause is essentially permanent.   The recent attempt
was put down with ease; but the apathy of the nation is
alarming; for it did not arise from dislike of the existing
government, but from the absolute indifference of the
French to any form of government whatever.   I am sure
that at the present time three fourths of the nation either
have never heard, or never bestow a thought upon, what
has happened.   Trade and manufacturers are prosperous,
that is enough for them; and they have such an imbecile
love of comfort, that they seem to fear to think of the
causes that procure it, and maintain it, lest they should
endanger it.

You will see in my letter to Berlin, the almost personal interest which I take in your inquiries. Your journey, full of interest for you, is a piece of luck to me. You will come back with a number of ideas and of reflections which will be new to me; for I have never set foot in Germany. We shall find it an inexhaustible mine of useful and agreeable conversations. I cannot tell you how much pleasure I felt in reading your last letter to see your eagerness to examine and to understand everything before you, and your lamentations that you cannot be in two places at once, or prolong your visit. You know, too, what I think ought to be the turn of mind of a traveller. How rare it is, and how little can be done without it. I never believed that the scheme, of which we so often talked, of making our letters during your tour a sort of biography, could be realized. In a foreign country every instant has its demands. One must catch one's impressions flying, and record them without trying to reflect on them. That must be done afterwards. Pray attend, if you have time, to the municipal institutions of Prussia. Do not hurry back. You cannot be better employed as respects yourself, or as respects the world, than you are at present.

I am here on my return from Normandy, and shall probably remain till the 15th of December. I work seven hours a day and make little progress, for I feel that my second book will find the world and critics ready to pounce on it. I must therefore do my best. There is not a day when I do not feel your absence. A crowd of ideas remains undefined in my mind, from my inability to talk them over with you, and hear how you would oppose them, or observe the new form that they would assume if you admitted them. I pass a short portion of every day with three men, Pascal, Montesquieu, and

Rousseau ; I miss the presence of a fourth, and that is you. Although we often differ even upon serious points, there is so much resemblance in our general views and impressions, that your society always rouses and animates me. You alone have habitually this effect upon me, and this is the chief proof that I have of some remarkable or at least peculiar quality in you ; for most people leave me more or less cold, while you almost always excite me. Good-by. I leave you to resume my work. Besides I shall wait for your first letter from Germany, before I write to you at length.

Paris, December 26, 1836.

I received, two days ago, your letter No. 1. It suggested to me several ideas which I will not allow to vanish before I utter them. You return to the subject of the revolution of July. To speak freely, I fear lest politics should in the end cool our friendship, which I should consider as one of the greatest misfortunes that could happen to me. I am not afraid of such an event on my side, but on yours. When politics are in question you have an instinct independent of your reason, secretly forcing you to act and to feel without being under the control of your will. It is on this rock that I fear the shipwreck of our intimacy ; for though we sympathize in many things, we are separated on one that is important, and that time will render of still more consequence ; this cannot be denied. Every day I deplore the events of July ; on this we are agreed. I should see without much regret the restoration which you think essential. Here our minds diverge. You believe that we ought from this instant to endeavor at any risk to bring about this restoration by every honest means. I do not think so. At present I see no chance of a restoration except by foreign aid. If the restoration were effected in that or in any other way, by force and against the wish of the majority of the nation, I see no chance of its lasting; nor do I think that it would be able or willing to establish amongst us certain liberal principles to which I attach as much importance as to the restoration itself.

You see things in a different light, and you think and act accordingly. But you must feel that such being my sincere impression I cannot conscientiously assist in the overthrow of the existing government. I shall never ask a favor from it, I shall oppose its encroachments all my life; but I cannot wish to upset it till I am convinced that I have found some good and permanent substitute. This is the gulf between us. I am sure that your reason will appreciate the train of ideas that I have suggested, even though you may think that I am mistaken. I am confident, too, that you will always think me sincere ; but as I said in the beginning of my letter, I fear your instinct ; I feel impelled to caution you. If ever I imagined that in consequence of some difference of opinion you would change towards me in any way, I should grieve deeply. For in our friendship there is an element that nothing could replace, that coldness would kill ; it is a pure, free, fine, and manly feeling, and it has always elevated us. — If once it were to become an ordinary friendship, a mere habit, the charm would disappear. Let us therefore struggle with all our might against the common enemy, the only enemy whom we have to fear — political difference on the points that I have just considered.

I turn now to the other subjects in your letter. All that you tell me of the centralizing, pedantic tendency of European democracy seems to me to be perfectly true.

But after fully developing your ideas, you add that on these points we are *nearly* agreed; that is not saying enough. Those ideas are interwoven with my life, they occupy my mind every day and every moment in the day. To show men if possible how in a democracy they may avoid submitting to tyranny, or sinking into imbecility, is the theme of my book, and the attempt will be repeated in every page of that which I am now writing. To labor for such an object is, in my mind, a sacred calling, in which one must grudge neither one's money, one's time, nor one's life.

I am as great a partisan as you are of public education, and for the same reasons; and I much wish you to examine the subject in Prussia, where the system is said to be better than elsewhere. My curiosity is at present excited principally on these points: 1. Is the law obliging parents to send their children to school still in force? what are its effects and how is it applied? 2. What part do the local authorities take in education? Do the schools excite any local interest? By what means has the public been induced to take an interest in education? 3. Is there any intermediary instruction between the primary and principal education? 4. Is the chief education given in schools, or in universities?

Good-by — Marie desires to be remembered to you. Scarcely a day passes without our talking of you.

Paris, January 26, 1837.

Your letter, No. 2, which I received four or five days ago, gave me even more pleasure than your former ones. I read attentively, over and over, what you say upon the means of preventing our political opinions from jarring with our friendship. I have often had the same thoughts,

but you make them clearer to my mind than they ever
were before. I think with you that the past is a guaran-
tee for the future, and that we shall achieve the difficult
task of uniting entire independence to perfect intimacy.
Few men could do this, but experience shows that we
differ from most men. And we have one great safeguard
— differing as to the means, we agree as to the ends of
government. Our minds are like two lines, that however
long asunder, always find some points of meeting. To
finish the subject, I must tell you once for all, that there
is nothing in the world that I hold so precious as your
friendship. For me it is a never-failing source of energy
and high-mindedness, of elevated feeling and generous
resolution ; it is a world in itself, perhaps an ideal world,
but still a resting-place to which I escape, not from indo-
lence, but like a weary man, who stops for an instant to
recover strength, that he may be more active in the
fight. If ever it cooled or died, I should begin to doubt
of myself and of all that is good.

February 1*st.* — I was forced to leave off here by an
attack of influenza, which made me lose four days in bed.
I am up again, but very weak, and my head not in a
state to add much to this letter. At the end of yours,
however, is an observation which I must answer. You
ask me, if in America and England I find the same
prudery and affectation which so justly disgust you in
Berlin. Yes; and especially in England, where it is
easier to enter a woman's bedroom in order to make love
to her than for any other purpose. Still I must say, that
in those two countries, where the affectation of virtue
and propriety is carried by women to an absurd extent,
there is more real virtue than with us. Is this the case
in Berlin ? The discovery of this good result made me

indulgent towards the accompanying evil, though I naturally have not much indulgence in the matter, and at last I thought that all that external and conventional parade of propriety was, perhaps, to female virtue, what an established worship is to religion — a form which powerful minds, whether for good or for evil, break through, but which serves as a protecting barrier to the weak and ordinary. So I thought that all the pretence of modesty, and rules of affected delicacy, which are unnecessary for a really virtuous woman, may perhaps be of use to the majority. As to your remark upon Protestantism, I am much inclined to share your opinion. But it is a subject that one cannot discuss fasting as I am. . . .

Tocqueville, June 11, 1837.

Up to this time, dear friend, my journey has been a melancholy one. I had scarcely arrived, when I was seized by one of those frightful attacks of neuralgia in the stomach with which you are familiar. I had been free from them for nineteen months; but this attack has been so bad that it may count for two. It has left me in such a state of weakness and discomfort, that I can neither walk nor write long at a time, and I am condemned to idleness and dreaming, two things which, as you know, do not suit me at all. Life becomes a burden. I am excited and worn out by my own imagination, and when I attempt to escape from this state, physical fatigue drives me back to it. It is sad to have a mind that cannot exist without taking violent remedies, such as intellectual labor, physical activity, or strong emotions. During the last twelve days, Marie and I have often regretted your absence; your society would be enough for us if we could only have it, for I can talk

to no one and listen to no one so well as to you. I
delight in thinking over our conversations of last winter.
I have never enjoyed your society so much nor so long,
as during the last few months in Paris. I cannot tell
you how I prize our friendship ; it is to me a source of
light, and strength, and high aspirations. I am always
repeating this, for I am always feeling it. When in our
childish days we were so united, I could not help fearing
lest age, and the so-called realities of life, might loosen
the ties that were so dear to me ; but I find that every
day they draw us closer.

•   Tocqueville, July 5, 1837.

My dear Louis, — Our good friend * * * asks you
for my opinion of Mademoiselle ———. Here is what
I know and what I think of her. She is the daughter
of a clever selfish man, and of a foolish bigoted mother.
However, I do not think that either would wish to tease
or to domineer over a son-in-law. The young lady is
not more than sixteen or seventeen. The outside is
charming, the inside commonplace.· She is shy, amiable, gentle, and dull. Such is the impression that she
has left on my mind. I do not think that as yet she has
more in her than the materials for a strictly correct
woman, without any higher qualities. She is, as I have
said, extremely pretty; she is fond of dress, in spite of
the dull retirement in which she lives, and from her
earliest years, I am told, has excelled in turning every
scrap of finery to the best account, both for herself and
her sisters. This is the only talent that I have ever
heard attributed to her, and joined with her small capacity, it will probably cause her to turn into a very
pretty and equally insignificant little creature. . . .
I own, that to me, her family would also be a great

obstacle. An atmosphere of commonplace pervades the whole house. * * * has escaped from it by his resemblance to his father, who, together with his feebleness, has given to him his pure and earnest heart. In all the rest of the family, the influence of * * * predominates. They have the virtues of the middle class, combined with the narrowest possible range of ideas, and are quite free from all aristocratical extravagances, such as the love of one's country, and enthusiasm for bold and brilliant actions.

These are exactly my impressions. It is hard to form a final opinion on so young a girl. She may be, to a certain extent, modified by the continual influence of a husband. Still I should never recommend a young man of the character of * * * to undertake the task of such an education; and I cannot help thinking with pain, of the way in which marriages are made in France. * * * is as likely to have such a wife as any other; for it is a great chance if, before he marries, he finds again a man who can give him as much information.

I am obliged to hurry away from you my dear Louis, for I must return to my work; I get on so slowly that I am out of patience. We are most anxious for your arrival; I cannot tell you how glad we shall be to see you. We shall have a better opportunity of enjoying each other's society, than we have had for the last ten years. I would have given a great deal, if you could have carried out your intention of spending six or eight months with us; such a long period of intimate companionship would have been an epoch in our lives; it would have closed our youth and launched us into maturity.

Tocqueville, September 4, 1837.

I have put off answering you because I am constantly expecting an afternoon of perfect leisure, which will enable me to communicate to you ideas and feelings which are crowding into my mind. I have waited in vain, and at last I have resigned myself to writing you a trifling letter, lest you should be too long without news of me.

The other day I met Madame —— at Caen; in the course of conversation I told her that I had just received from you a letter of ten pages, and that I hoped to answer it with one as long. She opened her eyes as wide as a park gate. She knew of our friendship, but a friendship producing letters of ten pages seemed to her to be supernatural. You would, I know, have been annoyed, you would have taken it for another proof that we live among those who do not understand us; but I laughed heartily. I should be sorry to be too well understood by such people, though they are highly respectable in their way, for it would prove that I am more like them than I care to be. I never quite enter into your displeasure when people whom you love and esteem misunderstand you. It gives me some pain, but not the pain which it gives to you; and the pain rather excites than depresses me. It makes me eager to justify my eccentricities by success, which is the only valid argument in such cases.

I cite myself, as I know myself; when I began to write, my family, it is true, encouraged me, but I relied little on that, for I thought them blinded by affection. One's relations are always in extremes, sometimes they are disposed to exaggerate one's merits, at others to make the most of one's faults. I was, therefore, not elated by the praise of my own family; the world thought of me just as it does of you. I passed for a poor eccentric young man, who, having no profession, wrote in order to kill time; at any rate, a respectable occupation, for it is better to write a bad book than to live in bad company.

I began surrounded by these difficulties. I remember well that they depressed, annoyed, and irritated me; but far from discouraging me, they kindled a fire within me. I felt that a man must either live quietly like other men, or show that he has in him something more than they have. Now that my book has obtained almost as much. success as I desired, I see that I am allowed to go my own way without interference. Why should you not attain the same exemption? for though I do not wish to compliment you, I feel that you are my superior.

I must repeat what I have often said to you. You exaggerate every difficulty: first, as to that of allying yourself to a family that will leave you free to follow your own tastes. Probably your new connections will not appreciate you, still they will be charmed by your studious habits, for it is better to write stupid books than to gamble. A father's first wish is that his daughter's husband should be steady, and with plenty of occupation. Of what sort? No matter whether he collects stones like * * * or ideas. What is wanted is, that he should not fold his arms and sit still.

Your second error is as to the difficulty of interesting your wife in your work, for I fancy that the sort of approbation which I have described would not satisfy you from her. Believe me, dear friend, you are mistaken. There are such women as you imagine, but many less than you suppose. On the contrary, I am amazed at the number of women, ordinary enough in other respects, whom I see taking a passionate and often exaggerated interest in the literary labors of their husbands. It is easily explained ; for fame of whatever kind is still fame, and the woman who bears your name is, at least, as much affected by it as yourself. You must think then that she would have a low opinion of you and your talents. But is this possible ? Is a wife often deceived on these points ? If in no other way, is she not enlightened upon them by what she hears, and by the opinions which her husband's friends have of him ? No one can be mistaken about you who has once heard you talk freely upon a serious subject. Madame de B—— who has just left us, told us, that in a long conversation which you had had with her husband, in her presence, she had been struck by your superiority, and that she could not believe that you were the " good fellow," she had heard of from the * * *. Your own wife could still less fail to receive a similar impression, for, however frivolous they may be, women soon discover the remarkable qualities of their husbands, and are generally willing to recognize a superiority in which they may almost be said to have a personal interest. Still I own that there are in the world some cold, silly, female fools, over whom one can have no influence, and who very likely would speak of their husbands as Madame —— did to me of Bonaparte, whom she saw frequently before his Italian campaigns : " I never knew such a tiresome man with his eternal politics ; so I always ran away when I saw him coming in." But these are exceptions.

P. S. Beaumont has brought back excellent materials

from Ireland. He has given me some curious details on England. It seems that there the democratic movement has stopped for the present. Though too late it is a great lesson for the continental aristocracies, who after placing themselves under the protection and guidance of the crown, are at this instant being hurried by that power to destruction; while the only aristocracy which has retained the management of its affairs and has dared to look the enemy in the face, still stands and will stand for some time longer.

Tocqueville, November 14, 1837.

I believe that I have already told you that, although I did not offer myself, a considerable number of the electors of the *arrondissement* of Valognes wished to propose me as deputy; the attempt has been made. My friends, who belonged to every shade in the opposition, failed, but by only a few votes; and on the whole I recollect the struggle with pleasure, on account of the ardor with which a portion of the people embraced my cause. A great tie, in consequence, unites us, and I shall return to this place hereafter with delight. In the course of the election, I was induced to publish a little pamphlet, which I send to you. In general our difference of opinion on an essential point, makes me avoid talking to you of my political occupations. But I must not leave you in ignorance of my important actions, and in my eyes the putting forth of this pamphlet is one.

As I was not elected, I am out of public life at least for several years. I am, I assure you, far from complaining of it. I shall quietly set to work again, and it will not be my fault, if you do not share my labors. You know that this has always been a dream of mine.

We yet have time, you see, to philosophize like two Greeks. . . .

I take, as you do, unceasing, and perhaps even more interest than I acknowledge to myself, in Lamoricière, whom I am inclined to think somewhat indifferent to every one of us, and only, and passionately, attached to his profession. He carries me away in spite of myself; and when I read the assault of Constantine, I fancied that I saw him standing alone on the top of the breach, and for an instant my whole soul was with him. I love him, too, for the sake of France : for I cannot help thinking that a great general is contained in that little man.

Baugy, March 21, 1838.

I have just received a letter from you ; but first I must answer the one that I carried away with me the other day.

Your letter is interesting, and on the whole I think that you are right. You would entirely satisfy me, if I were merely a reasonable being ; but I have within me powerful instincts, which your words cannot pacify. I own that it is unreasonable to long for a better fate than that of man. But such is my involuntary and irresistible impulse. There are some views of humanity so mean, that I feel contempt for the whole affair creeping over me in spite of myself. This impression would be unfortunate, if it were frequent, and, if it became permanent, would paralyze instead of stimulating my exertions. I should have too much to say on this subject, so as time passes, I turn to your second letter.

I reply to the first part of it by telling you, that during the last few days I have been reading the life of Mahomet and the Koran. The Koran is the most annoying and the most instructive of books; for, on looking closely, one sees all the threads by which the prophet held, and still holds, his votaries. It is a complete compendium of the art of prophecy, and I strongly advise you to read it. I cannot imagine, how ———— could say, that that book was an advance upon the gospel. In my opinion there is no comparison between them, and I think that reading it is enough to explain the difference between Mussulmans and Christians. The Koran seems to me to be no more than a clever compromise between materialism and spiritualism. Mahomet has opened the door to the coarsest passions of our nature, in order to introduce with them certain highly refined notions ; so that, one set balancing the other, human nature may hang tolerably suspended between heaven and earth.

This is the philosophical and disinterested part of the Koran ; as for the selfish part it is still more evident. The doctrine that "faith saves;" that "the first of religious duties is to believe blindly in the prophet;" that "the sacred war is the best of God's works;" and many other doctrines, of which the practical result is easily seen, are found in every page, and almost in every sentence in the Koran.

The violent and sensual tendencies of the Koran are so striking, that I cannot conceive their escaping the observation of a reasonable man. It is an advance on polytheism, inasmuch as it contains clearer and truer ideas of the Divine Being, and a more intelligible and wider analysis of certain duties common to man. But the passions which it excites have made it more mischievous to mankind than polytheism, which, having no unity in doctrine or priesthood, never had much hold over men, and left them considerable freedom of action ; whilst Mahom-

etanism has exercised over the human race an immense,
and on the whole a far from salutary influence. I should
like to say more about Mahometanism in particular, and
religion in general. But of late my head soon tires, and
forces me to think as little as possible on serious and en-
grossing topics. I stop, therefore, though with regret.
It makes me sad, to think of the long period of separation still before us : nearly two months. I feel the wish
and almost the necessity of conversing with you. I cannot understand why it should be impossible for you to
spend Easter-week with us. Neither society nor business engages people in our world at that period. Besides
the extreme pleasure it would give us to have you to en-
liven our solitude, we should have more leisure than we
have ever enjoyed to clear up some ideas of practical importance, which discussion only can render less obscure.
Come then, I pray.

Tocqueville, August 8, 1838.

I wish you to hear once more from me before you return, and I direct to Rennes as the safest place. . . . I
pass immediately, and, as we often do, without transition
from you to your antipodes, that is to Plato. Your view
of him seems to me to be admirable, because it exactly
coincides with my own. The epithet " puerile," which
you apply to the bearded old philosopher, especially
pleased me ; I smiled at it approvingly, for it is precisely
the appropriate adjective. There is, indeed, something
childish in the ideas, and still more in the arrangement,
sometimes methodical, and sometimes irregular peculiar
to Plato. But on several occasions he is more than man,
especially if one considers the time when he lived. On
the whole, I consider him a poor politician ; but as a
philosopher superior to any, and I admire his attempts to

introduce, as much as is possible, morality into politics. There is a high and spiritual aspiration about that man, which excites and elevates me. I think that it is to this more than to anything else that he owes his glorious immortality. For, after all, men in every age like to hear about their souls, though they seem to care only for their bodies. Adieu; I go back to work. We are looking forward to seeing you again.

Nacqueville, October 9, 1838.

I have lately been leading such an exciting and wandering life, dear friend, that I have not been able to answer your last letter. Yet I was much moved by it. Its expressions of attachment to me are very touching. Pray forgive me for having told you of my fears and doubts; my only excuse is the great value that I set upon our intimacy. Although I differ from you on several important points, still there is no mind to which I am so bound, or with which I have such real sympathy, as yours. Only with you can I give full vent to my highest instincts, which I am forced to control or to suppress in my habitual intercourse with men. With you I yield freely to every impulse of my head and of my heart. With you I can sift every idea and every feeling without fear of hurting either you or myself. With no one else is this the case, and the effect is delightful. It is the greatest and most manly enjoyment that I know. Nothing could pain me more than its loss. . . .

I must say that I approve and understand the urgent endeavors of your family to prevent your visit to Africa at the present moment. Such a journey would not be well-timed. But if you are not in Africa, why do you not write? You know how impatiently Marie and I long for news of you. . . .

. . . . I have already tried to resume my work, but I find great difficulties in satisfying myself. My ideas seem to flit before me like *tableaux vivans;* there is always some gauze before them which prevents my seeing them distinctly. I do not know if it be my fault, or that of my subject: probably, it is the fault of both. The subject is the concluding chapter, of which we have talked so much without coming to a decision. If any new thoughts occur to you about it, pray let me know. You are aware that I want an idea so general, that the mind of the reader, after going through the whole book, may rest on it; and yet so simple, as not to require a long development, which might exhaust an attention already fatigued. Perhaps in a few days I may write to you a very long letter on this subject; at present, I am too much in the dark to discuss it advantageously. I am sent for to ride, so good-by.

Algiers, May 23, 1841.

Thank you, dear friend, for your letter, which I received here ten days ago. I see that you expect much benefit for me from this journey. I hope so, too; but I doubt its lasting long enough to restore mind and body, both of which have been for some time in rather a poor way. I have but little to tell you of either. So as I have not much leisure, I will talk to you about Algiers. I am only beginning to see what are the questions connected with this country; but my view is a little clearer than it was in France. The situation is difficult and complicated; still I think that we should manage it if it were not for faults inherent in our character and in our institutions. But these faults, joined to the nature of the undertaking, will, perhaps, cause us to fail. The state of things is this.

We are every day gaining ground in the province of
Constantine, and we soon shall have turned out the
Turks, and established there a government somewhat
similar to theirs. In this there is nothing very glorious.
But there is reason to hope, that by holding the population of the interior in quiet and subjection, we may be
permitted to colonize the environs of Bona in peace.
However, I doubt whether the time has come to make
this attempt.

In the province of Algiers the enemy's marauders
chop off heads even as near as the hills above the town.
The plain of Mitidja is a desert. The colonists are
gone, and so are its old inhabitants, the Arabs. Still
Algiers is a large, and looks like a prosperous town.
The energy shown by the inhabitants in the midst of so
much danger and misery is surprising. There is evidently a higher and firmer tone of feeling here than in
France. All the province of Oran, and that of Tittery,
with the exception of those towns, is in the hands of the
Emir. From all that I hear, he is stronger in some
respects, and weaker in others, than formerly. His
government has acquired consistency and a better organization; more obedience is paid to him than was paid
to the Turks. Like them he has created a permanent
and regular army, which he instantly directs on a rebel-
lious tribe and crushes it. He uses hatred towards
Christians, the only feeling common to all Arabs, with
more skill than the Turks did. But it seems certain,
that the population, in spite of its fanaticism, is growing
tired of war, which destroys property and trade. We
may, therefore, hope that a war of "razzias," well managed, may in the end force Abd-el-Kader to ask for
peace, or may induce some of his tribes to desert him.

The provinces of Algiers and Oran would then resemble
that of Constantine, French dominion would be established with more or less security in the interior; a result
of little importance in itself, but which would render
possible the colonization of the environs of Algiers —
the real object of France. Our dominion here is only a
means.

There are two things which as yet I think I see
clearly. The first and most important is, that if we
allow a real Arab power to establish itself in the interior
of Africa, to organize itself, and every day to profit by
our example, to accustom more and more the tribes to
act together, and in case of a war between France and
a European nation, to be ready to receive from that
nation instruction, men, money, and arms; if we permit this, our African possessions will have no future
existence, colonization will be difficult, and the result
always precarious. Those who expect a permanent
peace with the Emir are mistaken. He cannot maintain
it if he would, for two reasons. I have said that the
only feeling which the tribes have in common, is fanaticism. His strength depends on his encouraging this
feeling, and he can do so only by war. In the second
place, all who are acquainted with Arabs are strongly
impressed by their cupidity, which is almost equal to
their fanaticism. A long peace would establish between
them and us relations so advantageous to them, that Abd-
el-Kader will never permit it to subsist, or if it should
last he would accompany it by commercial restrictions
that would destroy its usefulness. To destroy his rising
power is, therefore, what we must try to do and succeed
in doing.

The second point which seems to me clear is this, that

such success is not impossible, and is more easy now than it will be later. You must be aware that Abd-el-Kader does not rule over individuals, but over groups of individuals, whom we call tribes. Some of these can furnish 6,000 horsemen. Such a government, especially if you consider the wandering life of these tribes, is essentially difficult and precarious. You will feel this if you remember that each of these great tribes contains great aristocratic families, naturally as fit to take the command as that of Abd-el-Kader, who therefore submit to his dominion with impatience. I may say, however, by the way, that Abd-el-Kader is as active as a European king would be in diminishing this evil, by getting rid as fast as possible of these great families. On some pretext he has already cut off the heads of almost all the chiefs. I return to my system. A government of this kind is always difficult and precarious. We may hope that by flattering the vanity or stimulating the avarice of the chiefs of some of the powerful tribes, we may gain them over, or that by ravaging by war we may indispose them towards the Emir, and so bring about his fall. If this result, of which, for want of time, I have rudely sketched the means, be possible, it must be easier now that the power of Abd-el-Kader is only beginning than it will be when time shall have added to its strength. We ought then to continue our exertions, however painful, and to prosecute the war in every direction without giving the Arabs breathing time. As to the mode of making war on such people, I am beginning to have some clear ideas which I will explain to you at another time. To-day I will only say, that it has been proved to me that 6,000 infantry, even without artillery, might march all over the hostile country without fear; that they ought not to attempt any more great expeditions, but to go in every direction, now here and now there, as long as they have any provisions left, in order to surprise and astound the enemy ; and to show that destruction no longer follows straight lines and fixed plans, but falls unexpectedly everywhere.

Hitherto colonization has appeared to me to be easy, especially if protected by earthworks, and if we build fortified villages instead of solitary houses. It has been proved that a mere loop-holed wall is impregnable to the Arabs; they could never get over one of our Norman fences. At a little distance from Oran, I saw a fossé * nine feet wide, which Lamoricière made his troops dig in three months. It cost nothing, and is quite enough to insure perfect security within it. As for the soil, it is admirable, and only wants hands. When I have studied the subject further, I will tell you how I think that labor might be attracted and kept here.

I saw Lamoricière for two days at Mostaganem, just as he was starting with the army for Tagdempt. . . . He is already the first man in the country ; he succeeds here admirably ; he has the confidence of his soldiers, and at the same time satisfies the people. His system of *razzias* is excellent. His professional talents seem to me to increase.

Here is a letter, as in old times ; let me have an answer as in old times ; that is to say, of interminable length, and let me have it quickly. Why do we write less to each other ? and yet our attachment is as great as ever. As for me, experience of the world and of

* A " fossé " is a mound, from four to eight or nine feet wide, and about four or five feet high, generally raised round a farm in Normandy, and planted. — TR.

public affairs makes me turn every day more and more to you; and when I search my heart I find that on the whole I am more really bound to you, and that I set a higher value on your friendship than I did even twenty years ago. Chance united us: the more I see of other men the more I feel that our intimacy ought to have been the result of choice.

Good-by, write to me at Algiers; I intend to leave it for a short time for a tour in Constantine, which is open to us, and where one sees the Arabs at home. Try to put all sorts of questions to me in your letter, that my mind may be set to work.

Tocqueville, October 25, 1841.

Time goes on, my dear friend, and yet I do not hear that you are preparing to join us. Till now I have not regretted your absence, because we have had friends constantly with us or have been interrupted by visits; but at last, thank God, we are on the point of being alone. This is when I like to have you, the only time when we can really enjoy each other's society. Pray then come, if you can. You would give us real and great pleasure. Such a meeting is as useful as it is agreeable; for in Paris, though we see each other we have no intimate communion, and for myself, I shall always consider it essential to renew every year our valuable habit of close companionship. It is still more necessary now that I am about to enter the political arena. Your mind, in fact, is the only one on which I rely, and that has a real influence over mine. Many others have some effect on my actions, but none has the influence possessed by you over the ruling opinions and principles of which they are the result. It is when laying this first foundation of my conduct that I often want to consult you, especially in the moment of calm and reflection that precedes the struggle. I then feel the necessity of reviewing with you the chief principles which ought to guide me in the details of practice. Experience teaches me that in this world success and greatness depend much more on a good choice of these general principles, than on the skill with which you every day solve the petty problems of life.

I have passed a very pleasant summer. I have not been so happy for many years. I have enjoyed something which, if not contentment, is at least very like it. Will it last, or will it be lost in the political excitement of Paris? I shall not know till I try. You know with what incurable folly men attribute to reason a state of mind which is the accidental result of health, of place, of opportunities, of a thousand causes, which, forming no part of their being, must and will change. I hesitate, therefore, to attribute the comparative peace and contentment which I have enjoyed for the last few months to any real change in my views of life; and yet it does seem to me as if these views were somewhat modified.

I expect less from life. I aspire less. This is what I think that I have gained. Domestic happiness seems to me more desirable than formerly, and public applause and power less essential than till now I had thought them. I contemplate more calmly the possibility of passing my life like the ordinary run of mortals; and I no longer resist as intolerable the idea that I shall have no exalted destiny. In short, my desires, as far as I can see, are more moderate, and I have become more patient; what can be the cause? This is what, as yet, I cannot quite make out, and consequently I tremble for the future.

What can have curbed the ambition which, though peculiar, was so strong and so boundless? As I said before,
I cannot yet tell, and time alone will teach me. Is it
that this violent ambition has subsided on meeting the
obstacles presented by my own character and by external
circumstances? I think so. These obstacles are, in fact,
very great; perhaps insurmountable. The impossibility
of attaining anything satisfactory is evident. Is this the
reason of my tranquillity, and will this tranquillity follow
me into action? Not in the measure that I now enjoy it.
But, though I may not be calm, it would be a great gain
to be, at least, less excitable. To this I confine my hopes
for the winter. In the mean-while I experience a singular
phenomenon, of which I leave the explanation to your
perspicacity. As life appears to me less noble and less
valuable, I am better pleased to live. . . .

Tocqueville, August 23, 1842.

I received your letter this morning, dear friend, and I
hasten to give you a line in reply. I hold * * * to be
an excellent fellow and a very honorable man. His
family is good. As he is obliged to work for his bread,
he is forced to fill rather an inferior position. I quite
believe, that whenever he may have an opportunity of
associating with such men as you are, he anxiously seizes
upon it. He has, besides, great vivacity in conversation:
there is even a sort of irritability in his manner. All
this is sufficient, without any other cause, to explain his
eagerness to make himself agreeable to you, and to cultivate your society. It is not impossible, too, that, without
entertaining any profound and Machiavellian plot for getting at your thoughts, he may be charmed to profit by
your reflections on the subject which at present occupies

him. This may be one motive of his conduct, but it is not the only one. Rest assured, however, that this motive is common to all men who turn ideas to account by making books or speeches. Above all, it is irresistible to newspaper writers, who, forced for three parts of their time to write without having leisure to think, steal ideas ready-made wherever they find them. . . .

With regard to the talents of the man whom we are talking of, this is what I think : I believe his mind to be superficial and shallow, and therefore his opinions on a subject that you have studied would have little influence over me. Besides these natural defects, he has acquired others, proceeding from the period when he first entered society, and from the nature of his studies. He belongs, it must be acknowledged, to the crowd of pigmies who, coming after revolutions, imagine that manliness and profound thought are exhibited by a contempt for all political questions and passions, by seeing nothing very serious in the things which so much excited their fathers, fancying that they are nearer to Voltaire because they hold up his train. * * * certainly has this weakness, he even puts it on, thinking it becoming; and this is what at first made me take a dislike to him. But on nearer acquaintance, I found that his heart was worth more than his head; and that the principles which regulate his actions are safer and more upright than those that govern his pen and his tongue. . . .

Tocqueville, October 25, 1842.

I have not written to you during the six weeks that I have spent here ; and, indeed, I should not have had much to tell you. I have been leading a wandering and barren life — barren, at least, as regards ideas, still I hope that I have not wasted my time. Just now it is not by political

speeches or actions that one secures constituents; but by
making personal friends of them.   It is a vicious system
I own, but may be used for good purposes.   It is only
by submitting to this species of slavery that one obtains
liberty in great things.   However, I have just gone
through it, not without fatigue, but without being disgusted.   I have learnt to find pleasure in my relations
with these men, whom I sought at first from political motives; I now feel for many of them sincere regard and
esteem.   Personal contact with this class shows me that
the country is worth more than its rulers.

A few days ago I returned home.   I ought to be happy
and contented; I am uneasy and anxious.   For what
reason?   It is not easy to say; for after all I am not to
be pitied.   I possess as much domestic happiness as ever
falls to the lot of man; and as to external goods, I am
not worse off than my neighbors.   Yet I am habitually
gloomy and irritable.   I attribute this wearisome unproductive state of mind, sometimes to one cause, and sometimes to another.   But I believe, that in truth, there is
but one, and that is deep and lasting — dissatisfaction with
myself.   You know that there are two distinct species of
pride, or rather pride takes two forms, one grave and the
other gay.   There is a pride that revels in the advantages
that it enjoys, or thinks that it enjoys.   This is called
conceit.   As it pleased God to give me a large dose of
the vice of pride, he might at least have let me have this
kind.   But my pride is of a quite opposite nature.   It is
always uneasy and discontented; not, however, envious,
but gloomy and melancholy.   Every instant it is remind-
ing me of the faculties that I want, and driving me into
despair at not possessing them.   The fact is, that my
abilities, if I have any, are not those which are specially

wanted in such a career as mine; and those that I have not are precisely those which would be of every-day use to me; prompt conception, ease in execution, a clear perception of details, calmness, &c. I might add many others, if I wished to paint my portrait as it is constantly rising before my eyes; but it is unnecessary to the man in the whole world who knows me best. . . .

Did you ever read the History of England after the Revolution of 1688? I am at this moment studying it, and I find it very attractive, although Smollett is the sorriest writer that ever cumbered the ground. I own that this history inclines me to think that we often judge our own country and our own times with excessive severity. We often imagine as peculiar to ourselves and to our age, certain errors, weaknesses, and vices, which are caused by the form of our institutions, and by their special action on the corrupt side of human nature. The part played by selfish venal passions, the want of principle, the veering about of opinions, the degradation and the almost universal corruption of public men, in this History of Constitutional England, are enormous. The power of personal intrigues, the littleness and deformity of the passions that flourish in tranquil times, when the occasions that evolve great exertions and great characters no longer occur, are infinite. When one enters into these details, one can hardly believe, that at the time when all this meanness and vice were prevalent, or rather were allowed full play by free institutions, the nation began and carried through the great deeds with which it astonished the world in this century. It is striking in this history to see to what an extent quarrelling and passionate discussion belong to the very essence of a free country. The consequence is, that when no occasion is afforded for a grand debate, they squabble about nothing, and torment themselves to find some subject of disagreement and discussion. . . . There are more than ten periods in the history of the last century in England which afford this spectacle. I should be curious to have your opinion on this book. Among. other things you would see some curious points of resemblance between the times immediately following the Revolution of 1688 and our own; with this distinguishing feature, however, that as the Revolution of 1688 restored England to her natural allies and to her proper position among nations, the appearance which she presented to foreign countries immediately became more important. With us since 1830, the contrary has taken place, and for opposite reasons.

Enough of politics and history. What are you about? You have given up too much the habit of writing to me. I know that it is very difficult to write satisfactory letters at long intervals, but still it is better than silence. . . . Have you passed all the time since I saw you at Fosseuse? and have you done more than attend to your own affairs? I believe not; and I fear, that to induce you to do anything else with animation and perseverance, you require nothing less than the shock of some great public event, of another revolution, or of some similar disturbance. In the mental temperament that one knows best, there are secrets which one cannot penetrate, in spite of all one's efforts. I am sure, that during three parts of my time I am in a state of intellectual excitement that you cannot understand; and, in the same way, the slumber of your intelligence for the last few years is a problem which I cannot solve. That with such a mind as yours, you should not be determined to prove, at least to

yourself, by some great work, your own capacity; and
that as you have no political career, you should not try
your powers in the only arena open: this is so mysterious to me, that I give up the attempt to throw any light
upon it, or even to speak of it; for, as I said just now,
even to those who know and love each other best, there
are certain instincts and feelings, so peculiar to the possessor, that words are worth nothing in expressing or in
arguing against them. Language, which is adapted only
to the ordinary wants of men, in such cases tells nothing.
There is no one who, on some subjects, does not share
the fate of the deaf and dumb.

. . . . Contrive to pass a week with us, that we may
at least once a year communicate freely with each other.
Let us not allow public or private business, absence or
age, to freeze up our sympathies.

Tocqueville, October 19, 1843.

You are quite right in what you say of my disposition.
It is true that from a momentary impulse I am capable
of the most inconsistent behavior, and of suddenly turning away from the road which was leading me to the
object of my most passionate desires. Many people do
not understand me, and I am not surprised; for I do not
understand myself. There are two opposite elements in
my nature; but how have they become united? I know
not. I am the most impressionable of men in my every-
day actions, the most easily drawn to the right or to the
left, and at the same time the most obstinate in my aims.
I am constantly oscillating, and yet never lose my equi-
librium. All the principal objects that I have proposed
to myself in life I have pursued, and with unceasing and
often painful endeavors. I have preserved all my affec-

tions.   There is some inflexible principle which governs my versatile and excitable nature; I cannot understand it in the least myself, and therefore I have no right to blame another for not being able to explain it.

However interesting this subject may be to me, I must quit it, for my time is limited, and there is something about which I want to talk to you. . . .

Clairoix,* near Compiègne.

. . . . I am delighted to hear that the politicians whom you meet share in general your opinions on the affairs of Germany.†   Two days ago I saw in Paris a distinguished Englishman, Mr. Senior, who has just returned from Germany.   I talked with him, and was glad to find that his impressions on the state of Prussia resembled yours; at least I thought so.   This proves to me that you are in the right, and increases my wish that you would make up your mind some day to write about the country with which you are so well acquainted.   If you should do so, I would give you this advice.   The difficulty would lie in drawing a picture intelligible to a French reader of a state of society and of mind so different, not only from our own, but from what our experience of ourselves would lead us to imagine.   The prejudices arising from what we see at home, and from what our history tells us, stand in our way more than our ignorance.   Unfortunately I can give you no advice on this point, except to recall constantly your own earlier impressions, asking yourself what you expected to find in Germany before you studied the country, trying to retrace the path which led you from your preconceived

---

* A country-house then occupied by his father.

† Louis de Kergorlay was then in Germany.

notions to your matured opinions, and to induce your readers to follow in your footsteps.

I am sure that this is the object that you should propose to yourself; but by what means will you be able to attain it? The author alone can judge in this matter. Should you explain the resemblance and the difference between the two countries, or write so as to enable the reader to find them out? I cannot tell. In my work on America, I have almost always adopted the latter plan. Though I seldom mentioned France, I did not write a page without thinking of her, and placing her as it were before me. And what I especially tried to draw out, and to explain in the United States, was not the whole condition of that foreign society, but the points in which it differs from our own, or resembles us. It is always by noticing likenesses or contrasts that I succeeded in giving an interesting and accurate description of the New World. I do not quote this as an example to be followed, but as a useful piece of information. I believe that this perpetual silent reference to France was a principal cause of the book's success.

On the subject of religious enthusiasm you put me a question which I think insoluble, except upon general and fixed principles. To me it is incontrovertible that political liberty has sometimes deadened and sometimes animated religious feeling. That has depended on many circumstances: on the nature of the religion itself, and of the age attained, at the moment when they came in contact, by the two passions, religious and political. For passions, like everything else in the world, have their periods of growth, maturity, and decline. If religious excitement be in its decline, and political excitement just beginning, the latter passion will extinguish the former. These causes and many others that I do not mention may help to explain the great diversities, according to time and place, observable on these subjects. If, however, setting aside particular cases, one seeks to discover the truth most generally applicable, I should be more inclined to share the opinion of your German friends than your own. I believe that, as a general principle, political freedom rather increases than diminishes religious feeling. There is a greater family likeness than is supposed between the two passions. Both have in view universal, and, on the whole, immaterial blessings; both aim at a certain ideal perfection of the human race, the contemplation of which lifts the mind above the consideration of petty personal interests. For my part, I can more easily understand a man full of both religious and political fervor, than I can one possessed at the same time by the love of liberty and of material comfort. The two first may exist side by side, and unite in the same heart; but not the other two. There is another reason, less comprehensive and less high-sounding, but perhaps in fact more efficient, which makes these passions coexist and excite one another. It is that they often help one another. Free institutions are often the natural and sometimes the indispensable instrument of religious enthusiasm. Almost every effort made by the moderns towards liberty has been occasioned by the desire to manifest or to defend their religious convictions.

Religion drove the Puritans to America; and when there, made them insist on governing themselves. The object of the two English revolutions was to acquire liberty of conscience. The same necessity inclined in France the Huguenot nobility of the sixteenth century

towards republican ideas. Religious excitement on all
these occasions produced political excitement, and political passions in turn helped to develop religion. If religious convictions met with no obstacle, this effect would
probably not be produced. But they almost always do.
When they have obtained all that they wanted, this effect
may again cease. Your theory may be applicable to a
society which is religious without being agitated by con-
troversy or fanaticism. It is possible that public affairs
may then gradually and almost entirely absorb the attention of society: and yet I do not feel certain of this, unless politics happened to be in a very interesting state.
It is more likely that the excitement of mind created and
sustained by political liberty will stir up all the religious
elements remaining in the country.

This seems to me to be what is going on in America.
Time and prosperity have there deprived the religious
element of three fourths of its original power. Still what
remains is in vehement agitation. The religious world
in the United States assemble, speak and act together
more than anywhere else. I think that the habits induced by political freedom, and the impulse given by it
to everything, count for a great deal in the religious fer-
ment still observable in the country. I think that, though
they cannot restore its former omnipotence, these circumstances maintain its influence and are the causes of all its
present strength.

We must be careful not to confound political liberty
with certain effects that it sometimes produces. When
once it is well established and undisturbed in its exercise
it inclines men to enjoy luxury, to desire and labor to acquire wealth; and these tastes, wants, and cares kill religious enthusiasm. But these tardy and secondary results

of liberty deaden political passions as much as they do religious ones.

This is all that I had to say on this particular point; which, however, I am far from having examined with all the care that its importance deserves. The only universal truth that I see in the matter is, that there is no universal truth. I therefore conclude that the wise plan is to examine particular cases.

You tell me at the end of your letter, that our correspondence is no longer either so frequent or so full as it used to be. I have made the same remark. But though I am sorry for it, I do not allow it to distress me too much, because I think I see clearly that it is not caused by any change in our mutual sentiments. When I consider my attachment for you, our friendship seems to me as firm and as close as ever. Some of the enthusiasm of early youth has gone from it, but it has acquired a steadfastness, resulting from experience of life and of men, which could not formerly belong to it. The longer I have lived, and the nearer I have seen the political world, the more I have felt that I could place absolute reliance on you; for your mind is incapable of admitting the petty passions which in the long run loosen the ties of all ordinary friendships. Therefore, I may say, that I set as high, and indeed a much higher value upon our intimacy than ever, and I believe that you feel as I do. And now, why do we less often desire to pour out our hearts to each other? For two reasons: the actual business in which our lives are spent leaves us less time and less interest for the long discussions which almost always turned upon some general question; and still more the difference of our occupations. . . . Still, I agree with you, we must try to resist these influences. . . .

July 22, 1852.

I do not like to answer your wife's letter, dear friend, without adding a line for you. I can write nothing amusing, however, for to-day I am very sad. I have just heard of the death of our excellent friend, Stoffels! Although his death had been long foreseen, and the last letters left in doubt only the exact hour, the news has deeply agitated and distressed me. What a character was his! What a high moral tone he preserved in the narrow circle to which his life was confined. He is the first intimate friend whom I have lost, and though the separation was foretold it is no less bitter! . . . . and what will become of his family? I know none more estimable and interesting. Happily his children have inherited his great qualities. . . I cannot describe to you the gloom that this event has shed over me, nor the melancholy reflections that occur to me on youth that has passed away so quickly, on old age which is approaching, and on the sad destiny of man.

Since I have been here I have set seriously to work on the book that I mentioned to you. One or two chapters are sketched already. I am most anxious to know if it is worth anything. I have not begun by what ought to be the beginning of the book. I took it up at the part to which the notes that I made in Paris chiefly referred, and which I was most inclined to write. For the difficulty is to warm to one's work, and for this purpose one must begin with what one most fancies. The part that I have written is a description of the state of things before the eighteenth Brumaire, and of the moral causes of that *coup d'état.* . . . A great question which has often occurred to me, fell in my way: what material advantages did the people derive from the Revolution? In other words, at what should we estimate the value of the confiscated estates that were abandoned to them, of the feudal rights that were abolished, of the galling and oppressive taxes that were removed, and lastly, of the debts and rents that were fictitiously paid by means of assignments. . . . If you have ever turned your mind to these questions let me know what you think of them. To act in concert will stimulate our minds. If we do not profit by the years still remaining to us, while our intellects are in their prime, we shall have wasted, if not a treasure, still a capital of which we were intended to make a better use.

P. S. Just now I am annoyed by having to oppose my nomination to the *Conseil général.* I have more difficulty in avoiding it than most people have in obtaining it.

St. Cyr, near Tours, Sept. 9, 1853.

I write you a line, dear friend, to say that if it is the same to you, to make your little excursion in the beginning of October, instead of the latter end of September, I should prefer it. I am leaving home on a visit to the Beaumonts.

You have greatly encouraged me about my book. You always were, and still are, the man of all others most capable of understanding my undeveloped ideas, and of helping me to bring them out ; there is something in the contact with your mind, which makes mine fruitful. The two fit in somehow, and when pursuing the same idea, they keep step wonderfully. These conversations unfortunately have become very rare. You have such a variety of business, that naturally your thoughts are no longer disengaged, and you have lost the intense fondness for discussion that I used to notice in you in our youth. You are as much interested as ever in the friend, but not in the subject. It is sad that during the whole course of our life we have never been able to join in the same pursuits. When I was writing my first book, you were absorbed by politics. When your time and thoughts became free, I was buried in public affairs. And now that I am driven back to a life of conversation and reflection, you are absorbed in the necessary business of private life. Such has been our history during the last thirty years. It is a great pity; I think that each of us might have done better if we had been occupied at the same time with the same things.

Bonn, July 2, 1854.

I think I remember your telling me that you had met in the North of Germany a very great man, one of the nobles of Mecklenburgh, an old friend of your family, who had been very hospitable to you, and to whom you could introduce me. I forgot to mention the subject again to you when I passed through Paris, although I should have liked to make such an acquaintance. But since I have been in Germany, I attach still more im- portance to it. One of my principal studies, as you know, is the old system of Germany. I now find that there is nothing so difficult as to form a clear idea of it; the traces are entirely swept away in a great part of the country, and they are half effaced in the rest. To un- derstand it thoroughly, and perhaps to form a more accurate idea even of France one hundred years ago, it seems to me to be necessary to visit that portion of Germany where the institutions of the Middle Ages have not been entirely destroyed, and where they have left many vestiges in the customs, manners, society, and political economy of the country.   From all that I hear, the old kingdom of Prussia and Mecklenburgh are the most remarkable in this respect.   But as I especially wish to collect information from the old nobility and the peasantry, what would be most useful to me would be to visit for a few days a country-house.   Do you think that either directly or indirectly you could enable me to do any of these things? . . . .

We met with no accident on our journey.   In Belgium I saw Lamoricière, who talked to me of you, with real friendship.   I also saw Bédeau.   These visits pleased and distressed me for several days.   It is, indeed, melancholy to see such men, still so full of vigor, reduced to look on from afar while others act. Such is fate!

If I were to return to-day to France, and to be asked my impressions of this country, I should not have a word to answer.   I begin to have a glimmering of the state of ancient Germany, but as to modern Germany, I know nothing about it, I have lived so exclusively in the past.   I hope at last to come to my contemporaries, but at present I live only with their grandfathers.

Tocqueville, July 29, 1856.

I ought to have thanked you sooner for your letter, for it gave me great pleasure.   I consider you to be one of the very best literary judges that I know.   I even think it a sort of a phenomenon, that a man so full of ideas as you are, and whose ideas are often so profound and original, whom I should select among a thousand for these qualities — that this man, I say, should never have attempted a work that would mark his place and his name among his contemporaries and for posterity.

You have certainly one of the most remarkable minds that I have ever met with. Experience has only confirmed the opinion of my youth. Where then is the invisible spot, the hidden weakness, which has prevented such incontestable superiority from producing its natural fruits? No question has ever perplexed me so much as this. I have never been able to answer it to my own satisfaction. My wife and I, for she shares my opinion of you, have often discussed it, but always in vain. God has endowed you with great and rare abilities. By what strange inconsistency has he denied you the means, or rather the will, to make use of them, and to make the world appreciate what is so obvious to a few chosen spirits? Nothing is more astonishing.

You have drawn me from my book.* I return to it. I repeat that your opinion of it charmed me. Both before and after your letter I received numerous proofs of sympathy; but your judgment remains in my mind as the most solid basis of my satisfaction. I was so saturated with the facts and ideas contained in my book, that its originality had completely faded away. It struck you as well as others. I am delighted. I am also glad that you say that my style has become more simple. I have tried hard for it, but the effort did not always tend to simplicity, and I much feared that I had missed my object. I endeavored to be myself, and to imitate no one in particular; not even any of the greatest writers. I hope that in this I have succeeded. I shall be grateful if, when you are at leisure, you will mark in your copy the errors that you mention, that I may correct them in the next edition. The present edition will soon be sold. My editor tells me that the

* "L'Ancien Régime et la Revolution."

book is going off at an extraordinary rate. Almost all the papers have noticed it at length. Some praise and others blame; none speak of it with moderation. If I can believe the letters that I receive, my success has surpassed my expectations. But I am too well acquainted with my time and my country to exaggerate the value of my success. We have ceased to be what we were in a remarkable degree during two centuries — a literary nation. Still more important is the fact that power is now in different hands. The influential classes are no longer those who read. Whatever, therefore, may be the success of a book, it does not powerfully affect the public mind; nor can the writer hope to attract attention for any length of time, or indeed, ever to obtain that of the majority. Still, as even among the nations that read least, certain ideas, often indeed very abstract ideas, in the end govern society, it may be of some use to disseminate them. Besides, I do not see, in our day, any more honorable or more agreeable mode of employing one's time than in writing true and honest words that may draw the attention of the civilized 'world to their author, and serve, however humbly, the good cause.

We have been very well since our arrival; this place has rested and calmed us. It often reminds us of you; for we have spent here with you some of the happy days of our youth. Alas! will those days never return? and shall we never again be together for some time in the perfect quiet of the country, discussing all sorts of subjects, and stimulating each other to good thoughts and deeds?

Tocqueville, Aug. 28, 1856.

. . . . Of all the letters I have received since the publication of my book, from friends and also from strangers, almost enough to fill a volume, yours is incontestably the most striking as well as the most useful. I cannot sufficiently urge you to complete your criticism, and to amplify it as much as possible. You will thus render me an important service; for, thrown back, as I am, upon a literary life, I have more reasons than ever for attaining in it the highest eminence that I can. I was surprised at your finding on a first perusal so many errors as your first letter seemed to indicate; for though the book was written eagerly, in only two months, and without any interruption, I took, before I published it, great pains with the arrangement, and I attended very closely to the style. I was glad to see that the faults seemed to you fewer on the second reading than at first.

But now your criticism soars higher, and reaches what may be called the substance of the style, a matter which escapes the vulgar eye, and that all the grammatical talent in the world cannot discover. I was especially struck by the part of your letter relating to this. I have always had a vague suspicion of the defect that you point out : the inclination to include every shade of an idea in the same sentence, so that, in the endeavor to explain and to draw conclusions from the original thought, it is weakened, and the reader obtains a general impression, but not a distinct image. But no one has ever set this defect clearly before me; and indeed it belongs to those of which the inconvenience is felt without the cause being ascertained. You not only clearly mark it, but you offer to prove it by giving perspicuity to some of my sentences by suppressing portions of them. . . . You will do me a great service. By showing me examples of my fault, you will have done much to cure me of it ; for, as I said before, I know that I am subject to it. I know that between my style and that of the great writers there is some hitch that I must get over before I can take my place among them. But I seem to stumble against this impediment in the dark, without making out either exactly in what it consists or its extent, and, above all, without knowing how to overcome it.

It is, I think, in general, the result of the final touches. The first mould is often in a much better shape than that which the thought receives upon reflection. But the idea itself gains by reconsideration and trituration, by being taken up and laid down again, and looked at on all sides. Experience has taught me that thus it often acquires its real value. The difficulty is to combine freshness of expression with ripeness of thought. I know not if I shall ever attain it. It would be a great gain if I could only see clearly the means. As soon as you have written all your remarks on your copy, and added all the notes that may assist me in seizing your idea, send the whole back to me.

Tocqueville, Sept. 21, 1856.

The book which you announced has not arrived. I am impatient for it, though I am no longer in immediate want of it. The first edition being exhausted, and the demand continuing, the bookseller proposes to publish immediately a second edition of 2,000 copies, to be a reproduction of the first, with a few verbal corrections. I have consented, and it is already in hand. Michel Lévy hopes that we shall have to issue a third edition next summer. Before that comes out I shall have time to reconsider the subject, and remodel the whole work.

I shall employ your annotated volume for this purpose. Even now, I shall study it with the greatest interest. I shall seek in it, not so much the faults of the last book as the means of improving the next. I think that it is possible, during a whole life, to advance nearer and nearer to perfection. There is no more important maxim. Many eminent men make the contrary opinion an excuse for not becoming still more eminent. Above all, I am convinced that one may gradually eliminate all the faults that one *sees*. The real difficulty is in seeing them, and especially in seeing the way to attack them. Whenever I am pleased with my own performance, my satisfaction is mixed with uneasiness, as I know that it is a proof, not that I have reached perfection, but that I no longer see opening out beyond what I have done, new paths towards it. What is still worse, and happens to me still oftener, is to feel that I might do better, and yet not to see clearly what that better ought to be. . . .

Paris, Nov. 10, 1856.

. . . . The X * * * have been here for the last fortnight. They will stay ten days longer. We should have been very glad, for many reasons, to see you before they go. Your presence would have been agreeable, and also useful. These poor people are an example of one of the saddest of human miseries. They both are good-natured, refined, and full of high feeling ; but they are becoming unfit for one another, because each insists on finding in the other some small merits which are *not* possessed, losing sight of the good qualities which *are* there. The result has been a gradual alienation, which became so painful, that, at the time of their arrival here, X * * * was seriously contemplating a separation. Is not such

a sight enough to make one groan in despair, and to be
tempted to curse human nature, and the extravagance of
our expectations? There was only one way of treating
this disease, now perhaps incurable; it was to show to
each of them the excellent qualities of the other. This
always answers; for it is another contemptible fact in
our nature that the opinions of others have never so
much influence as upon our inmost feelings, that is, on
the subjects of which we ourselves ought to be the best
judges. Without previous concert, Marie and I have
tried to do this. It has already had some success; as
each of them has perceived the value which we set upon
the merits of the other, each has thought less of the
other's little deficiencies. This is better than direct advice. I am very sorry that you cannot take your share
in the good work. . . . .

You say truly that our two minds resemble a machine,
in which the moving power has lost its connection with
the working power, so that the one wastes its force, and
the other stands still. My mind is like the former. It
is in violent motion, and produces nothing. This is the
natural effect of the present state of our country, and of
the perpetual recurrence of small annoyances, without
great events or strong passions to stir up and absorb the
whole mind. The destiny of society is a problem forever present to my imagination; it shuts out every other
object of attention. And yet it does not excite in me
such intense interest as to force me to devote myself to
its solution. It prevents my thinking of other things,
and yet does not stimulate my mind; I brood over it
sadly and absently, and come to no conclusion. This is
the chief reason why it is so much less easy for me
to enter into ordinary conversation. There is another

which, though on the surface, you have never been able to understand.

. . . . At this point of my letter I was interrupted. I have not time to-day to finish the subject. I will in the next . . . .

Tocqueville, Feb. 2, 1857.

I quite understand, my dear friend, that, hurried as you were in your last journey, you could not come as far as this place.

You must have strangely mistaken my last letter, since you thought that I intended to give up Paris, and retire altogether to the country. Not only I never intended to do so, but it would be quite contrary to all my notions. It is true that I intend every year to spend at least eight months here, to make this my principal establishment, and to seek here for my chief sources of happiness. But to shut myself up here entirely, has never entered, and — I think I may answer for it — never will enter into my head. Your observations are true and are strikingly put, as you well know how to do, but they did not convince me, for I was convinced already.

You know that one of my firmest opinions is, that life has no period of rest; that external, and still more internal, exertion is as necessary in age as in youth — nay, even more necessary. Man is a traveller towards a colder and colder region, and the higher his latitude, the faster ought to be his walk. The great malady of the soul is cold. It must be combated by activity and exertion, by contact with one's fellow-creatures, and with the business of the world. In these days one must not live upon what one has already learnt, one must learn more; and instead of sleeping away our acquired ideas, we should seek for fresh ones, make the new opinions fight with the old ones, and those of youth with those of an altered state of thought and of society. Such have always been, and are now more than ever my maxims, and the longer I live, the more am I convinced of them. By observing them, I have seen men who were ordinary in youth, become agreeable and distinguished in old age. By neglecting them, I have seen eminent men fall into a torpor as heavy and unproductive as death. When strength decays, we may retire from the great struggles of the world. But absolute retirement away from the stir of life is right for no man, nor at any age.

We still intend to return towards the end of February. I hope, with you, that we shall see a great deal of each other in Paris. I shall be alone during most of the time, as Marie will have to go to Chamarande.* As I shall have no one at my home, I shall often go over to yours. I intend to go moderately into society, and a great deal to the museums and libraries. I am beginning to work again with considerable vigor, and I fancy that the ideal in my mind is well worth realizing. But the immensity of the task frightens me.

Tocqueville, Feb. 27, 1858.

. . . . We have returned to our first plan, which was not to be in Paris till the end of March. But I will not wait till then to ask for news of you, I have had none for such a long time. All I know is that you returned to Paris several months ago. I hope that you all have been well since then. We have had nothing to complain of till lately, when I have been suffering under influenza, an ailment difficult to shake off. With this exception, I have spent my time pleasantly. Since the autumn my life has been very retired, and even solitary, but

* The residence of her aunt. — TR.

suited to my taste. I take increasing interest in country pursuits; all that I ask is that God will grant me health to live here nine months out of every year.

I have not written so much as this long retirement would lead you to expect. This has been caused by the difficulty of setting my mind to work again after a long interval of repose, and of forcing it back to the subject whence it had escaped. There has been an obstinate struggle between will and inclination, in which, however, the will came off victorious. Much time was thus spent; I have got on very little with my work, but my interest in it has returned, and that was the hardest part. I have succeeded, after many trials and efforts, in finding the road that I ought to follow. I assure you that it was not easy. Am I, indeed, in the right path? Time will show. The first chapters of the new book are sketched out, but they are too unfinished for me to show them even to you. I am longing to have something ready to submit to you. All that I could say about my plan would be vague and difficult to understand. Half an hour spent in reading my MS. will make it evident to you, and you will not till then be able to tell me, if I am in the path that will lead to my object.

Six months ago, on my return from England, you wrote to me an interesting letter. On the spirit of self-government belonging to the English you say, that it can exist only when the local authorities are as good administrators as the central government, or even better. This is not always the case in England. In the local governments there are many faulty details which seem to me to be both seen and felt. The superiority of the central government in those things over which it has jurisdiction is acknowledged. Yet not only powerful private influence, but an insurmountable public conviction opposes itself to the extension of its sphere. There are many reasons, I think, for this: first, the aristocratic mould of English society. The aristocracy is wise enough to understand that, if the government took possession of the administration of the whole kingdom, on that day there would no longer be any reason for the existence of their body. There is also a vague but strong impression afloat that the system, though weak in many of its details, is the cause of so much life, activity, and variety; that, on the whole, it is the great cause which has made England the richest as well as the freest country in the world. Finally, the Englishman's great objection to allowing the government to do his business even well, is simply his wish to do it himself. This passion for being master at home, even to act foolishly, essentially characterizes the British race. " I had rather plough badly for myself than give up the stilts into the hands of the government." We ourselves have some of this feeling in private life. The English carry it to the greatest extent in municipal life. I am inclined, however, to think that centralization is gradually gaining ground in England, but so slowly that its encroachments are scarcely perceptible.

Tocqueville, May 16, 1858.

I was much annoyed at leaving Paris, dear friend, without having seen you; at least, without once having had an opportunity for full and unrestrained conversation after such a long separation, and before another separation which may be as long. I have no notion how we shall spend our summer and autumn. . . . .

Among the things that I wanted to talk over with you, my book was the first. I am beginning to be anxious about it. I am sure that I shall not make it long; but the way in which I set about examining facts and preparing for the final execution of my task, makes me fear that I shall never end it. Unfortunately, I know no rule by which to limit my researches. For the "literature of the Revolution," as a German would say, is so enormous, that a life might be spent in obtaining even a superficial acquaintance with it. You know that I am seeking less for facts than for the march of ideas and feelings. They are what I wish to describe. My subject consists in the successive changes in the social condition, the institutions, the public opinion and manners of the French, as the Revolution advanced. As yet I have discovered only one way of finding this out : it is to live over every moment of the Revolution with its contemporaries by reading not what has been said *of* them, or what they said afterwards of themselves, but what they themselves said at the time, and, as much as possible, what they really thought. Short pamphlets, and private letters, &c. are more useful for this purpose than the debates in the assembly. By these means I certainly attain my object, which is to live gradually through the period ; still my progress is so slow that I am often in despair. But is there any other way ?

There is also in the disease called the French Revolution, a peculiarity which I feel, though I cannot exactly describe it or explain its cause. It is a *virus* of a kind that was new and unknown. Many violent revolutions have taken place in the world : but the unrestrained, fierce, radical, desperate, fearless, almost mad behavior of the heroes of that time has, I think, no precedent in the great social earthquakes of past centuries. Whence came this new race? what produced it? what made it so effective ? how is it perpetuated ? For the same men are still with us, although circumstances are altered, and they have struck root over the whole civilized world. My mind exhausts itself in trying to form a true conception of these facts, and in endeavoring to reproduce it correctly. Besides all that can be explained in the French Revolution, there is a mysterious element in its motives and actions. I can perceive its presence, but I try in vain to lift the veil that hides it. A foreign substance seems interposed, which prevents me from feeling or seeing it distinctly.

Cannes, Nov. 29, 1858.

Since I last wrote my health has continued to improve, that is to say, the balance in the different functions is restored ; the traces left by the extreme fatigue of the journey have nearly disappeared, and strength at last seems to be gradually returning, though so slowly as to discourage me. In all these respects I am another man from the one I was when I arrived. As to the bronchial affection, I myself see no apparent change ; but this is in truth not extraordinary, since the state of my stomach has, till now, prevented any remedy from being tried, and the weather has also been unfavorable. It is mild, but there is incessant rain or wind, and the inhabitants do not recognize their own climate.

What you said in your first letter on the power that we fully retain, and which we ought to use, of discussing all the subjects, however abstract, that used formerly to interest and excite us, pleased me extremely. Although our lives are so different as to separate us, I still consider you as the only man in the world capable of thoroughly understanding the thoughts which I express, of completing them, and of rendering my mind still more fertile by

adding to it the fruits of a similar soil. You will understand, therefore, that, for me, whose greatest pleasures
now are intellectual, your communications are of infinite
value. . . . . .

Cannes, March 18, 1859.

You must not think, dear friend, that my silence is
caused by forgetfulness or indifference. The only causes
are sickness and solitude, the two things that most absorb the mind and take away all inclination for exertion,
even for the trifling exertion mixed with pleasure of
writing to so old and valued a friend.

I will describe to you our state; you will see that it
is not cheerful. The painful and, above all, tedious illness which I came here to cure is indeed, as the doctors
say, gradually yielding, but with an intolerable tardiness,
increased and sometimes interrupted by a thousand trifling accidents, produced by the disordered state of my
nerves. For instance, a slight return of the stomach
affection has, during the last week, deprived me of appetite, and with my appetite I have lost some of the
strength that I had regained, and which I want so
much.

Enough of myself. My wife arrived here ill. At
first she became much worse, so as to add anxiety for
her to that which I experienced on my own account. As
I got better her health improved. To-day she is infinitely better, but is still condemned for some time to silence.
We are now entirely alone, one of us can speak only in
a whisper, and the other cannot speak at all. Hippolyte
spent three months with us. It was a great comfort. . . .

Now let us turn to you. You also have been much
tried, but in another way. The terrible misfortune that
has happened to your sister — the no less cruel blow

that has fallen upon you — such trials are sad indeed.
Remember me to all your family, and tell them, pray,
that my own afflictions never make me indifferent to
those of my friends.   Good-by for to-day.   Do not wait
long before giving me news of you.

LETTERS TO EUGÈNE AND ALEXIS STOFFELS.

TO EUGÈNE STOFFELS.

Paris, Oct. 22, 1822.

I WILL not wait till my return to Metz to talk with you, my dear Stoffels. Our silence has lasted long enough. I will be the first to break it. I hope that after this you will not tell me that distance and the pleasures of Paris make me forget my old friends in the rhetoric class. At least, if I forget any of them, it will certainly not be you, you may depend upon it. We are too much united by the similarity of our opinions to be able to separate now, unless a total change took place in both of us, of which I have no fear. . . . Tell me how you spent the vacation; I hope more agreeably than I did, and that would not be difficult, for since I have been here I have led a quiet, monotonous life, which agrees neither with my disposition nor with my tastes. . . .

Paris, Aug. 7, 1823.

I did not intend to write to you till I reached Amiens, as I wished to tell you how we were established there.* But first one thing and then another have kept my father in Paris till now. As I thought every day that we should start on the next, I put off my letter. At last I

* The Comte de Tocqueville was Prefect of Amiens.

am tired of waiting, and I write to you from Paris. I arrived in good health but in bad spirits. One is not aware of the ties that bind one to a place where one has been happy. They are not felt till one breaks through all of them at once. At first it is very painful. Metz and some of its inhabitants will long be present to my memory, perhaps more than I could wish. . . . As for you, dear friend, we shall meet again in three months; and this thought is one on which I dwell with the most pleasure. We were very intimate at Metz, I hope that we shall be so in Paris. What are you doing now, my dear friend? Pray send me a full account. With your few friends, and the need that you have of sympathy, you must feel lonely. Take care of yourself in this respect, dear Stoffels; you know that you are inclined to give your friendship readily, and you may repent when it is too late. One loses nothing by keeping one's thoughts for a time to one's self, one almost always regrets having confided them too soon; at least I often have. I have longed to take back what I have told, and I have never repented my silence. Tell me about Metz, what is doing there, what is said there; you know that I am tolerably curious. Are you satisfied with your compositions? They must be finished. You would be a good fellow if you would send me your French composition. If by chance it is not yet done, remember when you are writing it to beware of enthusiasm.

Amiens, Sept. 16, 1823.

I am as indignant as you are, my dear Stoffels, at the way in which the " *Conseil* " has behaved to you. I see no motive for such a measure, and I can understand your first angry impulse. But, dear friend, you should be above all that. Two " *accessits*," followed by three others, are a better answer to the conduct of these gentlemen than all the eloquence in the world. Why throw the blade after the hilt? Why become desperate? There is no doubt of the existence of injustice and treachery in the world; but did you want this proof to be convinced of it? Certainly not. You must, therefore, live with your enemies, as you cannot always live with your friends; you must take men for what they are, be satisfied with their virtues; try to be as little annoyed as possible by their vices; confine yourself to a small circle of intimate friends, out of it expect only coldness and indifference, either hidden or apparent, and be upon your guard. Besides these considerations, I have known you, my dear friend, more than once prefer the voice of conscience to that of the world. Conscience cannot reprove you. Well, then, you are above everything. The part of the affair that most distressed me was that I feared lest this delay might prevent your journey to Paris. But you reassure me. I have already arranged in my mind a little excursion to the sea. We will go to my father's at Amiens for a few days, and from thence it is only a step to the coast.

Till then try to take exercise — shoot, dance, keep continually moving. Let bodily exertion take the place of mental activity. The first tires, but does not wear out the machine. But if the mind be unduly used, especially at our age, it will prey upon itself, and invent evils which, though without foundation, are no less painful. I am, unhappily, not without experience of this. . . . . .

Paris, Feb. 21, 1831.

It is a long time since I have had any talk with you, dear friend; yet I often think of you. Among other anxieties, I am anxious about your present and future position. I fancy that if, as seems probable, present events have their full swing, you have little chance of preserving the situation * which is of such importance to you. . . . . .

You have no doubt seen in the papers that my departure for America is at last fixed. I know not whether to be glad or sorry; there are reasons both for and against. Still I am generally approved. . . . . . I think that we shall start between the 20th of March and the 1st of April. In the way of travelling, it is impossible to imagine anything pleasanter than what we are about to do. Invested with an official character, we shall have a right to ask to see everything, and an entrance into the most exclusive circles. However, it will not be our business to look at great cities and fine rivers. We set forth with the intention of examining as fully and as scientifically as possible, all the springs of that vast machine — American society; everywhere talked of, and nowhere understood. And if public affairs at home give us time, we expect to bring back the materials for a valuable book, or at least, a new book; for there is nothing whatever extant on the subject.

Charles told me that you wished to read my " Tour in Sicily." When I go I will leave it out for you. You must keep it during my absence; and if (for one must provide for all chances) I should never return, you must keep it altogether. There are only a few pages in it that I think worth anything. I flatter myself that I should now do better. Good-by. Answer quickly.

New York, July 28, 1831.

We are very far apart, dear friend, and yet in spite of distance our hearts are united. As for me, I feel as

* That of a receiver of taxes at Metz.

much, perhaps even more, than when I was in France, that we are bound together for life, and that wherever fate may place us, we may each depend upon all the friendship and assistance that one man can give to another. . . . .

You know that we set sail on the 2d April, after midnight. The weather at first was in our favor; we seemed to glide over the ocean. I cannot tell you how imposing is the solitude of the Atlantic. For a few days flights of birds followed the ship; myriads of fishes covered the sea; not an hour passed without a sail appearing on the horizon. Soon all these things became rarer. At length birds, fishes, and vessels vanished. Above, below, and around reigned perfect solitude, and absolute silence. Our own ship, then indeed, became our world. You know that such a scene would please me; but constantly repeated, and every day the same, in the end jt oppresses and weighs on the spirits. When we neared Newfoundland, the sea sparkled all over. I believe that this effect is produced by the thousands of phosphorescent creatures which people the waters. Whatever be the cause, the effect is most extraordinary. I remember especially one evening; the weather was very stormy; our vessel, driven by a furious wind, pitched violently, throwing up on each side huge clouds of foam. This foam looked like fire. The ship seemed to be passing through one of the large furnaces for melting iron ore which I saw at Hayeuche. She left behind her a fiery track. The night was quite dark; we could scarcely see the rigging against the sky : the beauty of this scene was indescribable. A few days later we fell in with heavy gales; but there was no danger, for our vessel was too large to fear them. Thirty-five days had passed since our departure, when we heard the first cry of land. The

shores of America before us were low and barren : I can
believe that they did not enchant the Europeans who first
sighted them three centuries ago. We thought ourselves
in port, when a storm from the south-west forced us to
leave in haste the neighborhood of New York. As our
wood and sugar were exhausted, as our bread was failing,
and we had some sick on board, the attempt to land at
New York was given up. We chose instead a little harbor sixty leagues to the north, called Newport.* I can
assure you that it is a great pleasure to tread on *terra
firma* after crossing the immense chasm which separates
Europe from America. The next day we got on board
a steamer, which brought us to this place in eighteen
hours. These steamers are huge, much bigger than
houses, containing 500 or 600, and sometimes 1,000 passengers, who have vast saloons, beds, and a good´table
at· their disposal ; and thus quickly and imperceptibly
travel eight or ten miles an hour.

The situation of New York is one of the most beautiful that I know ; the harbor is immense, and at the
mouth of a river navigable for fifty miles by men-of-war.
It is the key of Northern America. Hither come every
year thousands of foreigners on their way to people the
wilds of the west, and all the European manufactures on
their road into the interior. The population, which fifty
years ago amounted to only 20,000, has now reached
230,000. It is a clean town, built of brick and marble,
but without remarkable edifices. It resembles little our
European capitals. The French are in general liked.
Our mission gave us a special claim, and both public and
private persons agreed in bestowing on us a flattering reception. All the public documents have been placed at

* In Rhode Island.

our disposal, and every information that we ask is immediately given.

. . . . You must feel that as yet I can have formed no opinion on this people. Like every other nation, it presents at first sight a combination of good and evil difficult to analyze, or to combine into a consistent whole. Morals are pure. The marriage tie, especially, is held more sacred than in any other country. Respect for religion is carried to an extreme. For instance, no one ventures to shoot, to dance, or even play upon an instrument on Sunday. Even strangers are bound by the same rules. I have seen chains across the streets in front of the churches during divine service. In this these republicans are very unlike our radicals. There are many other peculiarities in their opinions, manners, and material condition; but I have no time to point them out. This is the favorable view. The unfavorable is an immoderate desire to grow rich, and to do so rapidly; perpetual instability of purpose, and a continual longing for change; a total absence of established customs and traditions; a trading and manufacturing spirit which is carried into everything, even where it is least appropriate. Such, at least, is the external physiognomy of New York. . . .

To-day we plunge into the interior. We shall go up the Hudson as far as Albany. Thence we shall visit the falls of Niagara. After looking at the Indian tribes on the shores of Lake Erie, we shall return by Canada to Boston, and make our way to New York, whence we shall set out on another expedition. . . .

Philadelphia, Oct. 18, 1831.

It is a long time since I have written to you, dear friend, or heard from you, though you are among the

few who make me regret my exile, and attach me to
France. Since I last wrote, I have been running about
unmercifully. We embarked at Buffalo, a little town
situated at the lower extremity of Lake Erie. Our
voyage extended over 1,500 miles; we had a glimpse
of Lake Superior, and reached almost the farther end
of Lake Michigan. One look at the map will show you
our route. On our return to Buffalo we visited Niagara;
thence we went down the St. Lawrence and penetrated
into the two Canadas; we came back by Lake Cham-
plain, and went all over the states of New England, particularly the state of which Boston is the capital, and
thence to New York. At last we have reached Philadelphia, having done what no Frenchman had accomplished for many years. It is not that the journey is in
itself difficult, but that the opportunities of taking it are
rare. The shores of Lakes Huron and Michigan, which
in a hundred years will be covered with towns, are now
quite uninhabited. The forests have flourished undisturbed ever since the creation; even the pioneers have
not yet introduced the axe into them. It is nobody's
business therefore to go thither; and it was by a great
chance that we found a vessel bound for this route.

On one occasion, when alone with Beaumont and our
Indian guides in the midst of these forests, I suddenly
remembered that it was the 29th of July! I cannot
describe the effect of this recollection. . . . For an
instant I was carried back to the scenes of civil war
which we together witnessed. No past event was perhaps ever so vividly painted by my imagination. The
various feelings and passions by which at that time I
was agitated, from my mother's drawing-room till I
reached the little house at St. Cloud, seized on my mind

with violent and irresistible force. And when afterwards I looked round upon the strange scene about me, on the dark forest, the shattered remnants of previous generations of trees, and the wild faces of our guides, I for an instant doubted if I were the same man who had witnessed the events just recalled by my memory. At least, it seemed to me as if more than a year must have passed; and indeed I can scarcely yet believe that they are so recent. The midnight tocsin, the firing down the streets, our escape from Paris, our walks under arms in Versailles, the nights passed in the guard-house, all still appear a dream, a passage in some other life.

On my return from this adventure, I found awaiting me news of one of the greatest misfortunes which could have happened to me: the death of the friend of my whole life.* I own, dear friend, that this event has imbittered the rest of my journey. I looked forward to my meeting with him as one of the great pleasures of my return. It is an additional grief to me that he expired without any of us, whom he always treated like his children, having been able to receive his last breath. The two people in the world who, after my parents, have loved me best, are now separated from me forever. To see all the others pass away, it is only necessary to live. We pay this price for existence.

I hope that all your family are well. Edward tells me that his little girl already makes him very happy. I hope that you say the same. The more I see of the world, the more inclined am I to believe that domestic happiness is all that signifies. But will it ever be mine? To tell the truth, I doubt it. My reason says that it

---

* The venerable Abbé Lesueur, a second father to Tocqueville, for whom he had always a tender and filial regard.

ought to be sufficient for the human heart, but my passions contradict the assertion. When I am leading an agitated, wandering life, the idea of the tranquillity of home is delightful. When I return to regular habits, the monotony is fatal to me; I am possessed by an internal restlessness. I must have bodily or mental excitement, even at the risk of my life. The desire for strong emotions becomes irresistible, and my mind preys upon itself if it is not satisfied. In short, there is no one whom I do not know better than myself. I cannot find the clew to my own character. My head is cool, and my reason may even be called calculating; yet I am possessed by violent passions, which carry me away without persuading me, and conquer my will, though my judgment remains unconvinced.

I stay only a month here. In November we shall go towards the Mississippi, which will carry us down to New Orleans. We shall then return to New York by Savannah, Charleston, and Washington. It will be a tremendous journey, more than 4,000 miles.

Perhaps you will be disappointed by my telling you so little about this country, but I really do not know what to say. I should be obliged to send you a volume, and I have not time for that.

St. Germain, April 22, 1832.

I greatly fear lest you should fancy me dead, dear friend. You would be quite wrong, at least as to the present instant; one cannot answer for anything beyond in these times.* This pestilence carries off in a few hours the strongest and healthiest. So we must not boast. . . . Enough of this sad subject. You tell me that Charles accuses me of having the spleen.† There

---

* This was the year of the cholera.

† Sic in orig. — TR.

is some truth in the remark. He may have observed that I suffer from *ennui*, melancholy, and a sort of moral dejection. I believe that these are the ingredients of which spleen is composed. Many causes, some accidental, and others more permanent, have combined in producing this unpleasant state of mind. Have you never felt, after a change that has even been an improvement, an intellectual restlessness, caused, I think, by the alteration in one's habits? This is exactly what I experienced after my return home. I was delighted to get back, and yet I did not know what to do with my leisure after a whole year spent in almost feverish excitement. My mind was tired of quiet before my body had recovered from the fatigue. This impression has now nearly worn off, but I still have enough to make me serious. I am distressed at the condition in which I find my country. . . . Good-by! Believe that I am your old and attached friend. One can build on no other foundation in this world but a loving heart.

Paris, January 12, 1833.

I was beginning to be angry, when I received your letter. . . . You speak of what you call your "political atheism," and you ask me if I share it. On this we must understand each other. Are you disgusted with the parties themselves, or with the ideas which they profess? In the first case, you know that I have been always inclined to that opinion; but to the second I cannot in any way subscribe. There is now a growing indifference towards every idea that can disturb society, whether true or false, mean or ennobling. All seem agreed in considering the government of this country *sicut res inter alios acta.* All are becoming more and more devoted to their personal interests. Those only who desire power for themselves, and not the strength or glory of their country, can rejoice in such a spectacle. One must have but little penetration into the future to depend upon tranquillity so purchased. There is nothing healthy or manly in such repose. It is a kind of apoplectic torpor, which, if it lasted long, would infallibly lead to great disasters. No! I certainly do not laugh at political convictions; I do not consider them as indifferent in themselves, and as mere instruments in the hands of men. I laugh bitterly at the monstrous abuse that is every day made of them, as I laugh when I see virtue and religion turned to dishonest uses, without losing any of my respect for virtue and religion. I struggle with all my might against the false wisdom, the fatal indifference, which in our day saps the energy of so many great minds. I try not to have two worlds: a moral one, where I still delight in all that is good and noble, and the other political, where I may lie with my face to the ground, enjoying the full benefit of the dirt which covers it. I try not to imitate, after another fashion, the nobles of old times, who held that it was honorable to deceive a woman, but infamous to break one's word to a man. I try not to separate what is inseparable. Here, dear friend, is a long tirade, and as I have no more paper, I am forced to finish my letter.

Paris, February 16, 1835.

My dear Friend, —

I shall write only two lines this time. In the first place, because I am in a great hurry; and in the second, because I have no news for you. Hitherto the book is succeeding wonderfully. I am astonished at its popularity; for belonging to no party, I feared, if not a failure, at least a cold reception. I am welcomed everywhere, and receive advances that surprise me. M. Royer Collard, whom I did not know, asked to see me. I was with him last evening. He told me, with many compliments, that in his opinion my book was the most remarkable political work that had appeared for thirty years. I know that he has said the same thing to other people. So have M. de Chateaubriand and M. de Lamartine. At present, therefore, I am going on swimmingly; I am much astonished at my position, and quite confused by the praises sounding in my ears. There was a lady of Napoleon's court whom he one day chose to make a duchess. In the evening she went to a party, and hearing herself announced by her new title, she forgot that it belonged to her, and made way for the great lady to pass. I assure you that I feel like her. I ask myself if they really are talking of me; and when I can doubt no longer, I conclude that the world must be full of very insignificant people, if the work of my brain (of which I know so well the deficiencies) can produce such a sensation.

Paris, Feb. 21, 1835.

To return to the principal subject of your letters. I may say, dear friend, that the impression produced on you by my book, though in one respect stronger than I intended, is not of a kind that alarms or surprises me. This is the political object of the work:

I wished to show what in our days a democratic people really was; and by a rigorously accurate picture, to produce a double effect on the men of my day. To those who have fancied an ideal democracy, a brilliant and easily realized dream, I endeavored to show that they had clothed the picture in false colors; that the republican government which they extol, even though it may bestow substantial benefits on a people that can bear it, has none of the elevated features with which their imagination would endow it, and moreover, that such a government cannot be maintained without certain conditions of intelligence, of private morality, and of religious belief, that we, as a nation, have not reached, and that we must labor to attain before grasping their political results.

To those for whom the word democracy is synonymous with destruction, anarchy, spoliation, and murder, I have tried to show that under a democratic government the fortunes and the rights of society may be respected, liberty preserved, and religion honored; that though a republic may develop less than other governments some of the noblest powers of the human mind, it yet has a nobility of its own; and that after all it may be God's will to spread a moderate amount of happiness over all men, instead of heaping a large sum upon a few by allowing only a small minority to approach perfection. I attempted to prove to them that whatever their opinions might be, deliberation was no longer in their power; that society was tending every day more and more towards equality, and dragging them and every one else along with it; that the only choice lay between two inevitable evils; that the question had ceased to be whether they would have an aristocracy or a democracy, and now lay between a democracy without poetry or elevation indeed, but with order and morality; and an undisciplined and depraved democracy, subject to sudden frenzies, or to a yoke heavier than any that has galled mankind since the fall of the Roman Empire.

I wished to diminish the ardor of the Republican party,

and, without disheartening them, to point out their only wise course.

I have endeavored to abate the claims of the Aristocrats, and to make them bend to an irresistible future ; so that the impulse in one quarter and resistance in the other being less violent, society may march on peaceably towards the fulfilment of its destiny. This is the dominant idea in the book — an idea which embraces all the others, and that you ought to have made out more clearly. Hitherto, however, few have discovered it. I please many persons of opposite opinions, not because they penetrate my meaning, but because, looking at only one side of my work, they think that they find in it arguments in favor of their own convictions. But I have faith in the future, and I hope that the day will come when all will see clearly what now only a few suspect. . . . .

The material success of the book continues. . . . . From what you say of your arrangements for the summer, my dear friend, I greatly fear that I shall not be able to visit you this year. Beaumont and I intend, in a month's time, to go to England.

Paris, January 11, 1836.

I cannot allow you to learn from a formal announcement, my dear friend, the terrible blow which has just fallen upon us. My poor mother died on the evening before last. We had long seen the increasing probability of this event. I was not the less overwhelmed by it. There are some scenes for which one never can prepare one's imagination ; and this is one. The last two months of my poor mother's life were very painful ; but her last day was peaceful. After receiving the communion in the morning, she fell into a state of apparent insensibility, which lasted till half-past eight in the evening. She then seemed suddenly to awake from a deep sleep. She called us, Louis de Chateaubriand and ourselves, to her bedside. She blessed us in a distinct voice, and seemed to fall asleep once more. She had ceased to exist. Since then I have had complete experience of what I had often thought, that the only consolation in intense sorrow is in the heart of a loving wife. This is what I now feel, and the proof is present to me in my own home. Marie's own grief is great, for my mother was always full of kindness towards her, and she understands and does everything to soften my distress, naturally and without an effort. I shall add no more; you will, I hope, forgive me.

Berne, July 24, 1836.

. . . . You must indeed be demented if you think that I dislike or despise your counsels. Thank Heaven, I am not yet too old to' consider good and sincere advice as one of the greatest blessings of friendship. If it had been possible, therefore, your letters would have increased my affection for you. As for the letter itself, I candidly own to you that I think it surpasses all that you have ever said, and that it gives additional proofs of what you might do, if you would shake off the accursed misanthropical laziness which overpowers you. . . . .

I scarcely know how to answer you. If I am to be understood I must do so at length, and I have not time for a long letter; you must therefore take my answer only as a vague outline which requires much filling up.

You seem to me to have understood the general ideas

on which my programme is founded. What has always most struck me in my country, and especially of late years, has been to see ranged on one side the men who value morality, religion, and order, and on the other those who love liberty and legal equality. To me this is as extraordinary as it is deplorable; for I am convinced that all the things which we thus separate are indissolubly united in the eyes of God. They are all *sacred*, if I may use the expression; man can be great and happy only when they are combined. From the time that I found this out I believed that one of the greatest achievements in our time would be to prove it, to show that all these advantages are not merely compatible but necessarily connected. Such is the outline of my idea. You can quite understand it, for you share it. Still there is a shade of difference between us. My love for liberty is more ardent and more sincere than yours. You like it if it can be got without any trouble, but you are ready to do without it. Such is the case with many' excellent people in France. Such is not my feeling. I have always loved liberty instinctively, and the more I reflect, the more convinced am I that neither political nor moral greatness can long subsist without it. I therefore am as tenaciously attached to liberty as to morality, and I am ready to sacrifice some of my tranquillity to obtain it.

With this slight difference, we agree as to the object. But you say that we differ prodigiously as to the means; and in truth, I believe that on this point you do not perfectly understand me.

You think that I intend to put forward radical and even revolutionary theories. In this you are mistaken.

I have shown, and shall continue to show a strong and deliberate preference for liberty, for two reasons: first, because it is my fixed opinion; and, secondly, because I do not choose to be confounded with those friends of order who are indifferent to freedom and justice, provided that they can sleep quietly in their beds. There are quite enough of such people, and I venture to predict that they will never effect anything great and lasting; I shall therefore avow my attachment to liberty, and my desire to see it carried into every political institution in my country; but at the same time, I hope to show so much respect for justice, such sincere love of order and law, such a deliberate attachment to morality and religion, that I cannot but believe that I shall be discovered to be a liberal of a new kind; not to be confounded with our ordinary modern democrats. This is the whole of my plan. My account of it is incoherent, but I have kept back nothing. It is impossible for me to tell you beforehand how I shall attempt to illustrate these ideas. God alone knows if I ever shall be able to acquire any influence over my contemporaries, and perhaps it is presumption on my part to attempt it. But if ever I obtain any, it will be gradually and prudently, allowing my ideas to be inferred from my conduct, and to unfold themselves by degrees, instead of being thrown in a heap at the head of the public. If I have hitherto shown any qualities, I think that tact and prudence have been among them. I hope to continue to show them, but you must always bear in mind my starting-point.

My object, as I said in the beginning of my letter, is to combine the great principles that are now separate. For that purpose I must begin by proving, as is most true, that I am as passionately attached to one set of principles as to the other. You would have found this out long ago if you had been a demagogue. You would have heard me plead far more ardently the cause of religion and morality than that of liberty. But you are one of the excellent men whom I esteem highly, and cannot reason with calmly; for though they might direct the fate of their country, they will not stretch out their hands to help her. If these excellent men would love liberty as much as they love virtue, each principle would assist the other, and we should be saved.

This is a hasty sketch of what I had to say. Far from regarding such letters as your last with displeasure, I shall always consider them as the most precious results of our friendship, and you cannot make it closer than by often writing to me similar ones.

Tell me, if you please, that my undertaking is rash and above my powers; that it is a dream or a chimera; well and good. But leave me at least the belief that it is a great and noble attempt, and that it is worthy of the sacrifice of time, fortune, and even of life; that failure in it is better than success in any other cause. To persuade men that respect for law, both human and divine, is the best way to be free, and that to grant freedom is the best way to ensure morality and religion — such is my object. You will tell me that this is impossible; I am inclined to the same opinion; but it is the truth, and I will speak it at all risks. . . . I shall reach Geneva on the 15th of August. . . . .

Tocqueville, Oct. 5, 1836.

I found at Geneva your letter of the 18th of August; your arguments do not touch me, because I entirely share your opinion. We evidently are fighting in the dark. I expressed myself to you with a warmth that you took for a sign of a mind violently impelled to put its own ideas into action : this is not the case. You represent, with great reason, that revolutions are great evils, and give no good education to a people; that prolonged disturbance is, in itself, pernicious, and that respect for law can grow only out of the stability of the laws. . . . . All these things I firmly believe. I do not think that there is in France a man less favorable to revolution than I am, nor one that has a more intense hatred for what is called the revolutionary spirit, which spirit, by the by, is easily combined with the love of absolute government.

What am I then ? and what is it that I want ?

That we may understand each other better, let us distinguish the end from the means. What is the end ? What I want is not a republic, but. an hereditary monarchy. I would rather even that it were legitimate than elected as ours is, because it would be stronger, especially externally. What I want is a central government, energetic in its own sphere — an energetic central power is much more necessary in a democratic nation, where social influences are scattered, than in an aristocracy. Besides, our position in Europe makes what we ought to choose, if our ,choice were free, a necessity. But I desire that the sphere of this central power be clearly defined : that it may interfere only with what comes within its own jurisdiction, and that its principles may be always subordinate to public opinion as represented in the legislative bodies. I believe that the central power may be invested with high prerogatives, and exercise great authority in its sphere ; and at the same time, that ample room may be allowed to municipal liberties. I think that under such a government as this, the majority of the nation may share in the management of its affairs; that political life may animate almost the whole country; and that the direct or indirect exercise of political rights may be widely extended. I wish the general principles of the government to be liberal, that the largest possible margin should be left to individual action. I believe that all these things are compatible; I will even say that I am perfectly convinced that we shall never enjoy order and tranquillity till we shall have succeeded in combining them.

If this be admitted to be the end, I do not quarrel about the means. I should be among the first to admit that we must advance slowly, carefully, and legally. My impression is that the institutions which we now have give sufficient room for the result that I contemplate. Far from wishing to violate the laws, I respect them superstitiously. But I wish our laws to incline by slow degrees towards the ends that I have just mentioned, instead of making impotent and dangerous efforts to turn back. I wish the government itself to prepare the country for doing without it in many cases in which its intervention is still necessary, or thought necessary. I wish the people to be introduced into public life as soon as they appear capable of being of use, instead of banishing them from it at all hazards. Finally, I wish to proceed towards some definite end, and to choose the right path, instead of wandering about as we have been doing for the last twenty years. What else have I to say to you, dear friend? One might preach for a whole day upon this text without exhausting it. By this time you must understand my meaning without my attempting to dilute it, or to explain it by a thousand examples. . . . . To sum up, I have a clear conception of a government, neither revolutionary nor subversive, which I think might be established in our country. But I am as well aware as any one that such a government (which, however, would be only an extension of what we now have) could not be maintained without the aid of opinions, usages, and laws which we do not yet possess, and which must be introduced slowly, and with great precaution.

Valognes, March 7, 1839.

I was elected last Monday, dear friend — by a majority of eighty. Afterwards almost the whole population pressed round me, and accompanied me home with a complete uproar of acclamations. All this was very exciting, as you may think, and I thanked these good people from the window in a little speech, of which I send you the report. This is a great success, and, I may add, an honorable success; for I do not owe it to intrigue. I did not pay one visit; I have not promised one place. I confined myself to making an earnest appeal to the purest and most honorable feelings in the human breast, and I have succeeded. This proves that the race is not yet as depraved as it seems to be. However, I cannot conceal from myself that the hardest part is yet to come. The esteem in which I am held, the opinion entertained of me, impose on me obligations so formidable, that the thought of them already overpowers me. I greatly fear being unequal to my task. But if I am distinguished in no other way, I hope at least to be remarkable for honesty and political integrity. This will be easier for me than to be a great statesman, and it has its value. I have decided upon spending at any rate the whole of next session in the study of affairs and of men, within the chamber, as well as without. I feel the necessity of an apprenticeship, and I shall have strength of mind to submit to one.

Your last letter somewhat distressed me, dear friend. I fear lest I should have pained you unnecessarily by reproving too severely your depression. You have, indeed, great causes for grief; and fortune, I own, has not as yet given you reason to trust her. You say truly that my position does not qualify me for speaking to you in this way. Almost all that I have attempted has, as you say, succeeded for the last ten years. This ought to make me more tolerant towards you. But do not think that I am intoxicated by my success. It surprises me perhaps as much as it astonishes you; and far from relying on the future, I tremble when I think of it. I remember where I was after the revolution of 1830, and all that has since happened to me strikes me with astonishment. I should be mad. if I expected things always to go on in this manner. I am now entering a new stage, without knowing if I am fit to play my part on it, and obliged to try my powers in a way that perhaps neither my mind nor my body will be able to endure; for, it must be acknowledged, I have no longer at my disposal the iron constitution which you remember, and which lent itself so kindly to the strong emotions and extreme activity of my mind. Excitement, beyond a certain point, fatigues me, and I now and then feel that I require rest. I cannot help thinking that Providence, who has already bestowed on me so many keenly felt and elevated enjoyments, does not intend my life to be long. I am not strong enough to bear incessant work, yet inactivity kills me. But one must not think of such things. I own to you that of all the blessings which God has given to me, the greatest of all in my eyes is to have lighted on Marie. You cannot imagine what she is in great trials. Usually so gentle, she then becomes strong and energetic. She watches over me without my knowing it. She softens, calms, and strengthens me in difficulties which disturb *me*, but leave her serene.

Tocqueville, July 14, 1840.

You are quite right, dear friend, to complain of my silence; not that it has been voluntary, or that I had forgotten you, but because in truth there is a meanness in not writing to one's best friend, in order to give one's self up more completely to the political world, where in spite of all one's efforts, one meets only with cold hearts, capable of no enthusiasm, except for themselves. I have long been reproaching myself for not writing to you. But I must impress upon you that I have never been less indifferent to you. Public life seems to affect me in another way from most men. It makes me cling the more to old feelings, and to the friends whom I have left behind. Your friendship, and that of Louis, have never seemed to me to be such real blessings as now.

It is not that I have reason to complain of political men. I receive as much respect in the chamber, and enjoy as much influence as were to be gained in my short experience. But the side of human nature disclosed by politics is, indeed, miserable. Without a single exception, one may say that perfect purity and disinterestedness are unknown, that there is no real generosity or natural impulse. Even the youngest are no longer young. In moments of the highest excitement there is an undercurrent of cold selfishness and premeditation. Such a spectacle cannot fail to drive one back upon one's self; one seeks elsewhere for a purer mental atmosphere. I have entered public life, I like its excitement, and the great interests involved in it stimulate my mind; but there are many things absolutely wanting in it, without which I cannot live. And I can find them only in my wife and in two or three friends, who have remained much as we all were ten years ago. This is the explanation of what I before said on the increasing value that I set upon your friendship in the midst, and even in consequence, of the affairs that prevent my writing to you. . . .

I wrote from Tocqueville, which I reached only four days ago. I was kept in Paris by a report on prisons, which I will send to you. I cannot tell you how I enjoy the quiet of the country. You know that quiet is not in my line, nor do I take pleasure in rest. But rest and quiet occurring from time to time, and at long intervals, amid the turmoil of passions and politics, exercise a great charm even over my restless and anxious disposition. For a long while, I besought Heaven to give me *too* much to do. My prayers have been so well heard, that during the last few years I have often longed for time to take breath. Perhaps this may be the beginning of old age; for I cannot conceal from myself the fact, that for me youth is over, entirely over. I feel this much more mentally than physically. . . .

Do you think that the obstacles which prevented your coming this year will again stand in your way next year? The calm and even tenor of the life we lead here makes us still more anxious that you should share our retreat for a few months. . . .

P. S. This day fifty-one years, the French revolution commenced; and after the destruction of so many men and institutions we may say that it is still going on. Is not this encouraging to the nations that are only just beginning theirs? . . . .

Tocqueville, Nov. 30, 1841.

Before I quit this place, dear friend, I must have a little talk with you. I hoped to have been able to remain at Tocqueville till the end of December, perhaps even till the beginning of January; for it would have been soon enough if I had arrived in time for the discussion of the address. One of the many incidents that disturb my life and that prevent my ever settling anything definitely, forces me, against my will, to hasten my return. The friends who voted for me on the last vacancy in the Academy of France, think of proposing me again this time. I have, during the last fortnight, received letters upon letters, urging me to come and show myself. I cannot, without disobliging them, refuse any longer.

However, as I said before, this unexpected return costs me much. In the first place, I have not a very exalted idea of my chance in the Academy. Secondly, Tocqueville, even in this season, is so delightful to me that every day taken away from it seems to me a great and irreparable loss. Yet I must make up my mind to it. I start to-morrow. My stay at Tocqueville this year has been of great use. It has proved to me that I can be happy in the most retired life; that solitude, shared only by Marie, is, on the whole, not only the most agreeable, but the most useful mode in which I can pass my time. I repeat, that this experience is for me an important discovery. It makes me quite easy as to the future. I cannot hide from myself that, if I do not entirely regain my health, I shall sooner or later be obliged to give up politics, or at least to make them only a slight accessory to my existence. Bodily strength is as requisite in the chamber as in battle; and at present I have none.

But even admitting, and I will not yet despair, that I

may continue to make politics the business of my life, it still is a rare and inestimable comfort to feel that if it should be right or prudent for me to retire, either for a time or permanently, into private life, I should not be unhappy, and that if needful, I should return to it with pleasure. The power to quit without repining the political arena is, perhaps, the most essential qualification for acting independently and nobly. Almost all the meanness that we see in public men is caused either by the want of fortune, which makes them fear ruin if they should lose their places ; or, by such a concentration of all their passions in the pursuit of power, that they cannot contemplate quitting it without a horror which misleads their judgment, and makes them sacrifice the future to the present, and honor to place.

Paris, January 1, 1842.

Thank you, dear friend, for your last letter. I knew very well that you would be pleased at my election into the Academy, for I have as much confidence in your friendship as I hope that you have in mine. I had alarmed you too much as to the result of the contest. You know that I am not given to false hopes. I am more inclined to look on the dark than on the bright side of the future. When I wrote to you, too, my success was very doubtful. The king was acting openly in favor of M. Vatout, and it was difficult to say how much he might influence the event. Happily for me, public opinion, which in our day is more powerful than kings, was on my side. There was a large majority, as you saw. It would have been still larger if a succession of accidents had not occasioned the absence of four of my best friends from the Academy on the day of the battle.

I am delighted, and as you say, I have many reasons for so being, besides the Academy. It would be an injustice to Providence to deny it. Many external circumstances of happiness have been granted to me. But more than all, I have to thank Heaven for having bestowed on me true domestic happiness, the first of human blessings. I never appreciated it so highly as I now do. As I grow older, this portion of life, which in my youth I used to look down upon, every day becomes more important in my eyes, and would now easily console me for the loss of all the rest.

I hope, however, dear friend, to escape the danger that you mention, and which threatens all the happy in this world. If I am better off than others in many respects, I am worse off in the first requisite of all, and that is health. My health is the weight that drags me down. It is often very heavy. This year I have taken certain invalid precautions, which hitherto have answered. I never go out in the evening, and never dine out. By this means I am sure to be careful in my diet, and to sleep at night. It is, however, sad at my age to be forced to live like an old man : I do not say this to complain, but to show you that there are two sides to every picture. Another thorn in my flesh, is the state of politics : they affect me more than most people, for it is my duty to mix in them, and it is an ungrateful task, I assure you. There is no good to be done at present, nor probably in future.

Baugy, Jan. 3, 1843.

The letter which you sent to Tocqueville, dear friend, has been forwarded to me here, where I have been staying for the last month, but to-morrow I return to Paris. . . .

A misanthropy, which I think exaggerated, breathes in your whole letter. I am no longer a child. I have seen many countries, studied many men, mingled in many public transactions,˙and the result of my experience is very different from yours. You make human nature worse than it is. The truth lies between the dreams of your early youth and the dark impressions of your maturity. Men in general are neither very good nor very bad; they are indifferent. According to the view one takes, they exhibit both qualities. I never was thrown into close contact with the best, without discovering some weaknesses, and even vices, which at the first glance I had not seen. In the worst, I have always found some points on which they were accessible to good impressions. In every man there are two men, as Solomon truly said 3,000 years ago; if it be childish to see only the one, it is miserably unjust to fix one's eyes only on the other. This last, however, it seems to me that you do, and you are wrong. If to console you for having been born, you must meet with men whose most secret motives are always actuated by fine and elevated feelings, you need not wait, you may go and drown yourself immediately. But if you would be satisfied with a few men, whose actions are in general governed by those motives, and a large majority, who from time to time are influenced by them, you need not make such faces at the human race. Man with his vices, his weaknesses, and his virtues, strange combination though he be of good and evil, of grandeur and of baseness, is still, on the whole, the object most worthy of study, interest, pity, attachment, and admiration in the world; and since we have no angels, we cannot attach ourselves, or devote ourselves to anything greater or nobler than our fellow-creatures. These are the feelings that I wish to be yours in the year 1843. . . .

Tocqueville, Oct. 1843.

I have been here a month already, my dear friend, and that month has passed like a single day. I should like to know if the delight which I take in solitude and in the freedom of the country is natural, or arises from the fatigue of living in Paris for seven or eight months. Is it the place itself that makes me happy, or its contrast with another? Unfortunately, I fear that the latter hypothesis is nearer to the truth. In any case, I think that the life which I lead here would be agreeable to me; but it is delightful, because it follows the incessant and prolonged turmoil of Paris. I am much afraid that if I were compelled to give up the excitement which is often so trying to me, to bury myself forever in the retirement which I value so highly, it would end by becoming insipid. Is the fever of public life, then, essential to my temperament? I am inclined to think so; and yet I often suffer cruelly from it. What a miserable condition is that of man: plunged in such deep ignorance, that he knows no more of himself than of the most distant objects, and cannot see more clearly into his own heart than into the bowels of the earth!

Without wearying myself by trying to solve this riddle, I endeavor to enjoy, as much as possible, the present. I wish I could show you Tocqueville now. It is nearly finished. *Your* gate, the one whose removal to the top of the avenue you superintended, is already being covered with moss and ivy. The dirty court-yard has been converted into a beautiful green lawn. All along the walls that we want to hide, trees are growing, which as yet, it must be owned, are far from covering them. Why are you not here with Madame Stoffels, to see all these changes, and to listen indulgently to the admiration of the owners ? In spite of the lapse of time, we still think and say that the most agreeable month that we have ever spent here, and the most in accordance with our own tastes, was when you both were here. We cannot persuade ourselves that it is never to return, and our greatest wish is that you may be able to arrange to pay us another visit soon, not alone, this time, but with your children ; at least with several of them. You know that this is not a form of speech, but our most sincere desire.

Tocqueville, April 3, 1844.

I have been carrying about your last letter, dear friend, for a month, in my pocket, hoping to find time to answer it, and to have it at hand whenever I wanted to read it over again. The opportunity is always escaping me. I have just looked at the date, and am horrified by it. It is in last November, so that it came more than four months ago, and yet it seems as if I had only just received it. With what ill-omened rapidity life is beginning to pass ! If I am not mistaken, this is a proof that youth has fled forever, and that the impressions produced on the mind are becoming fainter ; for life is measured by the number of impressions that remain graven on the memory. When many are retained, time seems to pass slowly ; when they begin to escape us, time appears to fly ; every recollection of past emotion is a sort of landmark, like the objects which measure the road to the traveller. It is unfortunate for me that while I lose the impression of past feelings, I do not become more calm,

or at least much more calm. I have still too much of
the almost morbid irritability which makes me impatient
of the obstacles which stand in the way of every man ;
and yet I ought to accustom myself to them, for the
career which I have embraced is full of them. Political
life is an arena where not a day passes without one's
being forced to rouse one's self to fight, and the victory
gained is always far below one's anticipations.

One passage in your letter distressed me. You put
off indefinitely revisiting Normandy, and you talk of five
or six years ! ! Our ideas and habits may have become
so different in such a length of time, that we shall scarcely recognize one another. In such a long separation,
the ties of intimacy become looser and looser, and we
should both have to begin again. If you should be
really obliged to put off our meeting for five or six
years, I shall consider it as a serious calamity. For
ourselves, we seem to have no prospect of a long tour
which would enable us to take Metz in our way. Last
year I was nominated to the *Conseil général*, which
obliges me to spend next August in Normandy. I am
very sorry for this ; not only because I lose the episode
of our visit to you, but because I lose the tour itself. I
think that my taste for travelling grows by privation.
I long to extend the horizon, to see new countries, new
people, and new customs. But there is another obstacle
which prevents me, and that is money. It often limits
my wishes, which, however, are moderate enough. It
annoys me when I think of it, but I seldom do ; and the
slight inconvenience which I experience in this respect,
does not prevent my thanking God daily, and with all
my heart, for having permitted me to pay this price for
my admirable wife. I certainly cannot accuse Heaven

of having ill-treated me; but beyond every other blessing, I feel increasing gratitude to Providence for having
placed Marie in my path. I would willingly relinquish
every other gift in order to preserve this. Good-by,
dear friend; my heart becomes always tender and ex-
pansive when I get upon this subject. It is the source
of all the sweet and restorative influences of domestic
life. All the rest is a barren desert, where one is forced
to struggle from morning till night in the sun and dust.
Adieu.

Paris, November 14, 1844.

Your letters, my dear friend, notwithstanding my pleasure in hearing from you, always cause me some slight
annoyance. You always treat me as if my head were
so turned by politics as to make me almost forget my
friends. I have often told you that you were mistaken.
Politics often sever two friends when they are both engaged in the same sphere, because differences of opinion
and interests may bring collision. I own that there are
few friendships which entirely survive this trial; but this
is not your case, and the remembrance of you is all the
more valuable and refreshing in the heart-sickness caused
by public life. Before I entered it, I set a high value
upon my old and true friends; since that time they have
risen a hundred per cent. in my estimation. If I were
to lose them I feel that I should form no similar attachments. The time when such ties are contracted is now
forever past for me. Outside the small circle of my
affections, I look on men only as neutrals or as enemies;
as supporters or as adversaries; as people to be esteemed
or despised, but not as friends; and if those whom I still
possess die before me, I shall die alone; at least my heart
will be solitary. You must feel, that with this disposi-

tion, I am not tempted to forget my best and earliest friends ; and are you not at the head of them ? I never shall forget you nor become indifferent to your fate, nor to that of your children. But our intellectual sympathy may be diminished if years should pass without our meeting. . . . . You constantly speak of the impossibility of coming to see me at Tocqueville ; I cannot believe in it . . . . A week or ten days at Tocqueville, if you cannot spare more, would be enough to knit our minds together again, and to enable us to live apart for two years without misunderstanding each other. . . .

Paris, July 21, 1848.

I need not tell you, my dear friend, that I have been wishing to write to you sooner, but the events which have taken place since your letter came, have made a sufficient noise to serve as an excuse for me.

You ask me to write about politics. I would willingly do so if I had more time, but I have little, and must confine myself to a general summary.

Ever since February, I never doubted that a great battle was impending in Paris. I said it, repeated it, and wrote it a hundred times. The four days of June, therefore, only surprised me by their colossal proportions. Our victory restored some of the ground that social order had lost. For the first time for four months a regular government is possible ; and though I am convinced that both those who hold the reins of government, and the assembly itself, will be unequal to the difficulties of the position, and will not do all that they might towards the speedy and permanent accomplishment of this object, I think that it will be attained in spite of them by the irresistible impulse which the late events have given to the spirit of order; but great dangers are to be feared in the immediate present, and still more in the future.

The first will be caused by the state of our finances. If we continue to vote supplies, and the receipts continue to diminish, it will be impossible for us to escape a financial crisis, of which the consequences cannot be foretold. . . . This is the immediate danger. It is great and alarming. I am inclined, however, to think that it will not destroy us. I should not be surprised if, after these trials, the republican government were to become settled, and to go on for some time with regularity. But I have no confidence in the future. I feel a deep dejection, arising less from immediate apprehensions (though they are considerable), than from the absence of hope. I scarcely dare hope to see a regular government strong, and, at the same time, liberal, established in our country. This ideal was, as you know, the dream of my youth, and likewise of the portion of my mature age that has already passed. Is it possible still to believe in its realization? For a long time I thought (but long before last February this belief had been much shaken), that we had been making our way over a stormy sea, on which we still were tossing, but that the port was at hand. Was I not wrong? Are we not on a rolling sea that has no shore? or is not the land so distant, so unknown, that our lives, and perhaps those of our children, may pass away before it is reached, or at least before any settlement is made upon it? I do not expect a series of revolutions. I believe in tolerably long intervals of order, tranquillity, and prosperity; but how can one continue to hope for a good system of government firmly settled? In 1789, in 1815, even in 1830, France might still be supposed to be suffering under a sharp illness, after which the health of society would be restored to more than its former vigor and permanence. But do we not now see that the complaint is chronic, that the evil is more deeply seated; that though intermittent, it will continue longer than we ever expected ; that it is not only a single form of government which seems to be impracticable, but any sort of settled government; and that we are fated to oscillate between despotism and liberty, and to bear neither for a continuance ?

I am indeed alarmed at the state of the public mind. It is far from betokening the close of a revolution. At the time it was said, and to this day is perpetually repeated, that the insurgents of June were the dregs of the populace ; that they were all outcasts of the lowest description, whose only motive was lust of plunder. Such, of course, were many of them ; but it is not true that they were all of this kind. Would to God that they had been ! Such wretches are always a small minority, they never prevail ; they are imprisoned or executed, and all is over. In the insurrection of June, besides bad passions, there were, what are far more dangerous, false opinions. Many of the men who attempted to overthrow the most sacred rights were carried away by an erroneous notion of right. They sincerely believed that society was built upon injustice, and they wished to give it another foundation. Our bayonets and our cannon will never destroy this revolutionary fanaticism. It will create for us dangers and embarrassments without end.

Finally, I begin to ask myself whether anything solid and durable can be built on the shifting basis of our society ? whether it will support even a despotism, which many people, tired of storms, would, for want of a better, hail as a haven? We did not see this great revolution in human society begin; we shall not see it end. If I had children, I should be always repeating this to them, and I should tell them that in this age, and in this country, one ought to be fit for everything, and prepared for everything, for no one can count on the future. And I should add, that in France especially, men should rely on nothing that can be taken away; but try to acquire those things which one can never lose till one ceases to exist: fortitude, energy, knowledge, and prudence. Adieu! dear friend; believe that my gloomy views of the future are in part due to the melancholy produced by what is passing around me, and trust always in my warm regard.

Paris, April 28, 1850.

. . . . My strength has almost entirely returned, and except politics, which I have set aside for the present, I have almost resumed my ordinary life. But this illness is an unpleasant recollection. It came for no apparent cause; it may come again without my being able to guard against it. Happily, the doctors assure me that the lung is sound. The mischief, therefore, done already, is not much; but is it entirely got rid of ? . . .

You wish for political prognostications; who can venture to make any? The future is as black as night; the most far-sighted admit that they cannot look forward. As for me, I see a tolerably clear outline of what seems to be the future destiny of this country; but the details escape me, and the next turn that affairs will take is as much hidden from me as from one who has never been engaged in them. All I can say is, that I am more uneasy than I have been for a long time. What I see clearly is, that for sixty years we have been deceiving ourselves by imagining that we saw the end of the Revolution. It was supposed to be finished on the eighteenth Brumaire, and again in 1814; I myself thought, in 1830, that it might be over when I saw that democracy, having in its march passed over and destroyed every other privilege, had stopped before the ancient and necessary privilege of property. I thought that, like the ocean, it had at last found its shore.

I was wrong. It is now evident that the tide is rising, and that the sea is still enlarging its bed; that not only we have not seen the end of the stupendous revolution which began before our day, but that the infant just born will scarcely see it. Society is not in process of modification, but of transformation. Into what form? I have not the least idea, and I think that no one has. One feels that the old world is passing away; but what will be the new? The master spirits of the age can no more foresee it than the ancients could the abolition of slavery, the establishment of Christianity, the invasion of the barbarians, or any other of the great events which have changed the condition of the world. They knew that the institutions of their own day were crumbling, and that was all that they knew. . . .

To return to something nearer and more distinct, I do not think, as many do, that the present framework of society in France is in immediate peril. It yet contains far too much vital power to collapse; and I therefore disbelieve in the speedy and total overthrow with which we are threatened. . . .

Sorrento, December 30, 1850.

I am writing to you, dear friend, from a little town on the shores of the Bay of Naples, facing that city and

Mount Vesuvius. Our original destination was Palermo. . . . We have been forced to seek another wintering place. We found it here, and here we have been for the last three weeks, congratulating ourselves every day on having thought of coming. It would be impossible to find a more enchanting country, or, hitherto, a more delightful climate. We have taken a furnished house on the outskirts of Sorrento. We stand in the midst of olives and orange-trees, on a hill fronting Naples and the sea. It is true that we have no society; but I require it much less than I used. I have brought plenty of books, and I expect one of my dearest friends, Ampère, to spend the rest of the time with us. We intend to remain here till the middle of March, when we shall travel quietly home. As yet the climate and mode of life have agreed admirably with my health, and I hope to take back to Paris sufficient strength to enter actively into public affairs. My wife, too, has been very well since our arrival, and we are both experiencing the pleasure mingled with anxiety, perhaps all the greater on account of the admixture, that one feels in a safe and comfortable refuge in the midst of a storm, or rather between two storms.

You know that a mind as active as mine, and to which complete rest is as fatal now as it was in our youth, could not endure this life, in spite of its tranquil enjoyments, without some useful occupation. I am therefore not idle. My time is filled up with several interesting studies. I have long wished to begin writing again. For the last ten years politics have prevented my realizing this wish. But at the same time they have given to me a knowledge of men and of business which will enable me, when I have leisure, to write more easily and better. I profit

by the short respite which I am now enjoying, not to
write another book, but to choose a subject and to prepare materials. I do not know if I shall ever turn my
present labors to account, but at least they amuse me.

In this retirement the remembrance of public affairs
and public men gradually grows fainter, while my true
friends become more dear. It is not astonishing, therefore, that we have often thought and talked of you in our
hermitage. We long for news of you all, father, mother,
and children, and the sooner the better.

Good-by, dear friend. ˙ Here is the end of the year
1850. Remember that you have 1,500 miles off two
friends who heartily wish that the coming year will bring
all sorts of blessings to yourself and to your family. A
thousand kind remembrances to Madame Stoffels, and a
kiss for each child.

Versailles, July 23, 1851.

. . . . At length, dear friend, our great parliamentary
battle is over. The result is what was to have been expected. As for me, I still think that the revision would
have been, as I said, the least dangerous measure. But
it has now become nearly impossible, and we are almost
irresistibly impelled towards a reaction which will not
be constitutional. . . . .

Many members of the political world drew, like you,
from my report * an impression that I was opposed to
the revision. This is caused, I think, by the fact that to
complete my argument I must have said some things
that I could not mention in my official position, and
which I left the reader to infer. I am much annoyed
by this meaning being attached by yourself and by others

* On the Revision of the Constitution. An extract from it is given,
vol. ii. p. 162. — TR.

to my report, for I may be supposed to have been insincere, and to have pleaded for the purpose of losing my cause. This is false, and would be very injurious to me. On the contrary, I was perfectly convinced of the necessity of a revision, and I have become more so than ever during the last few days, when I have been calmly reconsidering my previous reasons. . . . .

My wife received a delightful letter from yours a few days ago. She intends to answer it soon. A postscript was added by your daughter, written in a style as natural and graceful as herself. She really is a charming girl. . . . .

, TWO LETTERS TO ALEXIS * STOFFELS

Tocqueville, January 4, 1856.

Thank you for your letter, my dear friend. It gave us great pleasure. We are touched by the affection which it proves, and to which ours, as you know, corresponds. We shall be delighted to see you again, and our house will always be open to you. You will be ever welcome. You know all this, so I need not dwell on it. I will only add that in spite of all that you have been told, we shall have opportunities of meeting, during four or five months, for we shall be in Paris towards the end of this month or the beginning of next at farthest, and as usual stay there till June.

Now, let us talk a little about yourself. You are plunged into all the horrors of Roman law. You find the subject difficult, perhaps even distasteful. I am not

---

* Eugène Stoffels died in July, 1852. Tocqueville's affection extended to his children, especially to the eldest, Alexis, his godson, to whom he often wrote. There is something paternal about his letters, as will be seen from these two specimens.

surprised, for it had the same effect upon me. But it is impossible to be a great lawyer without having studied it seriously. Roman law has played a most important part in almost all modern nations. It has done them much good, and in my opinion, still more harm. It has improved their civil laws, and spoilt their political laws; for Roman law has two sides.

The one concerns the relations between individuals, and in this respect it is one of the most admirable products of civilization ; the other part has to do with the relations between subjects and sovereign ; and then it is full of the spirit of the age when the last additions were made to its compilation — the spirit of slavery. Aided by Roman law and by its interpreters, the kings of the fourteenth and fifteenth centuries succeeded in founding absolute monarchy on the ruins of the free institutions of the Middle Ages. The English alone refused to adopt it, and they alone have preserved their independence. Your professors will not tell you this. But it is the most important part. Still the present is not the time for considering it, for your examination will not relate to it.

You tell me, without adding any explanation, that you are advised not to go far into the law. This surprises me. You would then have to renounce the degree of doctor, which seems to be now, the natural, and even indispensable complement to a magisterial or legal education. I wish that you had been more explicit on a point of so much importance, and that you would let me know the reasons which incline you to be satisfied with the degree of licentiate. Perhaps they are sufficient; I shall be sorry if this is the case. In all things one should aim boldly at perfection. However one tries, one never gets near enough to it. I wish, dear Alexis, that you had a stronger will. I have often told you so. One never succeeds, especially in youth, without a spark of the devil. At your age, I would have tried to jump over the towers of Notre Dame if I had expected to find what I wanted on the other side. You have distinguished and amiable qualities, but you have not enough enthusiasm; this is the only reproach which my friendship allows me to make to you; I hope that you will forgive it, as a proof of my affection. . . .

We have passed our time here tranquilly and agreeably. The duties of the proprietor have rather interfered with the labors of the writer. I hope however to return to Paris with a volume ready for publication. Shall I publish it? I am not yet certain. My subject is the French Revolution, considered from a point of view which, if I am not mistaken, is original. The book is written in a spirit now almost unknown to my contemporaries. I have remained an old superannuated lover of liberty in an age when almost every one wishes for a ruler. This want of sympathy between myself and the public alarms me, for past experience shows that the books whose appearance produces a sensation, are those in which the author swims with the current of public opinion, not those in which he attempts to stem it.

Adieu! dear friend; be brave. Do not go to sleep over "Usucaption," * and think of us sometimes.

Tocqueville, December 12, 1856.

I take advantage, my dear friend, of a moment's leisure to write a few words to you.

. . . Really you have no reason to complain. I own that the career embraced by you is not very delightful at

* A technical term in Roman law.

starting; but you enter it under favorable auspices, with a respected name, a good character, and friends that reflect honor upon you. How many have had to row against wind and tide, instead of, like you, being favored by both! I have so often discoursed to you in this fashion that I will say no more to-day. Allow me only to repeat, that one may spend one's life without success, or anything but disgust, in the languid, imperfect pursuit of a profession, but that every profession to which one gives one's self up produces success and pleasure. However toilsome the first efforts may appear, one becomes attached to every employment, if steadily persisted in. . . . . But enough of sermons for to-day.

I like better telling you that your last letter pleased us much; it is frank and natural. You should always treat me thus. Tell me all that happens to you, all that comes into your head, just as if I were not thirty years older than you are. You know that I like young people, provided that, though they have some of the faults incidental to their age, they be not without the corresponding virtues. It is not only the barrister or the future magistrate that interests me in you, but the *man ;* and nothing that excites or occupies your mind is indifferent to me. So you are fully warned : if your correspondence is to be pleasant to me and useful to yourself, it must be a true picture of all that happens to you, within and without.

I am very glad that you were not tired of Tocqueville; I need not tell you how pleased we were with your visit. You saw that yourself. Both husband and wife were of one mind on that point. . . . . .

P. S. Your essay appeared to me to be good. I do not mean as to the matter; I can no longer judge of that; but as to the style, which is easy and agreeable, like the author. It remains for him to prove that he has energy. This world belongs to the energetic.

[After the two correspondences with Count Louis de Kergorlay and Eugène Stoffels, his earliest friends, the letters of M. de Tocqueville are arranged by M. de Beaumont chronologically. — Tr.]

TO THE BARON* AND BARONESS DE TOCQUEVILLE.

Paris, August 8, 1829.

I intend to write to both of my dear friends at once to-day; I have not time for two letters, because we are in the middle of the assizes; and yet I wish to have a little talk with both. The difficulty is to know which to address first, for there are things which would not interest you equally. My heart puts neither first or last, so I will begin with the lady of the house; but she must be aware that it is out of pure politeness.

I will tell you, then, dear sister, that if my letter touched your heart, yours found its way straight to mine. I said so to your husband a few days ago. I cannot describe to you the impression that this proof of your friendship produced on me. One has constantly to thank people for their kind expressions, and one's thanks are often warmer than the feeling that inspires them; one returns bad money for good, and with a good conscience, for no one is deceived. Well, I wish you on

---

* His brother Edward, afterwards Vicomte de Tocqueville, who, with his bride, was travelling in Switzerland and Italy. During this time, Alexis de Tocqueville used to send them news of the progress of affairs in France, which every day became more serious till they ended in the revolution of July, 1830.

the contrary to take mine for what it represents, and at its real value ; but I know not how to manage this. I should like to tell you exactly what I felt, neither more nor less. I repeat, then, simply, and from the bottom of my heart, that your letter touched me ; moreover, that I believed in it without any restriction, because my own feelings reflected all that you expressed so well. I solemnly assure you that your friendship towards myself, and the happiness which you bestow, and I hope always will bestow upon Edward, are the two things most likely to contribute to mine, and to make me look forward with pleasure to the future.

It is not only I who have to thank you for your letter, — there is a *chorus* on this point. Whenever a letter from Switzerland reaches Paris, the whole clan is summoned ; the assembly is not very numerous, but it is unanimous. We do not read all at once, but little by little. We follow you upon the map. We make comments on your movements ; we share in your enjoyment of the splendid scenery that you describe. The account of the fatigue which you undergo almost terrifies us ; happily our fears are imaginary. At last, when we have finished reading, we allow ourselves to talk. Then come the remarks. If it were only true that the ears tingle when one is well spoken of, what a singing you would have in them ! We end by saying that your letters are a perfect picture of yourself, and to this we can add nothing. Sometimes we venture to remark that your style is excellent, and perfectly natural. But I ought not to tell you this, and we are angry with ourselves when it strikes us. Neither the reader nor the writer ought ever to pay attention to such things.

. . . . But it is time for me to turn to your husband.

You no doubt are already aware of the strange events that are happening here. The ministers have resigned in a body. A new ministry, composed of MM. de Polignac, La Bourdonnaye, Montbel, and others, has taken the helm. How will they manage to stand? God only knows. Or rather, He knows already what we only suspect, — that they will not stand. It seems that they intend, at first, to retain the present chamber; but it is highly improbable that it will go with them. If they summon another, all the chances will be against them, should the present election laws continue. To obtain the consent of this chamber to a change in those laws appears to me to be quite impossible. So, then, they will be driven to the system of *coups d'État*, of legislating by proclamations. Royal power and popular power being at war, there will be a pitched battle, in which the people will risk only the present, while the monarchy stakes both the present and the future. If this ministry falls, it will greatly damage the crown, whose child it is. Guarantees will be demanded by the people which will reduce to almost nothing a power which is already too weak. God grant that the House of Bourbon may not one day deeply repent what has just been done! ...

Adieu, dear friends; I embrace you as I love you, sincerely and affectionately.

TO M. GUSTAVE DE BEAUMONT.

Tocqueville,* August 30, 1829.

I have just received a second letter from you. I could not answer the first, as you did not tell me where to find you; but I thank you for remembering me twice. You seem to expect me to give an account of all that I have

* Then belonging to his father.

seen here. I shall do no such thing. 1st. Because it would be very long. 2dly. Because it would not in the least amuse *me*. 3dly. (This is my chief reason) because it would not amuse *you*. This last head may be subdivided. You would be bored. 1st. Because a description of a fine thing is almost always a bad thing. 2dly. (I kept this for the last) because you are the least curious of men as to all that has no actual or practical utility for you; a defect, by the by, which seems to me to be an abuse of your excellent abilities, and a real imperfection.

All I shall tell you is, that a great vessel of one hundred guns has been launched; that I managed to climb up to the poop, which is more than fifty feet high, and that I then felt myself glide into the sea amidst a flourish of trumpets, a discharge of artillery, and the cheers of an immense crowd collected round the harbor. This was indeed a fine sight, and one that your imagination will easily picture. When the captain called out to cut the last mooring, and we began to move, I myself was seized with a fit of enthusiasm such as I had not experienced for a long time. I must say, that the indescribable sensation which filled my breast and upset my mental balance gave me intense pleasure. . . .

I have not done much intellectually since our separation. However, we learnt this year, among other things, to employ our odd moments. I have turned this knowledge to account by reading the greater part of Guizot. We must read it again together next winter : its analysis of ideas and accuracy of language are wonderful. *Wonderful* indeed. This book sheds a light on the fourth century which was totally unknown to me; and yet it is full of interest, as exhibiting the decay of the great Roman system.

TO THE SAME.

Neufchâtel, October 4, 1829.

Allow me, my good friend, to offer you no congratulations.* Your happiness costs me so dear, that I have not the power of putting on a joyous air. I would have done all that man could do to bring about the event which has happened, but I cannot sincerely rejoice at it. . . . . I did not think our separation possible, and the more I think over it, the less can I accustom myself to the idea. We are now close friends, and friends for life I believe. . . . But our intimacy, dear Beaumont, the intercourse of every moment, the unlimited confidence, all that, in short, made our united lives so delightful, that is all over. This thought must be less sad for you, who will find great and immediate compensations; a boundless future is now open to you, the circle in which you are known may widen indefinitely. But for me, who lose everything at once, who will return alone to the lodging where I used not to be able to live a week without you — walking with you in the evening, studying with you in the day — for me, crushed now under the weight of my own thoughts, with no one of whom I may ask advice in the little difficulties and annoyances incidental to our profession; what future is in store for me? I am sick at heart. . . . Although a decline in our intimacy seems inevitable, still, dear friend, we must struggle against it with all our might. We must, therefore, continue to tell everything to each other, to study some things in common, and to meet on certain days. I cannot conceal from you that I have some fears on

* M. de Beaumont had just been appointed to the "parquet" in Paris.

your account, dear friend. I know no one more capable
of friendship, but your mind is so versatile. . . . As for
me, I have given my friendship to few, my confidence to
scarcely any; even my esteem is obtained with difficulty; but the man on whom I have once bestowed all
these, may depend on possessing them always. . . .

I have much to say to you about your new position,
but such things are better spoken than written. If the
government were to wish to make use of you now, your
position would be very delicate. . . . Be ruled by your
own opinion, and be the servant of no one. . . . Good-
by : forgive the involuntary sadness of this letter. You
are happy, so you will have plenty of congratulations :
but among all those who come to wish you joy, believe
that there is not one who at heart rejoices so much in
your success as I do.

Write to me at Geneva . . . . a long letter full of
plans for the preservation of our intercourse ; tell me
what you think of my own future, of the chances left to
me. . . .

TO THE SAME.

Gray, October 29, 1829.

At length, dear friend, here I am, sitting by the fire
with my table in front of me, and ready to talk to you.
This is just what I like, and yet I cannot be gay to-day.
On my arrival four days ago, I was seized with one of
the attacks in the stomach that you know, and so sharp
a one this time that fever followed. They were obliged
to bleed me. Now I am up again as usual able to walk
and talk and transact my business; but I still feel the
effects of my illness, and I am not yet quite recovered.
All this makes me gloomy ; and besides, it rains, the

wind whistles through my door, and my chimney smokes; a concentration of circumstances calculated to make one misanthropical, and reflect deeply on the faults, the vices, and the baseness of mankind.

Seriously, dear friend, my health is beginning to make me really uneasy. It seems to me as if years were far from improving it, that bodily fatigue affects me more than formerly. I fear that the life which we lead may increase the evil, so that in time I may become a valetudinarian. And this is not all. The hardest part to understand is, that I am afraid of being afraid: I mean, of my mind dwelling on the state of my body, and aggravating its importance. I am alarmed at the room that my physical evils occupy in my imagination, of the distaste with which they cause me to regard the future, and every sort of ambition — I might as well say, life itself. It is this moral weakness creeping over me, threatening to destroy the only virtue I really value in man, — energy, that I especially dread. And now, dear friend, what can you do? why have I told you all this? I really do not know; all I can say is, that these are the thoughts that press upon me; that my mind is more full of them than of any other; and that I felt the necessity of lightening my burden by shifting some of it on you. Now that I feel better, I will turn to something else.

Your letter, which reached me at Geneva five days ago, gave me much pleasure, and did me a great deal of good. Only you took too much to heart the hasty things I said to you about the instability of your friendships. You must allow something for first impressions, dear friend. When a man has just received a blow on the head, you should not reproach him for stepping unsteadily, provided that he is in the right direction. . . . It is quite true that I cannot yet reconcile myself to the impending change in our lives. From the first moment I perceived (with my imagination no doubt, rather than on reflection), that the tie which has united us so closely for the last two years must necessarily be loosened, I saw you launched into a different sphere. These considerations grieved me deeply ; more deeply, perhaps, than I can say. This is what I tried to express. If my words were ill-chosen, and I am willing to own it, you cannot at any rate complain of the intention.

However, I believe that I was wrong. I do not mean to admit that there is not a real change in our respective conditions, but that I feel persuaded that two men of our age, who understand each other, who have disclosed every corner of their hearts the one to the other, and whose mutual affection has grown with their intimacy, cannot greatly change. They cannot fail to be friends for life; and even if they have not frequent opportunities of meeting, they will still continue to confide in each other freely. These are the sage reflections which I had made before your letter came ; and that I imparted to Kergorlay in the long talks which we often have about you, in our walking expeditions, in places where your name was never before pronounced since the creation. But your letter did better than help to convince me ; it convinced something better than my head ; in short, it deeply touched my heart. I tell you this plainly, and the feeling is too serious for me to add any commentary. Yes, my friend, you are right in saying that we must have as many interests as possible in common. I quite enter into your plans. Some useful historical work might be our joint production. We must, of course, fit ourselves for political life, and for this purpose we must study the history of our race, and especially of the generations immediately preceding us.

General history is useful only in respect of the light which it throws upon human nature, and as a preparation. In that, my dear friend, I am almost as great a novice as yourself. I know more of the events themselves; but with regard to their causes, to the means furnished by men to those who have influenced them for the last two hundred years; to the state of the different nations before the outbreak of revolutions and afterwards; their classification, manners, and instincts; their present resources, the distribution and causes of these resources, of all this I am ignorant; and to this everything else is merely an introduction. There is one science which I long despised, but which I now own to be not only useful, but necessary; I mean Geography; not to learn the exact meridian of towns, but everything that relates to the knowledge which I have just mentioned; such as a clear understanding of the configuration of the earth as it influences the political condition and wealth of nations. Some countries are almost forced by their geographical position alone to adopt a certain form of government, to exercise a certain influence; their destiny even is caused by it. I confess that this is not the sort of geography that is taught in schools; but I fancy that it is the only kind which we can understand or recollect.

In conclusion, dear friend, let us hold fast to each other as much as we can. Especially let us preserve the habit of telling everything to one another, and we shall still have something like the time we spent at Versailles, which was one of the happiest periods of my past, and will be of my future, life.

TO THE BARON AND BARONESS DE TOCQUEVILLE.

Paris, April 6, 1830.

It was not without misgiving, dear friends, that I wrote to you in Rome. Something told me that I had better have directed my letters to Naples. But all our family went against me. Yet I was right. I thought that your calculations would be so exact, that we might be certain of your following your intended route, and that your silence ought to have been interpreted in my way. At length I yielded: my letter is in Rome with many others. No one can approve more strongly than I do your resolution to remain where you are. The holy week in Rome is finer seen from a distance than close; as in many other sights, there is more fatigue than real interest. Besides, it is said that the Pope will not officiate. Continue then to bask in the sunshine of Naples; content yourselves with enjoying the place you are now in, and the happiness that you find in each other. No one can appreciate better than I do your reasons for doing what many people will think extraordinary.

I was dining with some of my colleagues when Edward's long letter on the Neapolitan Constitution arrived. I read all the political part aloud; many compliments were paid to me which I transmit to the rightful owner. *I* shall pay you no compliments, dear Edward; but I thank you heartily for your letter. It taught me more about the country which you are now in, than I learnt in the six months I spent in Italy. How is it that two grown-up men, one of whom had completed his legal studies, can have travelled together for so long without directing their attention to the subject of most interest?

I am sorry that you did not get the letter which I sent to Rome; it would have given you all our political news. I confess that I am too idle to write it over again. Besides, by this time you must be acquainted with the outline. The address from the chamber, as might have been expected, was strong; the King showed, in his reply, that he was offended, and on the next day the chambers were prorogued till the 1st of September. Little has happened since. The ministry becomes more and more illiberal. It is supposed that M. de Chabrol and two other moderate members will resign. The King talks of nothing but force, the ministers of firmness. The wise royalists are uneasy; the fools — and they are the majority, are enchanted. They are always discussing *Coups d'État*, changes in the election laws by proclamations, &c., &c. In spite of all this, the French people are perfectly quiet. Newspaper writers on both sides are condemned every day by the tribunals. Nobody is satisfied with their decisions. The newspapers scream like seagulls, which is natural, since the decision is against them. The government is equally dissatisfied, since the grounds of the decision maintain the right of resistance to every unconstitutional measure. As for me, I own that I think that the judges do their duty in each case.

I am alarmed for the ministry, 1st, on account of the mediocrity of its members — there is but one opinion of their chief; 2d, the warmth and number of its enemies; 3d, the lukewarmness of most of those who think themselves obliged by conscience to support it; 4th, the arrogance of its most ardent upholders. They imagine that they are still at Coblentz. The royalists proper are only a small handful; and yet they try all they can to make themselves still fewer. They abuse each other with a virulence which would be amusing if it were not lamentable. One would think that they had only to share the prizes of victory. And so M. de Villèle's organ, *La Gazette* and *La Quotidienne*, the ministerial organ, attack each other every morning, to the great delight of the liberals.

In the midst of all this we are preparing for war with incredible activity (the expedition to Algiers). It is worth remarking, that since war has been resolved on, the liberal papers have in general ceased to criticise, both the end in view and the preparations. The unanimity of opinion upon this point shows the spirit of the nation.

You have heard, no doubt, of Hippolyte's endeavor to be allowed to join the campaign. He even stopped the Dauphiness as she was getting into her carriage. This was well received, and has made him popular; but as yet there is no positive result. Adieu.

TO THE BARON DE TOCQUEVILLE.

Versailles, May 6, 1830.

I see, my dear brother, from your last letter, that in reality we agree. You perceive the evil, but not the remedy. There are dangers, indeed, on every side. If we adhere to the constitution I do not think that the ministry can stand. It has no ardent supporters. All parties, even the ministers themselves, are aware of its instability. The Premier is an honest man, presumptuous and commonplace, who inspires no confidence. The royalists are undecided, disunited, without zeal; and what is worse, without much fear for the future, because they think that the House of Bourbon alone is threatened, and not monarchy itself; and that a revolution may take place without public disturbance.

Therefore if the charter be acted on, there is not much probability that the ministry will remain. If the King abandons it, there will be a reaction, and the royal authority will fall very low. Still this would be the safest course; for if the King sets his power above that of the charter, he will infallibly lose his throne. Such, at least, is my conviction. Let us consider, for a moment, how he would extricate himself if he were to set aside the law. What support would he have? Certainly not that of public opinion. There is scarcely a man who would approve of the measure. Almost the whole nation would rise up if it were attempted. That of the tribunals? But on the day that the King began to rule by proclamations, the tribunals would refuse to enforce them. I know them well enough to answer for this. He would have then to supersede them by executive commissions, to violate the laws more and more, to reign by military force, to fill the streets with soldiers. But could he be sure that they would long be satisfied with this employment? And then, and this reason is conclusive, is it possible that a man like Charles X., a man of seventy-two, with his kind and easy disposition, could face such consequences; and carry out persistently such a scheme? Is there among all the boasters round his throne one man brave enough to act under him, or skilful enough to act for him? What would happen then if force were resorted to? Perhaps the downfall of the present dynasty, or at any rate, an extreme diminution in the power of the crown. No one in France wants to be governed by proclamations. It is nobody's interest.

The judicial bodies would lose their importance; the peers their rank; men of talent their expectations; military men their promotion; and the lower classes all their security. If so, can he fight against the general will?

I have no private news for you. The expedition to Algiers must have sailed. I am anxious about Louis de Kergorlay, who told me, as a secret, that he is to be the first to land with a light portable battery, which is to open fire long before the arrival of the heavy artillery, and to protect the disembarkation.

TO M. GUSTAVE DE BEAUMONT.

Versailles, May 8, 1830.

I begin this letter at Versailles, dear friend, but I shall finish it in Paris, whither I start in half an hour. I am unwilling to lose any time in answering the kind, long letter which I received yesterday.

You have a remarkable power of moulding hearts according to your will. Your letter set me on my legs again. I mean that it has restored me to my previous state, neither happier nor more anxious than usual. The fact is, that you are the only man whose judgment I trust. Kergorlay would be well able to give an opinion; but he is not of our profession. You alone have the power and the means of judging.

When I reflect upon it, I think that we are not sufficiently grateful for the happiness of having stumbled upon each other amid the crowd. It is especially fortunate for me; not that I mean to affect modesty, and say that I am inferior to you, although I think so in many respects; but that you had more chances of being known and appreciated than I had, with my icy and

unattractive manners. You have already many friends.
Sooner or later, you would have found one who would
have been as much attached to you as I am. But among
the calculating minds who wear black gowns, I know not
where I could have found a friend, if I had not met with
you. Whatever might have been our fate, the thing is
done. We are friends, and I think for life. The same
studies, the same plans, the same places unite us, and
may unite us throughout our lives. What rare and in-
appreciable good fortune! Each of us finds in the other
the man most capable of giving him good advice, and
the most resolved not to spare him. Believe me, that
the longer we live the more we shall see that we cannot
depend upon hearing the truth except from each other.
Nothing is rarer than to meet a man who is qualified for
speaking it, except to find a man who is willing to speak
it. As for him who both can and will, where is he to be
found? I am frightened sometimes when I feel how sus-
picious I have grown. There is scarcely any praise
which I do not suspect; and I often put an unfavorable
interpretation on blame. On you alone I depend entirely.

TO THE VICOMTE DE TOCQUEVILLE. *

Versailles, August 18, 1830.

My dear Brother,

We all approve of your plan; none of us will ever
advise you to resign your commission. With your lively
mind and disposition you would soon find idleness intolerable. One may try a quiet life, but not throw one's

---

* His eldest brother Hippolyte, since Count de Tocqueville. He
was then captain in a cavalry regiment. This letter was written three
weeks after the Revolution of July, 1830.

self into it headlong and irrevocably. For the last two days my father has been in Paris acting for you. He has asked the *Directeur du personnel* for an audience. He probably obtained one yesterday. I can quite imagine that you would like to keep an opening in case of war; it would, in fact, be the path where you would most clearly see your duty. We must not allow invasion under any pretext! This is the cry even of the royalists. The nation would rise as one man if any interference were attempted with its internal affairs. . . .

I took the new oath of allegiance yesterday; it was an unpleasant moment. Not that it went against my conscience, but my pride suffered from the thought that others might fancy that I was acting from interested motives against my convictions. I remain, therefore, but will it be for long? I know not. The magistracy as well as the army is humiliated. But we cannot, as you can, regain our position at the point of the sword. I feel this so much, that I think I should abandon this career if I saw an opening in any other, but I do not, so I stay till I am sent away. See what it is to be moderate! If the Polignac ministry had triumphed, I should have been dismissed for resisting the proclamations. It has lost, and I shall perhaps be set aside by the conquerors; for I cannot approve all that is going on.

We hear from Emilie * almost every day. It would be impossible to show us more affection than she does. My father was quite touched by it the other day, and he said that his only consolation in these sad circumstances was the attachment shown by his sons and his daughters-in-law. For my part I have been much pleased at the calm with which he has contemplated all these changes.

* The Vicomtesse de Tocqueville.

If I allowed myself, I should have a great deal more to tell you. What I have seen during this revolution would fill a volume. We shall soon talk about it, which will be better.

TO M. GUSTAVE DE BEAUMONT.

London, August 14, 1833.

At last I have reached England, dear friend; I assure you not without trouble. First I sailed from Cherbourg to Guernsey, in a yacht, whose owner offered me a passage. There I found a steamer which took me in ten hours to Weymouth, a little town on the south coast of England, whence I made my way to London. I arrived last Saturday. It would be difficult to describe my impressions since I set foot in this huge metropolis. I feel in perpetual confusion, and deeply conscious of my insignificance. We were great people in America. We are not much in Paris. But one must fall below zero, and take what the mathematicians call minus quantities, to calculate what I am here. There are two reasons for this: first the enormous size of the town, which is beyond all that Paris can give an idea of, and the number of remarkable men to be found in it; secondly, the position occupied by the aristocracy, of which I had no previous conception. The advantages bestowed by fortune, when it is added to high birth, seem to me to be a thousand times greater than any others. Of course I cannot yet speak of the character of the English nation; I can only tell you what strikes me most in their manners: it is their aristocratic form; the aristocratic spirit seems to me to penetrate all classes. . . . I find nothing at all like America. . . . I wander all over London like a midge over a haystack. . . . All the people to whom I have access receive me kindly, but the difficulty is to get sight of them. . . . The hardest part is to confine one's curiosity within certain limits; the multitude of interesting objects (intellectually speaking), weigh one down; I want to be directed in my choice. . . . Write to me as soon as possible.

TO THE SAME.

Paris, July 5, 1834.

I received from you the other day, my dear friend, just such a letter as I like — long and full of details. I thank you for it, and beg you to go on in the same way. I will try on my part to be a punctual correspondent. You, indeed, are the only person to whom I can write without wasting time. All I say to you flows so naturally, that my letters take me only the time that is occupied in tracing the characters. Independently of our friendship, which however is the primary cause, this is occasioned by my conviction that, knowing me so well, I have nothing to lose or to gain with you. So I go on without thinking of consequences.

On the day before yesterday I went again to Gosselin.* If he had read my MS. the result of my visit would not have been flattering; for the more questions of his I answered about the book, the more frightened he became. He ended by telling me that he would print 500 copies. I wondered, and then he explained his motives. It does not, indeed, cost much more to print 1,000 than 500 copies. But if the work does not sell, the surplus is lost. When, on the other hand, a second edition is called for, it costs, of course, more than if the necessary number had been printed at first, but one is tolerably safe. By the first plan one risks loss, by the second diminution of gain.

* His publisher.

Now in publishing one must be satisfied with aiming at small but safe profits. All this seemed to me to be very sensible. It is no less true that Gosselin is horribly afraid of losing, or at least of gaining very little by my book. This was the moral that I drew from my visit.

It is a humiliating part of an author's profession to be obliged to have to treat with one's publisher as if he were one's superior.

I still am determined, or rather I am more than ever determined, to go to you towards the 15th of next month. I shall arrive with my MS. under my arm, and my gun across my shoulders. Prepare yourself beforehand for every exercise of mind and body.

TO THE SAME.

April 1, 1835.

I shall write to you, dear friend, only a few hurried lines. It seems as if you had been a month away, so many things, little things I mean, have taken place. Yesterday morning I went to Gosselin. He received me with the most beaming face, and said, " Ah ! so it appears that your book is a masterpiece ! " Does not this paint the tradesman? I sat down. We talked about the second edition. We were obliged to make a bargain, which I did as awkwardly as possible, and looking like a little boy before his master. In short, I found no objections to make to any of his proposals ; and after putting on my head the hat that I had been twirling in my hand for the last quarter of an hour, I went away convinced of two things : — first, that Gosselin intended to behave well ; and, secondly, that though a little man, I am, in business, a great dunce. . . .

On the day before you left I went to see Madame

Récamier, who invited me to come on the day after, which was yesterday, at three o'clock, to hear the *great man* * read a portion of his memoirs. So I went. I found a troop of budding and full-blown celebrities; a well-selected circle. At the head, Chateaubriand, Ampère, Ballanche, St. Beuve, the Duc de Noailles, and the Duc de Laval; the same whom I heard say ten years ago in Rome, " By Jove ! I have spent some delightful hours with that woman ! " Chateaubriand introduced me to all these people in terms calculated to make a few of them my friends, and the greater number my sincere enemies. They all paid me many compliments. When this little piece was over, the real play began. It would take too long to tell you all about it. It was on the First Restoration and the One Hundred Days. Some bad taste, some very bitter feeling, some profound views in his picture of the perplexities experienced by Napoleon when on the throne, all with great spirit, and full of poetry. Napoleon's march on Paris after his return from Elba, told as it would have been by Homer and Tacitus in one; the battle of Waterloo described so as to make every nerve vibrate, though the booming of the cannon is now so distant. . . . How shall I repeat it to you ? I was deeply moved, excited, and agitated; and when I expressed my warm admiration, I was perfectly sincere. Madame Récamier, and afterwards M. de Chateaubriand, desired me to say that they regretted your not being present.

I returned home after this reading, transported to that region midway between earth and heaven, in which one finds one's self after any great excitement, while the impression still lasts. . . .

* M. de Chateaubriand.

TO N. W. SENIOR, ESQ.

Paris, February 21, 1835.

MY DEAR MR. SENIOR,

I thank you much for the kind letter which you have just sent to me. There is no approbation that I was more anxious to gain, and I am proud of having obtained it. How much I wish that the book could be read by a large majority of your countrymen, and that the opinion which you have formed of it could become general. Its success here much surpasses my expectations. But I shall not be satisfied unless it extends to a country to which I am intellectually indebted almost as much as to my own.

I am about to remark upon your objections, which gave me almost as much pleasure as your praise; because they prove the attention with which you read my book, and because I intend to make use of several of them in preparing the second edition.

You tell me, with much truth, respecting a note on page 77, that a poor-law is no proof of a republican government; but my reason for quoting America in this respect, was to give French readers an instance of the expense willingly incurred by a democracy. There are many causes which may induce any government to relieve the poor at the expense of the public, but a republican government is, from its nature, forced to do so.

In page 115, I said that in English legislation, the *bien du pauvre, had in the end been sacrificed to that of the rich.* You attack me on this point, of which you certainly are a competent judge. You must allow me, however, to differ from you. In the first place it seems

to me that you give to the expression *le bien du pauvre,*
a confined sense which was not mine; you translate it
wealth, a word especially applied to money. I meant
by it all that contributes to happiness; personal consideration, political rights, easy justice, intellectual enjoyments, and many other indirect sources of contentment.
I shall believe, till I have proof of the contrary, that in
England the rich have gradually monopolized almost
all the advantages that society bestows upon mankind.
Taking the question in your own restricted sense, and
admitting that a poor man is better paid when he works
on another man's land, that when he cultivates his own,
do you not think that there are political, moral, and
intellectual advantages attached to the possession of
land, which are a more than sufficient, and above all,
a permanent compensation for the loss that you point
out?

I know, however, that this is one of the most important questions of the age, and perhaps the one on which
we differ most entirely. Soon I hope that we shall have
an opportunity for discussing it. In the mean while, I
cannot help telling you how dissatisfied I was at the way
in which Mr. McCulloch, whose talents, however, I acknowledge, has treated this question. I was astonished
at his quoting us Frenchmen in support of his arguments
in favor of the non-division of landed property; and at
his asserting that the physical well-being of the people
deteriorated in proportion to the subdivision of property:
I am convinced, that up to the present time, this is sub-
stantially false. Such an opinion would find no echo
here, even from those who attack the law of succession
as impolitic and dangerous in its ultimate tendency.
Even *they* acknowledge that as yet the progress of our

people in comfort and civilization, has been rapid and uninterrupted; and that in these respects, the France of to-day is as unlike as possible to the France of twenty years ago. I repeat, however, that such questions cannot be treated in writing. They must be kept for long conversations.

END OF VOL. I.

☞ Any Books in this list will be sent free of postage, on receipt of price.

BOSTON, 135 WASHINGTON STREET,
JANUARY, 1862.

A LIST OF BOOKS

PUBLISHED BY

TICKNOR AND FIELDS.

Sir Walter Scott.

ILLUSTRATED HOUSEHOLD EDITION OF THE WAVER-
LEY NOVELS. 50 volumes. In portable size, 16mo. form. Now
Complete. Price 75 cents a volume.

The paper is of fine quality; the stereotype plates are not old
ones repaired, the type having been cast expressly for this edition. The Novels are illustrated with capital steel plates en-
graved in the best manner, after drawings and paintings by the
most eminent artists, among whom are Birket Foster, Darley,
Billings, Landseer, Harvey, and Faed. This Edition contains
all the latest notes and corrections of the author, a Glossary and
Index; and some curious additions, especially in " Guy Mannering" and the "Bride of Lammermoor;" being the fullest
edition of the Novels ever published. *The notes are at the foot
of the page,*—a great convenience to the reader.

Any of the following Novels sold separate.

WAVERLEY, 2 vols.
GUY MANNERING, 2 vols.
THE ANTIQUARY, 2 vols.
ROB ROY, 2 vols.
OLD MORTALITY, 2 vols.
BLACK DWARF,
LEGEND OF MONTROSE, } 2 vols.
HEART OF MID LOTHIAN, 2 vols.
BRIDE OF LAMMERMOOR, 2 vols.
IVANHOE, 2 vols.
THE MONASTERY, 2 vols.
THE ABBOT, 2 vols.
KENILWORTH, 2 vols.
THE PIRATE, 2 vols.
THE FORTUNES OF NIGEL, 2 vols.
PEVERIL OF THE PEAK, 2 vols.
QUENTIN DURWARD, 2 vols.

ST. RONAN'S WELL, 2 vols.
REDGAUNTLET, 2 vols.
THE BETROTHED,
THE HIGHLAND WIDOW, } 2 vols.
THE TALISMAN,
TWO DROVERS,
MY AUNT MARGARET'S MIRROR, } 2 vols.
THE TAPESTRIED CHAMBER,
THE LAIRD'S JOCK,
WOODSTOCK, 2 vols.
THE FAIR MAID OF PERTH. 2 vols.
ANNE OF GEIERSTEIN, 2 vols.
COUNT ROBERT OF PARIS, 2 vols.
THE SURGEON'S DAUGHTER,
CASTLE DANGEROUS, } 2 vols.
INDEX AND GLOSSARY,

TALES OF A GRANDFATHER. Illustrated. 6 vols. $4.50.

LIFE. By J. G. Lockhart. *In Press.* Uniform with Novels.
Vols. 1 and 2 now ready. Cloth. $1.50.

Thomas De Quincey.

CONFESSIONS OF AN ENGLISH OPIUM-EATER, AND SUSPIRIA DE PROFUNDIS. With Portrait. 75 cents.

BIOGRAPHICAL ESSAYS. 75 cents.

MISCELLANEOUS ESSAYS. 75 cents.

THE CÆSARS. 75 cents.

LITERARY REMINISCENCES. 2 vols. $1.50.

NARRATIVE AND MISCELLANEOUS PAPERS. 2 vols. $1.50.

ESSAYS ON THE POETS, &c. 1 vol. 16mo. 75 cents.

HISTORICAL AND CRITICAL ESSAYS. 2 vols. $1.50.

AUTOBIOGRAPHIC SKETCHES. 1 vol. 75 cents.

ESSAYS ON PHILOSOPHICAL WRITERS, &c. 2 vols. 16mo. $1.50.

LETTERS TO A YOUNG MAN, AND OTHER PAPERS. 1 vol. 75 cents.

THEOLOGICAL ESSAYS AND OTHER PAPERS. 2 vols. $1.50.

THE NOTE BOOK. 1 vol. 75 cents.

MEMORIALS AND OTHER PAPERS. 2 vols. 16mo. $1.50.

THE AVENGER AND OTHER PAPERS. 1 vol. 75 cents.

LOGIC OF POLITICAL ECONOMY, AND OTHER PAPERS. 1 vol. 75 cents.

Thomas Hood.

MEMORIALS. Edited by his Children. 2 vols. $1.75.

Alfred Tennyson.

POETICAL WORKS. With Portrait. 2 vols. Cloth. $2.00

POCKET EDITION OF POEMS COMPLETE. 2 vols. $1.50.

POEMS. Complete in one volume. With Portrait. $1.00.

THE PRINCESS. Cloth. 50 cents.

IN MEMORIAM. Cloth. 75 cents.

The Same. Holiday Edition. With Portraits of Tennyson and Arthur Hallam, and Biographical Sketch. $2.50.

MAUD, AND OTHER POEMS. Cloth. 50 cents.

IDYLLS OF THE KING. A new volume. Cloth. 75 cents.

Charles Dickens.

[ENGLISH EDITION.]

THE COMPLETE WORKS OF CHARLES DICKENS. Fine Library Edition. Published simultaneously in London and Boston. English print, fine cloth binding, 22 vols. 12mo. $27.50.

Henry W. Longfellow.

POETICAL WORKS. 2 vols. Boards, $2.00. Cloth, $2.25.

POCKET EDITION OF POETICAL WORKS. In two volumes. $1.75.

POCKET EDITION OF PROSE WORKS COMPLETE. In two volumes. $1.75.

THE SONG OF HIAWATHA. $1.00.

EVANGELINE: A Tale of Acadia. 75 cents.

THE GOLDEN LEGEND. A Poem. $1.00.

HYPERION. A Romance. $1.00.

OUTRE-MER. A Pilgrimage. $1.00.

KAVANAGH. A Tale. 75 cents.

THE COURTSHIP OF MILES STANDISH. 1 vol. 16mo. 75 cents.

Illustrated. editions of EVANGELINE. POEMS, HYPERION, THE GOLDEN LEGEND, and MILES STANDISH.

Charles Reade.

PEG WOFFINGTON. A Novel. 75 cents.

CHRISTIE JOHNSTONE. A Novel. 75 cents.

CLOUDS AND SUNSHINE. A Novel. 75 cents.

"NEVER TOO LATE TO MEND." 2 vols. $1.50.

WHITE LIES. A Novel. 1 vol. $1.25.

PROPRIA QUÆ MARIBUS and THE BOX TUNNEL. 25 cts.

THE EIGHTH COMMANDMENT. 75 cents.

James Russell Lowell.

COMPLETE POETICAL WORKS. In Blue and Gold. 2 vols. $1.50.

POETICAL WORKS. 2 vols. 16mo. Cloth. $1.50.

SIR LAUNFAL. New Edition. 25 cents.

A FABLE FOR CRITICS. New Edition. 50 cents.

THE BIGLOW PAPERS. New Edition. 63 cents.

FIRESIDE TRAVELS. *In Press.*

Nathaniel Hawthorne.

TWICE-TOLD TALES. Two volumes. $1.50.

THE SCARLET LETTER. 75 cents.

THE HOUSE OF THE SEVEN GABLES. $1.00.

THE SNOW IMAGE, AND OTHER TALES. 75 cents.

THE BLITHEDALE ROMANCE. 75 cents.

MOSSES FROM AN OLD MANSE. 2 vols. $1.50.

THE MARBLE FAUN. 2 vols. $1.50.

TRUE STORIES. 75 cents.

A WONDER-BOOK FOR GIRLS AND BOYS. 75 cents.

TANGLEWOOD TALES. 88 cents.

Edwin P. Whipple.

ESSAYS AND REVIEWS. 2 vols. $2.00.

LECTURES ON LITERATURE AND LIFE. 63 cents.

WASHINGTON AND THE REVOLUTION. 20 cents.

Charles Kingsley.

TWO YEARS AGO. A New Novel. $1.25.

AMYAS LEIGH. A Novel. $1.25.

GLAUCUS; OR, THE WONDERS OF THE SHORE. 50 cts.

POETICAL WORKS. 75 cents.

THE HEROES; OR, GREEK FAIRY TALES. 75 cents.

ANDROMEDA AND OTHER POEMS. 50 cents.

SIR WALTER RALEIGH AND HIS TIME, &c. $1.25.

NEW MISCELLANIES. 1 vol. $1.00.

Mrs. Howe.

PASSION FLOWERS. 75 cents.
WORDS FOR THE HOUR. 75 cents.
THE WORLD'S OWN. 50 cents.
A TRIP TO CUBA. 1 vol. 16mo. 75 cents.

George S. Hillard.

SIX MONTHS IN ITALY. 1 vol. 16mo. $1.50.
DANGERS AND DUTIES OF THE MERCANTILE PROFES-
SION. 25 cents.
SELECTIONS FROM THE WRITINGS OF WALTER SAVAGE
LANDOR. 1 vol. 16mo. 75 cents.

Oliver Wendell Holmes.

ELSIE VENNER : a Romance of Destiny. 2 vols. Cloth. $1.75.
POEMS. With fine Portrait. Cloth. $1.00.
ASTRÆA. Fancy paper. 25 cents.
THE AUTOCRAT OF THE BREAKFAST TABLE. With Il-
lustrations by Hoppin. 16mo. $1.00.
The Same. Large Paper Edition. 8vo. Tinted paper. $3.00.
THE PROFESSOR AT THE BREAKFAST TABLE. 16mo.
$1.00.
The Same. Large Paper Edition. 8vo. Tinted paper. $3.00.
SONGS IN MANY KEYS. A new volume. $1.25.
CURRENTS AND COUNTER-CURRENTS, AND OTHER MEDI-
CAL ESSAYS. 1 vol. Cloth. $1.25.

Ralph Waldo Emerson.

ESSAYS. 1st Series. 1 vol. $1.00.
ESSAYS. 2d Series. 1 vol. $1.00.
MISCELLANIES. 1 vol. $1.00.
REPRESENTATIVE MEN. 1 vol. $1.00.
ENGLISH TRAITS. 1 vol. $1.00.
POEMS. 1 vol. $1.00.
CONDUCT OF LIFE. 1 vol. $1.00.

Goethe.

WILHELM MEISTER. Translated by *Carlyle.* 2 vols. $2.50.

FAUST. Translated by *Hayward.* 75 cents.

FAUST. Translated by *Charles T. Brooks.* $1.00.

CORRESPONDENCE WITH A CHILD. *Bettina.* 1 vol. 12mo. $1.25.

Henry Giles.

LECTURES, ESSAYS, &c. 2 vols. $1.50.

DISCOURSES ON LIFE. 75 cents.

ILLUSTRATIONS OF GENIUS. Cloth. $1.00.

John G. Whittier.

POCKET EDITION OF POETICAL WORKS. 2 vols. $1.50.

OLD PORTRAITS AND MODERN SKETCHES. 75 cents.

MARGARET SMITH'S JOURNAL. 75 cents.

SONGS OF LABOR, AND OTHER POEMS. Boards. 50 cts.

THE CHAPEL OF THE HERMITS. Cloth. 50 cents.

LITERARY RECREATIONS, &c. Cloth. $1.00.

THE PANORAMA, AND OTHER POEMS. Cloth. 50 cents.

HOME BALLADS AND POEMS. A new volume. 75 cents.

Capt. Mayne Reid.

THE PLANT HUNTERS. With Plates. 75 cents.

THE DESERT HOME: OR, THE ADVENTURES OF A LOST FAMILY IN THE WILDERNESS. With fine Plates. $1.00.

THE BOY HUNTERS. With fine Plates. 75 cents.

THE YOUNG VOYAGEURS: OR, THE BOY HUNTERS IN THE NORTH. With Plates. 75 cents.

THE FOREST EXILES. With fine Plates. 75 cents.

THE BUSH BOYS. With fine Plates. 75 cents.

THE YOUNG YAGERS. With fine Plates. 75 cents.

RAN AWAY TO SEA: AN AUTOBIOGRAPHY FOR BOYS. With fine Plates. 75 cents.

THE BOY TAR: A VOYAGE IN THE DARK. A New Book. With fine Plates. 75 cents.

ODD PEOPLE. With Plates. 75 cents.

The Same. Cheap Edition. With Plates. 50 cents.

BRUIN: OR, THE GRAND BEAR HUNT. With Plates. 75 cts.

Rev. F. W. Robertson.

SERMONS. First Series, $1.00.
" Second " $1.00.
" Third " $1.00.
" Fourth " $1.00.

LECTURES AND ADDRESSES ON LITERARY AND SOCIAL TOPICS. $1.00.

Mrs. Jameson.

CHARACTERISTICS OF WOMEN. Blue and Gold. 75 cents.
LOVES OF THE POETS. " " 75 cents.
DIARY OF AN ENNUYÉE. " " 75 cents.
SKETCHES OF ART, &c. " " 75 cents.
STUDIES AND STORIES. " " 75 cents.
ITALIAN PAINTERS. " " 75 cents.
LEGENDS OF THE MADONNA. " " 75 cents.
SISTERS OF CHARITY. 1 vol. 16mo. 75 cents.

Grace Greenwood.

GREENWOOD LEAVES. 1st and 2d Series. $1.25 each.
POETICAL WORKS. With fine Portrait. 75 cents.
HISTORY OF MY PETS. With six fine Engravings. Scarlet cloth. 50 cents.
RECOLLECTIONS OF MY CHILDHOOD. With six fine Engravings. Scarlet cloth. 50 cents.
HAPS AND MISHAPS OF A TOUR IN EUROPE. $1.25.
MERRIE ENGLAND. 75 cents.
A FOREST TRAGEDY, AND OTHER TALES. $1.00.
STORIES AND LEGENDS. 75 cents.
STORIES FROM FAMOUS BALLADS. Illustrated. 50 cents.
BONNIE SCOTLAND. Illustrated. 75 cents.

Mrs. Mowatt.

AUTOBIOGRAPHY OF AN ACTRESS. $1.25.
PLAYS. ARMAND AND FASHION. 50 cents.
MIMIC LIFE. 1 vol. $1.25.
THE TWIN ROSES. 1 vol. 75 cents.

Samuel Smiles.

LIFE OF GEORGE STEPHENSON, ENGINEER. $1.00.
SELF HELP; WITH ILLUSTRATIONS OF CHARACTER AND
    CONDUCT. With Portrait. 1 vol. 75 cents.
BRIEF BIOGRAPHIES. With Plates. $1.25.

Miss Cummins.

EL FUREIDIS. By the Author of "The Lamplighter," &c.
    $1.00.

Thomas Hughes.

SCHOOL DAYS AT RUGBY. By *An Old Boy.* 1 vol. 16mo.
    $1.00.
The Same. Illustrated edition. $1.50.
THE SCOURING OF THE WHITE HORSE, OR THE LONG
    VACATION HOLIDAY OF A LONDON CLERK. By *The Author
    of " School Days at Rugby."* 1 vol. 16mo. $1.00.
TOM BROWN AT OXFORD. A Sequel to School Days at
    Rugby. 2 vols. 16mo. With fine Steel Portrait of the Author.
    $2.00.

François Arago.

BIOGRAPHIES OF DISTINGUISHED SCIENTIFIC MEN.
    2 vols. 16mo. $2.00.

Bayard Taylor.

POEMS OF HOME AND TRAVEL. Cloth. 75 cents.
POEMS OF THE ORIENT. Cloth. 75 cents.
A POET'S JOURNAL. *In Press.*

John Neal.

TRUE WOMANHOOD. A Novel. 1 vol. $1.25.

Hans Christian Andersen.

THE SAND-HILLS OF JUTLAND. 1 vol. 16mo. 75 cents.

R. H. Dana, Jr.

To Cuba and Back, a Vacation Voyage, by the Author of "Two Years before the Mast." 75 cents.

Miscellaneous Works in Poetry and Prose.

[POETRY.]

Alford's (Henry) Poems. 1 vol. 16mo. Cloth. $1.00.
Angel in the House: The Betrothal. 1 vol. 16mo. Cloth. 75 cents.
"   "   The Espousals. 1 vol. 16mo. Cloth. 75 cents.
Arnold's (Matthew) Poems. 1 vol. 75 cents.
Aytoun's Bothwell. A Narrative Poem. 1 vol. 75 cents.
Bailey's (P. J.) The Mystic. 1 vol. 16mo. Cloth. 50 cents.
"   "   The Age. 1 vol. 16mo. Cloth. 75 cents.
Barry Cornwall's English Songs and Other Poems. 1 vol. $1.00.
"   "   Dramatic Poems. 1 vol. $1.00.
Boker's Plays and Poems. 2 vols. 16mo. Cloth. $2.00.
Brooks's German Lyrics. 1 vol. $1.00.
"   Faust. A new Translation. 1 vol. $1.00.
Browning's (Robert) Poems. 2 vols. $2.00.
"   "   Men and Women. 1 vol. $1.00.
Cary's (Alice) Poems. 1 vol. $1.00.
Cary's (Phœbe) Poems and Parodies. 1 vol. 75 cts.
Fresh Hearts that Failed. By the Author of "The New Priest." 1 vol. 50 cents.
Hayne's Poems. 1 vol. 63 cents.
"   Avolio and Other Poems. 1 vol. 16mo. Cloth. 75 cents.
Hunt's (Leigh) Poems. 2 vols. Blue and Gold. $1.50
"   "   Rimini. 1 vol. 50 cents.
Hymns of the Ages. 1 vol. Enlarged edition. $1.25
Hymns of the Ages. 2d Series. 1 vol. $1.25.
The Same. 8vo. Bevelled boards. Each volume, $3.00.
Johnson's (Rosa V) Poems. 1 vol. $1.00.
Kemble's (Mrs.) Poems. 1 vol. $1.00.

LOCKHART'S (J. G.) SPANISH BALLADS. With Portrait.
1 vol. 75 cents.
LUNT'S (GEO.) LYRIC POEMS. 1 vol. 16mo. Cloth.
63 cents.
"   "   JULIA. 1 vol. 50 cents.
MACKAY'S POEMS. 1 vol. $1.00.
MASSEY'S (GERALD) POEMS. 1 vol. Blue and Gold. 75
cents.
MEMORY AND HOPE. A Collection of Consolatory Pieces.
1 vol. $2.00.
MOTHERWELL'S POEMS. 1 vol. Blue and Gold. 75 cts.
"   MINSTRELSY, ANCIENT AND MODERN.
2 vols. $1.50.
MULOCH'S (MISS) POEMS. (By Author of " John Hali-
fax.") 1 vol. 75 cents.
OWEN MEREDITH'S POEMS. 1 vol. Blue and Gold. 75 cts.
PARSONS'S POEMS. 1 vol. $1.00.
"   DANTE'S INFERNO. Translated. *In Press.*
PERCIVAL'S POEMS. 2 vols. Blue and Gold. $1.75.
QUINCY'S (J. P.) CHARICLES. A Dramatic Poem. 1 vol.
50 cents.
"   "   LYTERIA : A Dramatic Poem. 50 cents.
READ'S (T. BUCHANAN) POEMS. New and complete edi-
tion. 2 vols. $2.00.
REJECTED ADDRESSES. By Horace and James Smith.
New edition. 1 vol. 63 cents.
SAXE'S (J. G.) POEMS. With Portrait. 1 vol. 75 cents.
"   "   THE MONEY KING AND OTHER POEMS.
With new Portrait. 1 vol. 75 cents.
"   "   POEMS — the two foregoing vols. in one.
$1.25.
"   "   POEMS. Complete in Blue and Gold. With
Portrait. 75 cents.
SMITH'S (ALEXANDER) LIFE DRAMA. 1 vol. 50 cents.
"   "   CITY POEMS. 1 vol. 63 cents.
"   "   EDWIN OF DEIRA. With Por-
trait. 75 cents.
STODDARD'S (R. H.) POEMS. 1 vol. 63 cents.
"   "   SONGS OF SUMMER. 1 vol. 75 cts.
SPRAGUE'S (CHARLES) POETICAL AND PROSE WORKS.
With Portrait. 1 vol. 88 cents.
THACKERAY'S BALLADS. 1 vol. 75 cents.
THALATTA. A Book for the Seaside. 1 vol. 75 cents.
TUCKERMAN'S POEMS. 1 vol. 75 cents.
WARRENIANA. 1 vol. 63 cents.

[PROSE.]

ALLSTON'S MONALDI. A Tale. 1 vol. 16mo. Cloth.
75 cents.

ARNOLD'S (DR. THOMAS) LIFE AND CORRESPONDENCE. Edited by A. P. Stanley. 2 vols. 12mo. Cloth. $2.00.

ARNOLD'S (W. D.) OAKFIELD. A Novel. 1 vol. 16mo. Cloth. $1.00.

ALMOST A HEROINE. By the Author of " Charles Auchester." 1 vol. 16mo. Cloth. $1.00.

ARABIAN DAYS' ENTERTAINMENT. Translated from the German, by H. P. Curtis. Illustrated. 1 vol. $1.25.

ADDISON'S SIR ROGER DE COVERLEY. From the " Spectator." 1 vol. 16mo. Cloth. 75 cents.

The Same. 1 vol. 16mo. Cloth, gilt edge. $1.25.

ANGEL VOICES; OR, WORDS OF COUNSEL FOR OVERCOMING THE WORLD. 1 vol. 16mo. Cloth, gilt, 38; gilt edge, 50; full gilt, 63 cents.

The Same. Holiday Edition. Tinted paper. 50 cents.

AMERICAN INSTITUTE OF INSTRUCTION. Lectures delivered before the Institute in 1840–41–42–43–44–45–46–47–48–49–50–51–52–53–54–55–56–57–58–59–60. 21 vols. 12mo. Sold in separate volumes, each 50 cents.

BACON'S (DELIA) THE SHAKSPERIAN PROBLEM SOLVED. With an Introduction by Nathaniel Hawthorne. 1 vol. 8vo. Cloth. $3.00.

BARTOL'S CHURCH AND CONGREGATION. 1 vol. 16mo. Cloth. $1.00.

BAILEY'S ESSAYS ON OPINIONS AND TRUTH. 1 vol. 16mo. Cloth. $1.00.

BARRY CORNWALL'S ESSAYS AND TALES IN PROSE. 2 vols. $1.50.

BOSTON BOOK. Being Specimens of Metropolitan Literature. Cloth, $1.25; gilt edge, $1.75; full gilt, $2.00.

BUCKINGHAM'S (J. T.) PERSONAL MEMOIRS. With Portrait. 2 vols. 16mo. Cloth. $1.50.

CHANNING'S (E. T.) LECTURES ON RHETORIC AND ORATORY. 1 vol. 16mo. Cloth. 75 cents.

CHANNING'S (DR. WALTER) PHYSICIAN'S VACATION. 1 vol. 12mo. Cloth. $1.50.

COALE'S (DR. W. E.) HINTS ON HEALTH. 1 vol. 16mo. Cloth. 63 cents.

COMBE ON THE CONSTITUTION OF MAN. 30th edition. 12mo. Cloth. 75 cents.

CHAPEL LITURGY. Book of Common Prayer, according to the use of King's Chapel, Boston. 1 vol. 8vo. Sheep, $2.00; sheep, extra, $2.50; sheep, extra, gilt edge, $3.00; morocco, $3.50; do. gilt edge, $4.00; do. extra gilt edge, $4.50.

The Same. Cheaper edition. 1 vol. 12mo. Sheep, $1.50.

CROSLAND'S (MRS.) LYDIA: A WOMAN'S BOOK. 1 vol. 75 cents.

"   "   ENGLISH TALES AND SKETCHES. 1 vol. $1.00.

CROSLAND'S (MRS.) MEMORABLE WOMEN. Illustrated. 1 vol. $1.00.

Dana's (R. H.) To Cuba and Back. 1 vol. 16mo. Cloth. 75 cents.

Dufferin's (Lord) Yacht Voyage. 1 vol. 16mo. Cloth. $1.00.

El Fureidis. By the author of "The Lamplighter." 1 vol. 16mo. Cloth. $1.00.

Ernest Carroll; or, Artist-Life in Italy. 1 vol. 16mo. Cloth. 88 cents.

Fremont's Life, Explorations, and Public Services. By C. W. Upham. With Illustrations. 1 vol. 16mo. Cloth. 75 cents.

Gaskell's (Mrs.) Ruth. A Novel. 8vo. Paper. 38 cts.

Guesses at Truth. By Two Brothers. 1 vol. 12mo. $1.50.

Greenwood's (F. W. P.) Sermons of Consolation. 16mo. Cloth, $1.00; cloth, gilt edge, $1.50; morocco, plain gilt edge, $2.00; morocco, extra gilt edge, $2.50.

"   History of the King's Chapel, Boston. 12mo. Cloth. 50 cents.

Hodson's Soldier's Life in India. 1 vol. 16mo. Cloth. $1.00.

Howitt's (William) Land, Labor, and Gold. 2 vols. $2.00.

"   "   A Boy's Adventures in Australia. 75 cents.

Howitt's (Anna Mary) An Art Student in Munich. $1.25.

"   "   A School of Life. A Story. 75 cents.

Hufeland's Art of Prolonging Life. 1 vol. 16mo. Cloth. 75 cents.

Jerrold's (Douglas) Life. By his Son. 1 vol. 16mo. Cloth. $1.00.

"   "   Wit. By his Son. 1 vol. 16mo. Cloth. 75 cents.

Judson's (Mrs. E. C.) Alderbrook. By Fanny Forrester. 2 vols. $1.75.

"   "   The Kathayan Slave, and other Papers. 1 vol. 63 cents.

"   "   My two Sisters: A Sketch from Memory. 50 cents.

Kavanagh's (Julia) Seven Years. 8vo. Paper. 30 cents.

Kingsley's (Henry) Geoffry Hamlyn. 1 vol. 12mo. Cloth. $1.25.

Krapf's Travels and Researches in Eastern Africa. 1 vol. 12mo. Cloth. $1.25.

Leslie's (C. R.) Autobiographical Recollections. Edited by Tom Taylor. With Portrait. 1 vol. 12mo. Cloth. $1.25.

LAKE HOUSE. From the German of Fanny Lewald. 1 vol. 16mo. Cloth. 75 cents.

LOWELL'S (REV. DR. CHARLES) PRACTICAL SERMONS. 1 vol. 12mo. Cloth. $1.25.

" " OCCASIONAL SERMONS. With fine Portrait. 1 vol. 12mo. Cloth. $1.25.

LIGHT ON THE DARK RIVER; OR, MEMOIRS OF MRS. HAMLIN. 1 vol. 16mo. Cloth. $1.00.

The Same. 16mo. Cloth, gilt edge. $1.50.

LONGFELLOW (REV. S.) AND JOHNSON (REV. S.) A book of Hymns for Public and Private Devotion. 6th edition. 63 cents.

LABOR AND LOVE. A Tale of English Life. 1 vol. 16mo. Cloth. 50 cents.

LEE'S (MRS. E. B.) MEMOIR OF THE BUCKMINSTERS. $1.25.

" " FLORENCE, THE PARISH ORPHAN. 50 cents.

" " PARTHENIA. 1 vol. 16mo. $1.00.

LUNT'S (GEORGE) THREE ERAS IN THE HISTORY OF NEW ENGLAND. 1 vol. $1.00.

MADEMOISELLE MORI: A Tale of Modern Rome. 1 vol. 12mo. Cloth. $1.25.

M'CLINTOCK'S NARRATIVE OF THE SEARCH FOR SIR JOHN FRANKLIN. Library edition. With Maps and Illustrations. 1 vol. small 8vo. $1.50.

The Same. Popular Edition. 1 vol. 12mo. 75 cents.

MANN'S (HORACE) THOUGHTS FOR A YOUNG MAN. 1 vol. 25 cents.

" " SERMONS. 1 vol. $1.00.

MANN'S (MRS. HORACE) PHYSIOLOGICAL COOKERY-BOOK. 1 vol. 16mo. Cloth. 63 cents.

MELVILLE'S HOLMBY HOUSE. A Novel. 8vo. Paper. 50 cents.

MITFORD'S (MISS) OUR VILLAGE. Illustrated. 2 vols. 16mo. $2.50.

" " ATHERTON, AND OTHER STORIES. 1 vol. 16mo. $1.25.

MORLEY'S LIFE OF PALISSY THE POTTER. 2 vols. 16mo. Cloth. $1.50.

MOUNTFORD'S THORPE. 1 vol. 16mo. Cloth. $1.00.

NORTON'S (C. E.) TRAVEL AND STUDY IN ITALY. 1 vol. 16mo. Cloth. 75 cents.

NEW TESTAMENT. A very handsome edition, fine paper and clear type. 12mo. Sheep binding, plain, $1.00; roan, plain, $1.50; calf, plain, $1.75; calf, gilt edge, $2.00; Turkey morocco, plain, $2.50; do. gilt edge, $3.00.

OTIS's (MRS. H. G.) THE BARCLAYS OF BOSTON. 1 vol.
Cloth. $1.25.
PARSONS's (THEOPHILUS) LIFE. By his Son. 1 vol. 12mo.
Cloth. $1.50.
PRESCOTT's HISTORY OF THE ELECTRIC TELEGRAPH.
Illustrated. 1 vol. 12mo. Cloth. $1.75.
POORE's (BEN PERLEY) LOUIS PHILIPPE. 1 vol. 12mo.
Cloth. $1.00.
PHILLIPS's ELEMENTARY TREATISE ON MINERALOGY.
With numerous additions to the Introduction. By Francis Al-
ger. With numerous Engravings. 1 vol. New edition in press.
PRIOR's LIFE OF EDMUND BURKE. 2 vols. 16mo. Cloth.
$2.00.
RAB AND HIS FRIENDS. By John Brown, M. D. Illus-
trated. 15 cents.
SALA's JOURNEY DUE NORTH. 1 vol. 16mo. Cloth.
$1.00.
SCOTT's (SIR WALTER) IVANHOE. In one handsome vol-
ume. $1.75.
SIDNEY's (SIR PHILIP) LIFE. By Mrs. Davis. 1 vol.
Cloth. $1.00.
SHELLEY MEMORIALS. Edited by the Daughter-in-law
of the Poet. 1 vol. 16mo. 75 cents.
SWORD AND GOWN. By the Author of "Guy Living-
stone." 1 vol. 16mo. Cloth. 75 cents.
SHAKSPEAR's (CAPTAIN H.) WILD SPORTS OF INDIA.
1 vol. 16mo. Cloth. 75 cents.
SEMI-DETACHED HOUSE. A Novel. 1 vol. 16mo. Cloth.
75 cents.
SMITH's (WILLIAM) THORNDALE; OR, THE CONFLICT
OF OPINIONS. 1 vol. 12mo. Cloth. $1.25.
SUMNER's (CHARLES) ORATIONS AND SPEECHES. 2 vols.
16mo. Cloth. $2.50.
ST. JOHN's (BAYLE) VILLAGE LIFE IN EGYPT. 2 vols. 16mo.
Cloth. $1.25.
TYNDALL's (PROFESSOR) GLACIERS OF THE ALPS. With
Illustrations. 1 vol. Cloth. $1.50.
TYLL OWLGLASS's ADVENTURES. With Illustrations by
Crowquill. 1 vol. Cloth, gilt. $2.50.
THE SOLITARY OF JUAN FERNANDEZ. By the Author of
"Picciola." 1 vol. 16mo. Cloth. 50 cents.
TAYLOR's (HENRY) NOTES FROM LIFE. 1 vol. 16mo.
Cloth. 50 cents.
TRELAWNY's RECOLLECTIONS OF SHELLEY AND BYRON.
1 vol. 16mo. Cloth. 75 cents.
THOREAU's WALDEN: A LIFE IN THE WOODS. 1 vol.
16mo. Cloth. $1.00.
WARREN's (DR. JOHN C.) LIFE. By Edward Warren,
M. D. 2 vols. 8vo. $3.50.
    "   "   THE PRESERVATION OF HEALTH.
1 vol. 88 cents.

WALLIS'S (S. T.) SPAIN AND HER INSTITUTIONS.   1 vol.
16mo.   Cloth. $1.00.
WORDSWORTH'S (WILLIAM) BIOGRAPHY.   By Dr. Chris-
topher Wordsworth.   2 vols.   16mo.   Cloth. $2.50.
WENSLEY: A STORY WITHOUT A MORAL.   1 vol. 16mo.
Paper.   50 cents.
The Same.   Cloth.   75 cents.
WHEATON'S (ROBERT) MEMOIRS.   1 vol.   16mo.   Cloth.
$1.00.

In Blue and Gold.

LONGFELLOW'S POETICAL WORKS.   2 vols. $1.75.
  "   PROSE WORKS.   2 vols. $1.75.
TENNYSON'S POETICAL WORKS.   2 vols. $1.50.
WHITTIER'S POETICAL WORKS.   2 vols. $1.50.
LEIGH HUNT'S POETICAL WORKS.   2 vols. $1.50.
GERALD MASSEY'S POETICAL WORKS.   1 vol.   75 cents.
MRS. JAMESON'S CHARACTERISTICS OF WOMEN.   75 cts.
  "   DIARY OF AN ENNUYEE.   1 vol.   75 cts.
  "   LOVES OF THE POETS.   1 vol.   75 cts.
  "   SKETCHES OF ART, &c.   1 vol.   75 cts.
  "   STUDIES AND STORIES.   1 vol.   75 cts.
  "   ITALIAN PAINTERS.   1 vol.   75 cents.
  "   LEGENDS OF THE MADONNA.   1 vol.
             75 cents.
OWEN MEREDITH'S POEMS.   1 vol.   75 cents.
       "   LUCILE: A Poem.   1 vol.   75 cents.
BOWRING'S MATINS AND VESPERS.   1 vol.   75 cents.
LOWELL'S (J. RUSSELL) POETICAL WORKS. 2 vols. $1.50.
PERCIVAL'S POETICAL WORKS.   2 vols. $1.75.
MOTHERWELL'S POEMS.   1 vol.   75 cents.
SYDNEY DOBELL'S POEMS.   1 vol.   75 cents.
WILLIAM ALLINGHAM'S POEMS. 1 vol. 75 cents.
HORACE.   Translated by Theodore Martin.   1 vol.   75 cts.
SAXE'S POETICAL WORKS.   With Portrait.   1 vol.   75 cents.

Works Lately Published.

SIR THOMAS BROWNE'S WRITINGS.   A New and Elegant
Edition, comprising " Religio Medici," " Urn-Burial," " Chris-
tian Morals," &c.   With fine Portrait.   1 vol. $1.50.
SPARE HOURS.   By John Brown, M. D.   1 vol. $1.50.
MEMOIRS, LETTERS AND REMAINS OF ALEXIS DE
TOCQUEVILLE, Author of " Democracy in America."   2 vols.
$2.50.

Works Lately Published.

CECIL DREEME. By Theodore Winthrop. With Biographical Sketch of the Author by George W. Curtis. 1 vol. $1.00.

SERMONS Preached in Harvard Chapel. By James Walker, D. D. 1 vol. $1.50.

EDWIN OF DEIRA. By Alexander Smith, Author of " A Life Drama," &c. 1 vol. With fine Portrait of the Author. 75 cents.

THE AUTOBIOGRAPHY, LETTERS, AND LITERARY RE-MAINS OF MRS. THRALE PIOZZI. Edited by A. Hayward, Esq. 1 vol. $1.50.

THE LIFE AND CAREER OF MAJOR JOHN ANDRÉ. By Winthrop Sargent. 1 vol. $1.50.

THE SABLE CLOUD. By Nehemiah Adams, D. D., Author of " A South-Side View of Slavery." 1 vol. 75 cents.

FAITHFUL FOREVER. By Coventry Patmore, Author of " The Angel in the House." 1 vol. $1.00.

OVER THE CLIFFS : A Novel. By Charlotte Chanter, (a sister of Rev. Charles Kingsley.) 1 vol. $1.00.

THE RECREATIONS OF A COUNTRY PARSON. 2 vols. $1.25 each. Sold together or separately.

REMINISCENCES OF SCOTTISH LIFE AND CHARACTER. By Dean Ramsay. From the Seventh Enlarged Edinburgh Edition. With an American Preface. 1 vol. 16mo. $1.00.

POEMS BY REV. WM. CROSWELL, D. D. Edited, with a Memoir, by Rev. Arthur Cleveland Coxe, D. D. 1 vol. $1.00.

PERSONAL HISTORY OF LORD BACON. From Original Letters and Documents. By Hepworth Dixon. 1 vol. $1.25.

POEMS. By Rose Terry. 1 vol. 16mo. 75 cents.

THE AUTOBIOGRAPHY OF THE REV. DR. ALEXANDER CARLYLE. Containing Memorials of the Men and Events of his Times. Edited by John Hill Burton. 1 vol. $1.50.

FAVORITE AUTHORS : A Companion Book of Prose and Poetry. With 26 fine Steel Portraits. $2.50.

HEROES OF EUROPE. A capital Boy's Book. With 16 Illustrations. 1 vol. 16mo. $1.00.

BONNIE SCOTLAND. By Grace Greenwood. Illustrated. 75 cents.

THE SEVEN LITTLE SISTERS, who live in the Round Ball that floats in the Air. Illustrated. 63 cents.

www.ingramcontent.com/pod-product-compliance
Lightning Source LLC
Chambersburg PA
CBHW031028030726
47497CB00004B/1046